FAITH
SECRETS

Scripture quotations are taken from the Holy Bible, King James Version. The King James Version is public domain in the United States of America. All bolding and emphasis are added by the author.

Cover Illustration and Design by: M. Kaleem

Formatting by: Deborah Ling

Printed in thFe United States of America

Table of Contents

Dedication

I dedicate this book to God the Father, Jesus, His Son, and the Holy Spirit. I attribute all that I am and anything I have accomplished to the Godhead. All three of the Godhead have played an integral part in my life. You revealed yourselves to me when I was young and have always been there for me throughout my whole life. I love you with all my heart, mind, soul, body, and strength. I will never forget what you have done for me. I THANK YOU from the bottom of my heart!

I also dedicate this book to my wonderful wife, Eunice. The way you love me and take care of me does not go unnoticed. You also played a significant role in getting this book out. Thank you for always supporting me, my walk with God, and the ministry God has given me. You are not only my wife, but you are my companion and friend.

Introduction

The subject of *Biblical Faith* found in the Holy Scriptures is one of the most fascinating studies from the Word of God that can dramatically change your life. When you discover what true *Biblical Faith* is, your life will never be the same. The Bible says that without faith, it is impossible to please God. Anyone who wants to please the Lord will want to learn as much as they can about faith. In this book, I will reveal what I call **Faith Secrets** that God, by His Spirit, has taught me from the Word of God. These **Faith Secrets** have transformed my life, and I believe they will change the life of anyone who hears, understands, and lives what the Lord has shown me in His Word about faith.

When Jesus Christ walked this Earth, He healed many people and performed many miracles. But, whenever He healed someone or performed a miracle, He always pointed right back to the person's faith. Jesus never said the power of God healed someone or that He healed them. Instead, Jesus made statements like this: *"Go thy way; thy faith hath made thee whole,"* or *"If thou canst believe, all things are possible to him that believeth."* He also told two blind men He healed, *"According to your faith, be it unto you."* Jesus made statements like these repeatedly the whole time during His ministry.

When you read the four Gospels, it is amazing to see how much Jesus was looking for faith and teaching about faith to His disciples. Jesus worked all of His miracles by faith. No one in the history of the world has performed as many miracles as Jesus, and Jesus taught that faith was the key to all the miracles He was performing. I cannot express enough how important faith is to God and why it should be important to you.

Faith is the secret key to accessing all the blessings of God. All you have to do to inherit the promises of God is believe. Our faith is the simplest yet most profound way to please God. We don't have to beat our bodies, climb high mountains, or crawl on our knees to please God. All we have to do is have faith in God to please Him. However, as simple as this seems, it can still be the hardest thing for people to do.

It has taken me years to develop my faith. One of the biggest keys I found that helped my faith grow was a deeper understanding of the Word of God. The Bible says that God's people perish for lack of knowledge. Your faith in God will grow as you understand what true *Biblical Faith* is.

The Word of God reveals we cannot receive healing, have our prayers answered, please God, or go to Heaven without faith. Faith is the most important thing God is looking for in those people He calls believers. In this book, I will reveal many **Faith Secrets**, but to start I want to reveal 10 important truths every believer needs to know about faith.

Below is the list of 10 important truths we need to know about faith found in the Word of God.

1. You Cannot Be Saved Without Faith

2. It is Impossible to Please God Without Faith

3. God Won't Answer Your Prayers Without Faith

4. You Cannot Be Healed Without Faith

5. Mustard Seed Size Faith Can Make Mountains Move

6. The Just Shall Live by Their Faith

7. Whatsoever is Not of Faith is Sin

8. Christians Walk by Faith and Not by Sight

9. Nothing is Impossible to Them That Believe

10. Faith is the Substance of Things Hoped For

IMPORTANT FAITH TRUTHS

1. You Cannot Be Saved Without Faith

Jesus died for everyone, but the only people who will experience salvation are those who believe.

> *John 3:16 (KJV)*
> *16 For God so loved the world, that he gave his only begotten Son, **that whosoever believeth in him should not perish**, but have everlasting life.*

The only way to access God's unmerited favor of salvation is by faith and faith alone.

> *Ephesians 2:8 (KJV)*
> *8 **For by grace are ye saved through faith**; and that not of yourselves: it is the gift of God:*

People receive salvation when they believe God raised Jesus from the dead and confess Jesus as their Lord.

Romans 10:8-10 (KJV)
*8 But what saith it? The word is nigh thee, even in thy mouth, and in thy heart: that is, the word of faith, which we preach; 9 **That if thou shalt confess with thy mouth the Lord Jesus, and shalt believe in thine heart that God hath raised him from the dead, thou shalt be saved.** 10 For with the heart man believeth unto righteousness; and with the mouth confession is made unto salvation.*

Confessing Jesus as your Lord means He is your supreme Master, and you will obey Him in all things.

Luke 6:46 (KJV)
46 And why call ye me, Lord, Lord, and do not the things which I say?

2. It is Impossible to Please God Without Faith

There is only one way to please God, and that is by faith.

Hebrews 11:6 (KJV)
*6 **But without faith it is impossible to please him:** for he that cometh to God must believe that he is, and that he is a rewarder of them that diligently seek him.*

It is impossible to please God without faith because God lives by the same faith He expects us to live by. Faith is also how God spoke everything into existence by His Word.

Hebrews 11:3 (KJV)
*3 **Through faith we understand that the worlds were framed by the word of God,** so that things which are seen were not made of things which do appear.*

When God spoke from Heaven, declaring Jesus to be His Son at His baptism, God also proclaimed Jesus was well pleasing to Him. Now that you know you can only please God with faith, you can see the hidden message of the Father in declaring Jesus was His Son, in whom He was well pleased. God, The Father, said that Jesus had a faith that pleased Him.

> *Matthew 3:16-17 (KJV)*
> *16 And Jesus, when he was baptized, went up straightway out of the water: and, lo, the heavens were opened unto him, and he saw the Spirit of God descending like a dove, and lighting upon him: 17 And lo a voice from heaven, saying, **This is my beloved Son, in whom I am well pleased.***

Jesus revealed His faith in all the miracles He performed and always pointed to people's faith when they received a miracle from Him. Jesus pleased the Father the same way we can please God, and that is by faith.

3. God Won't Answer Your Prayers Without Faith

God only hears us when we pray with unwavering faith. The Bible teaches that a double-minded, wavering person will receive nothing from God. Many prayers go unanswered because they are not offered in faith. God is a God of faith and only hears and responds to the language of faith.

> *James 1:5-8 (KJV)*
> *5 If any of you lack wisdom, let him ask of God, that giveth to all men liberally, and upbraideth not; and it shall be given him. 6 **But let him ask in faith,** nothing wavering. For he that wavereth is like a wave of the sea driven with the wind and tossed. 7 **For let not that man think that he shall receive any thing of the Lord.** 8 A double minded man is unstable in all his ways.*

Don't expect God to hear or answer your prayers if they are filled with fear, doubt, and unbelief. When you pray to God, how is He supposed to answer you? He will answer your prayer by using His faith to work a miracle for you. So, He cannot connect with your prayer if you are in fear, doubt, and unbelief. Faith only connects with faith. Your faith-filled prayer authorizes God to work in this world on your behalf.

4. You Cannot Be Healed Without Faith

We know God anointed Jesus with the Holy Spirit and power, but whenever He healed someone, He always pointed back to their faith as to why they were healed.

> *Matthew 15:28 (KJV)*
> *28 Then Jesus answered and said unto her, **O woman, great is thy faith: be it unto thee even as thou wilt.** And her daughter was made whole from that very hour.*

> *Mark 5:34 (KJV)*
> *34 And he said unto her, **Daughter, thy faith hath made thee whole; go in peace, and be whole of thy plague.***

The Apostles also pointed to people's faith when they performed miracles in the New Testament.

> *Acts 3:16 (KJV)*
> *16 **And his name through faith in his name hath made this man strong,** whom ye see and know: yea, **the faith** which is by him hath given him this perfect soundness in the presence of you all.*

God is a God of faith and can only operate with faith. When God sees faith, He uses His faith to perform the miracle. Therefore, you must have faith to be healed. The Holy Spirit, the Third Person of the Trinity, is the One who anoints people and performs miracles, and the Holy Spirit will only operate by faith. When the Holy Spirit sees faith,

He uses His power to heal people. Therefore, God wants us to put our faith in the power of God.

> *1 Corinthians 2:4-5 (KJV)*
> *4 And my speech and my preaching was not with enticing words of man's wisdom, but in demonstration of the Spirit and of power: 5* **That your faith should not stand in the wisdom of men, but in the power of God.**

5. Mustard Seed Size Faith Can Make Mountains Move

Jesus taught that it only took faith the size of a mustard seed to move a mountain. There are two ways to look at what Jesus meant by referring to faith as a mustard seed. First, it could mean it only takes a small pure dose of faith, with no unbelief, to speak to a mountain and make it move. The second way to look at the mustard seed is that it could grow so big that you can speak to mountains and make them move with your faith. I believe both are true. Faith can be small but must be free from all unbelief, and this kind of faith can grow to be exceedingly great.

> *Matthew 17:20 (KJV)*
> *20 And Jesus said unto them, Because of your unbelief: for verily I say unto you,* **If ye have faith as a grain of mustard seed,** *ye shall say unto this mountain, Remove hence to yonder place; and it shall remove; and nothing shall be impossible unto you.*

> *Matthew 13:31-32 (KJV)*
> *31 Another parable put he forth unto them, saying,* **The kingdom of heaven is like to a grain of mustard seed,** *which a man took, and sowed in his field: 32* **Which indeed is the least of all seeds: but when it is grown, it is the greatest among herbs, and becometh a tree, so that the birds of the air come and lodge in the branches thereof.**

6. The Just Shall Live by Their Faith

The just are called to live by faith and not by the law. The law is not of faith.

> *Romans 4:13-16 (KJV)*
> *13 For the promise, that he should be the heir of the world, was not to Abraham, or to his seed, **through the law, but through the righteousness of faith.** 14 For if they which are of the law be heirs, faith is made void, and the promise made of none effect: 15 Because the law worketh wrath: for where no law is, there is no transgression. 16 **Therefore it is of faith, that it might be by grace;** to the end the promise might be sure to all the seed; not to that only which is of the law, but to that also which is of the faith of Abraham; who is the father of us all,*

God ordained the just to live by faith because it only takes believing in the grace of God and not by works to be saved. God never ordained good works to save us. We are only saved by believing in the finished work of Christ on the cross. We do good works because we are saved and not to earn salvation.

> *Ephesians 2:8-10 (KJV)*
> *8 **For by grace are ye saved through faith;** and that not of yourselves: **it is the gift of God:** 9 Not of works, lest any man should boast. 10 **For we are his workmanship, created in Christ Jesus unto good works,** which God hath before ordained that we should walk in them.*

God prophesied in the Old Testament that the just would live by their faith before Jesus came to the Earth.

> *Habakkuk 2:4 (KJV)*
> *4 Behold, his soul which is lifted up is not upright in him: **but the just shall live by his faith.***

7. Whatsoever is Not of Faith is Sin

When the Bible teaches that whatsoever is not of faith is sin, it refers to someone living by their conscience. The passage where this statement is found is in the Book of Romans, Chapter 14. This passage of Scripture talks about someone feeling good or not feeling good about what they eat. So, what made something sinful was their faith or their conscience not feeling good or feeling good about what they were about to do. Strong Christians were also commanded not to offend a weak person's conscience. This means if they felt good about something, don't do it in front of someone who didn't feel good about it, so they weren't emboldened to go against their conscience.

> *Romans 14:19-23 (KJV)*
> *19 Let us therefore follow after the things which make for peace, and things wherewith one may edify another. 20 For meat destroy not the work of God. All things indeed are pure; but it is evil for that man who eateth with offence. 21 It is good neither to eat flesh, nor to drink wine, nor any thing whereby thy brother stumbleth, or is offended, or is made weak. 22* **Hast thou faith?** *have it to thyself before God. Happy is he that condemneth not himself in that thing which he alloweth. 23* **And he that doubteth is damned if he eat, because he eateth not of faith: for whatsoever is not of faith is sin.**

Christians are called to live by faith and obey what they believe is right in their heart. The conscience convicts people based on the Laws of God written in their hearts. The New Covenant has everything to do with the Laws of God being written in the believer's heart. The New Covenant was foretold through the prophecy of Jeremiah. God did away with the Old Covenant when the New Covenant was established through the finished work of Christ.

Jeremiah 31:31-34 (KJV)
*31 Behold, the days come, saith the Lord, that I will make **a new***
***covenant** with the house of Israel, and with the house of Judah: 32*
Not according to the covenant that I made with their fathers in the
day that I took them by the hand to bring them out of the land of
Egypt; which my covenant they brake, although I was an husband
*unto them, saith the Lord: 33 **But this shall be the covenant** that I*
will make with the house of Israel; After those days, saith the Lord,
I will put my law in their inward parts, and write it in their
***hearts;** and will be their God, and they shall be my people. 34 And*
they shall teach no more every man his neighbour, and every man
his brother, saying, Know the Lord: for they shall all know me, from
the least of them unto the greatest of them, saith the Lord: for I will
forgive their iniquity, and I will remember their sin no more.

In the New Covenant found in Christ, God writes His Laws in our hearts and minds. God created and designed our conscience to accuse or excuse us if we obey the moral law written in our hearts. Living by obeying your conscience is also called living by faith, which is why it says whatsoever that is not of faith is sin. We must live with a clean conscience for our faith to work for us. Those who live by a clean conscience have boldness toward God, and their prayers are answered.

1 John 3:19-22 (KJV)
*19 And hereby we know that we are of the truth, **and shall assure***
our hearts before him. 20 For if our heart condemn us, God is
***greater than our heart, and knoweth all things.** 21 Beloved, if our*
heart condemn us not, then have we confidence toward God. 22
***And whatsoever we ask, we receive of him,** because we keep his*
commandments, and do those things that are pleasing in his sight.

8. Christians Walk by Faith and Not by Sight

To walk by faith and not by sight means we don't look at what our eyes see to believe. Instead, our faith is in God and His Word. Our eyes can deceive us, but faith in God and His Word will never deceive us.

> *2 Corinthians 5:7 (KJV)*
> *7 (For we walk by faith, not by sight:)*

After Jesus rose from the dead, doubting Thomas said he would not believe unless he put his finger in the holes where Jesus was crucified. He also said he wouldn't believe Jesus rose from the dead unless he put his hand in the side where Jesus was pierced. When Jesus appeared to him, He told Thomas to put his finger in the holes in His hands and thrust his hand into His side. Then Jesus told Thomas not to be faithless but to believe. Jesus said that the ones who had not seen and believed were blessed.

> *John 20:24-29 (KJV)*
> *24 But Thomas, one of the twelve, called Didymus, was not with them when Jesus came. 25 The other disciples therefore said unto him, We have seen the Lord. But he said unto them, **Except I shall see in his hands the print of the nails, and put my finger into the print of the nails, and thrust my hand into his side, I will not believe.** 26 And after eight days again his disciples were within, and Thomas with them: then came Jesus, the doors being shut, and stood in the midst, and said, Peace be unto you. 27 **Then saith he to Thomas, Reach hither thy finger, and behold my hands; and reach hither thy hand, and thrust it into my side: and be not faithless, but believing.** 28 And Thomas answered and said unto him, My Lord and my God. 29 Jesus saith unto him, Thomas, because thou hast seen me, thou hast believed: **blessed are they that have not seen, and yet have believed.***

God wants us to believe Him and His Word without seeing anything with our naked eyes. This is called walking by faith and not by sight. True faith always believes without seeing. You may or may never see God manifest with your naked eye while you are alive, but you can still see the invisible God with your eye of faith. When you have faith, you will also see God manifest Himself through the miracles He performs.

9. Nothing is Impossible to Them That Believe

We know that with God, nothing is impossible because He has the power to do anything.

> *Luke 1:37 (KJV)*
> *37 For with God nothing shall be impossible.*

Jesus taught nothing was impossible with God, but those with faith believed nothing would be impossible for them either. All you need is faith for you to do the impossible with God.

> *Mark 9:23 (KJV)*
> *23 Jesus said unto him, **If thou canst believe, all things are possible to him that believeth.***
>
> *Matthew 17:20 (KJV)*
> *20 And Jesus said unto them, Because of your unbelief: for verily I say unto you, If ye have faith as a grain of mustard seed, ye shall say unto this mountain, Remove hence to yonder place; and it shall remove; **and nothing shall be impossible unto you.***

Faith is the key to doing the impossible. The mountain represents any impossible situation standing in your way. All you have to do is believe and speak to your mountain for it to move.

10. Faith is the Substance of Things Hoped For

Whatever you are hoping to receive from God, faith is the substance of what you are hoping for.

> *Hebrews 11:1 (KJV)*
> *1 Now faith is the substance of things hoped for,* the evidence of things not seen.

Hope always puts things in the future, whereas faith says you have it *NOW*. Faith believes it has received what it is hoping for. Faith brings all hope into the *NOW* and takes hope away from being in the future. When you understand that faith is in the *NOW*, it will become more evident how to receive answers to your prayers and communicate appropriately with God when you pray.

Understanding these 10 important truths about faith is important before I teach more about faith in the rest of this book. Your faith will grow as your understanding of what faith is from the Word of God grows. Understanding the secrets to real *Biblical Faith* could make all the difference in you receiving a miracle and answer to your prayers from God or not. For some people, this could be the difference between Heaven and hell, life and death, and blessings or cursings.

In conclusion, faith is very important to Jesus and God and should be important to us. The Bible is a Heavenly Book written to help us in our faith. God has granted me the privilege to see what true *Biblical Faith* is from the Word of God, and I will share many of the secrets God has revealed to me in this book. I believe these **Faith Secrets** will change your life as they have changed mine. I pray this book strengthens your *FAITH* and you receive all the *Precious Promises* of God found in His Word.

CHAPTER I

The Word of God

The Bible is the most profound and remarkable Book ever written, and there is no other Book like it. The Bible contains the very thoughts, mind, and will of God. The Bible describes itself as the written Word of God or the Holy Scriptures. The Bible teaches the truth about God, the history of the world, the future, and how to make it into Heaven. God gave the Bible to instruct humankind on what to believe and how to prepare for the afterlife. The Bible also lays the foundation of faith in all areas of the Christian life. We cannot know who God is and what He requires of us without the Word of God. In this chapter, I will reveal the origins of the Bible and how the Bible establishes our faith in God.

The word **BIBLE** comes from the Greek word *Biblios*, meaning *Scrolls*. The Scriptures contain the sacred Scrolls of both the Jewish and Christian faith. The Scriptures are made up of the Old Testament and New Testament Scrolls. Jews believe God wrote through holy men of God the Old Testament, and Christians believe God wrote through holy men of

God the Old and New Testaments. The Old Testament comprises 39 Books (Scrolls), and the New Testament contains 27 Books/Letters (Scrolls).

The Bible is a collection of writings from approximately forty authors, written on three continents and in three different languages. It is estimated that the Books of the Bible were written over a span of 1,600 years. The Bible has also sold more copies than any book in history. It is important to note that although the Bible has many authors, different languages, and a long span between Books, it maintains a Divine unity and coherency in all its passages. Later in history, men of God led by the Holy Spirit determined which Books and Scrolls would be included in the Holy Bible.

To understand what the Bible is, we must first look at what it says about itself. The Bible says that holy men of God spoke as they were moved by the Holy Spirit when writing the Scriptures. The word *moved* means to be under the influence as the wind drives a ship. As a ship is carried along by the wind to its final destination, so the Holy Spirit moved holy men of God to communicate exactly what He led them to write. The holy men who wrote the Bible did not write their own ideas or doctrines. The Holy Spirit wrote the sacred Scriptures through them. This sets the Bible apart from any other book.

> *2 Peter 1:19-21 (KJV)*
> *19 We have also a more sure word of prophecy; whereunto ye do well that ye take heed, as unto a light that shineth in a dark place, until the day dawn, and the day star arise in your hearts: 20 Knowing this first, that no prophecy of the scripture is of any private interpretation. 21 For the prophecy came not in old time by the will of man: **but holy men of God spake as they were moved by the Holy Ghost.***

The Bible also says that all Scripture is given by inspiration of God and can make us wise unto salvation through faith in Christ Jesus.

2 Timothy 3:15-16 (KJV)
15 And that from a child thou hast known the holy scriptures, which are able to make thee wise unto salvation through faith which is in Christ Jesus. 16 All scripture is given by inspiration of God, and is profitable for doctrine, for reproof, for correction, for instruction in righteousness:

The word *inspiration* means Divinely Inspired or God-breathed. *Inspiration* implies the infusion of the thoughts of God into the mind with the supernatural influence of the Divine Will by the Holy Spirit. The Holy Spirit wrote the Scriptures through chosen holy men of God, and this sets the sacred writings of the Holy Scriptures above any other book.

In the Book of Psalms, King David said his tongue was the pen of a ready writer. This means God spoke and wrote through King David's tongue. The Book of Psalms records the spiritual songs God spoke through him.

Psalm 45:1 (KJV)
1 My heart is inditing a good matter: I speak of the things which I have made touching the king: my tongue is the pen of a ready writer.

The Old Testament was first made up of the Pentateuch. The Pentateuch is comprised of the first five Books of the Bible written by Moses, called the Law of Moses. The first five Books of the Bible are Genesis, Exodus, Leviticus, Numbers, and Deuteronomy. God spoke directly to Moses on Mount Sinai, and Moses was the first holy man of God to write on Scrolls what God had spoken to him. These sacred Scrolls also give the account of the time when God spoke the Ten Commandments and engraved them on two stone tablets.

When God led the children of Israel to Mount Sinai, He came down and audibly spoke the Ten Commandments. This is the first and most holy account of humankind hearing the voice of God spoken from Heaven since the fall of Adam. It was so terrifying that the children of Israel asked God not to speak to them anymore. They wanted Moses to hear from God and then tell them what God said.

> *Deuteronomy 5:24-27 (KJV)*
> *24 And ye said, Behold, the Lord our God hath shewed us his glory and his greatness, and we have heard his voice out of the midst of the fire: we have seen this day that God doth talk with man, and he liveth. 25 Now therefore why should we die? for this great fire will consume us:* **if we hear the voice of the Lord our God any more, then we shall die.** *26 For who is there of all flesh, that hath heard the voice of the living God speaking out of the midst of the fire, as we have, and lived?* **27 Go thou near, and hear all that the Lord our God shall say: and speak thou unto us all that the Lord our God shall speak unto thee; and we will hear it, and do it.**

The Ten Commandments God spoke were engraved by the finger of God on two tablets of stone and placed in the Ark of the Covenant. The Ark of the Covenant was a box made of gold with two golden cherubims whose wings spread over the top of the Mercy Seat. The Mercy seat sat on top of the Ark of the Covenant. The Ark was placed in the Holy of Holies inside the Tabernacle of Moses and later in the Temple that King Solomon built.

The Tabernacle was a holy meeting place for the children of Israel to meet with God. It was comprised of the Outer Court, Inner Court, and Holy of Holies. Moses built the Tabernacle based on the pattern he saw in a vision of Heaven while meeting with God on Mount Sinai. The Temple of Solomon was later constructed after the pattern of the Tabernacle of Moses in the holy city of Jerusalem.

The Ten Commandments that God spoke to the children of Israel from Mount Sinai are so crucial to humankind that they changed the Laws of how people were to treat God and each other. The Ten Commandments and the Law of Moses also lay the foundation for all the laws in modern societies. Before the Word of God revealed the Laws of God, kings, rulers, and people were doing what was right in their own eyes. Most kingdoms had no real justice, and wickedness prevailed.

The Ten Commandments set the people of Israel apart from every other wicked nation. The Ten Commandments testify to the goodness of God and the authenticity of the Word of God. The Ten Commandments also play a fundamental role in Judaism and Christianity. Jesus summed up the Laws of God by saying that men should do to others what they would want to be done to themselves.

Matthew 7:12 (KJV)
12 Therefore all things whatsoever ye would that men should do to you, do ye even so to them: for this is the law and the prophets.

Below are the Ten Commandments that God spoke to the Children of Israel:

Deuteronomy 5:4-22 (KJV)
4 The Lord talked with you face to face in the mount out of the midst of the fire, 5 (I stood between the Lord and you at that time, to shew you the word of the Lord: for ye were afraid by reason of the fire, and went not up into the mount;) saying, 6 I am the Lord thy God, which brought thee out of the land of Egypt, from the house of bondage. 7 Thou shalt have none other gods before me. 8 Thou shalt not make thee any graven image, or any likeness of any thing that is in heaven above, or that is in the earth beneath, or that is in the waters beneath the earth: 9 Thou shalt not bow down thyself unto them, nor serve them: for I the Lord thy God am a jealous God, visiting the iniquity of the fathers upon

the children unto the third and fourth generation of them that hate me, 10 And shewing mercy unto thousands of them that love me and keep my commandments. 11 Thou shalt not take the name of the Lord thy God in vain: for the Lord will not hold him guiltless that taketh his name in vain. 12 Keep the sabbath day to sanctify it, as the Lord thy God hath commanded thee. 13 Six days thou shalt labour, and do all thy work: 14 But the seventh day is the sabbath of the Lord thy God: in it thou shalt not do any work, thou, nor thy son, nor thy daughter, nor thy manservant, nor thy maidservant, nor thine ox, nor thine ass, nor any of thy cattle, nor thy stranger that is within thy gates; that thy manservant and thy maidservant may rest as well as thou. 15 And remember that thou wast a servant in the land of Egypt, and that the Lord thy God brought thee out thence through a mighty hand and by a stretched out arm: therefore the Lord thy God commanded thee to keep the sabbath day. 16 Honour thy father and thy mother, as the Lord thy God hath commanded thee; that thy days may be prolonged, and that it may go well with thee, in the land which the Lord thy God giveth thee. 17 Thou shalt not kill. 18 Neither shalt thou commit adultery. 19 Neither shalt thou steal. 20 Neither shalt thou bear false witness against thy neighbour. 21 Neither shalt thou desire thy neighbour's wife, neither shalt thou covet thy neighbour's house, his field, or his manservant, or his maidservant, his ox, or his ass, or any thing that is thy neighbour's. 22 These words the Lord spake unto all your assembly in the mount out of the midst of the fire, of the cloud, and of the thick darkness, with a great voice: and he added no more. And he wrote them in two tables of stone, and delivered them unto me.

It is recorded in the Law of Moses that God would raise up a Prophet who would speak the Words of God. This Prophet would speak God's Word since they did not want to hear God speak from Heaven when He spoke the Ten Commandments. Moses prophesied that everything this Prophet spoke would be required of humankind. Let us read this prophecy foretelling of the Prophet to come found in Deuteronomy, Chapter 18.

Deuteronomy 18:15-19 (KJV)
15 The Lord thy God will raise up unto thee a Prophet from the midst of thee, of thy brethren, like unto me; unto him ye shall hearken; *16 According to all that thou desiredst of the Lord thy God in Horeb in the day of the assembly, saying, Let me not hear again the voice of the Lord my God, neither let me see this great fire any more, that I die not. 17 And the Lord said unto me, They have well spoken that which they have spoken. 18 I will raise them up a Prophet from among their brethren, like unto thee, and will put my words in his mouth; and he shall speak unto them all that I shall command him. 19 And it shall come to pass, that whosoever will not hearken unto my words which he shall speak in my name, I will require it of him.*

We know that this Prophet to come was Jesus Christ.

Acts 3:22-26 (KJV)
22 For Moses truly said unto the fathers, A prophet shall the Lord your God raise up unto you of your brethren, like unto me; him shall ye hear in all things whatsoever he shall say unto you. 23 And it shall come to pass, that every soul, which will not hear that prophet, shall be destroyed from among the people. 24 Yea, and all the prophets from Samuel and those that follow after, as many as have spoken, have likewise foretold of these days. 25 Ye are the children of the prophets, and of the covenant which God made with our fathers, saying unto Abraham, And in thy seed shall all the kindreds of the earth be blessed. 26 Unto you first God, having raised up his Son Jesus, sent him to bless you, in turning away every one of you from his iniquities.

After Jesus died and rose again, He opened His disciples' understanding that He was the fulfillment of the Old Testament prophecies. Jesus broke down the Old Testament Scriptures into the Law, the Psalms, and the Prophets.

> *Luke 24:44-48 (KJV)*
> *44 And he said unto them, These are the words which I spake unto you,*
> **while I was yet with you, that all things must be fulfilled, which**
> **were written in the law of Moses, and in the prophets, and in the**
> **psalms, concerning me. 45 Then opened he their understanding, that**
> **they might understand the scriptures, 46 And said unto them, Thus**
> *it is written, and thus it behooved Christ to suffer, and to rise from the*
> *dead the third day: 47 And that repentance and remission of sins should*
> *be preached in his name among all nations, beginning at Jerusalem. 48*
> *And ye are witnesses of these things.*

Jesus confirmed the Old Testament to be the Scriptures written by holy men of God that prophesied the coming of the Messiah and His sufferings. We know Jesus fulfilled these prophecies in His first appearance and will fulfill even more prophecies when He returns. Jesus fulfilled over 300 specific prophesies from the Word of God during His lifetime. This alone is astounding. Holy men of God in the Old Testament wrote these prophecies many years before Jesus was born.

Some of the prophesies Jesus fulfilled were Isaiah 53 and Psalms 22. They prophesied of a suffering Messiah, and Him being pierced, and refers to the crucifixion of Jesus. The Book of Daniel also accurately prophesied the exact time and date the Messiah would appear. Fulfilled prophesies found in the Scriptures prove that God Himself Divinely inspired the Bible. No group of men could accurately prophesy over a span of many years all the events of the life of Jesus Christ before He was born.

The New Testament is the recorded events of the life and ministry of Jesus the Christ as He fulfilled all the prophetic words written about Him in the Old Testament Scriptures. Jesus also told people during His ministry to search the Scriptures, for they testify of Him.

John 5:37-40 (KJV)
37 And the Father himself, which hath sent me, hath borne witness of
me. Ye have neither heard his voice at any time, nor seen his shape. 38
And ye have not his word abiding in you: *for whom he hath sent, him*
ye believe not. 39 **Search the scriptures; for in them ye think ye have**
eternal life: and they are they which testify of me. *40 And ye will not*
come to me, that ye might have life.

The four Gospels: Matthew, Mark, Luke, and John, record the life and Words of Christ. These Divinely spoken Words from Christ make up the first part of the New Testament and are a continuation of the Old Testament Scriptures. The rest of the New Testament is comprised of the Book of Acts, letters to the New Testament churches written by the holy Apostles, and the Book of Revelation. The men who wrote the New Testament lived during the time of Jesus and some were His first Apostles. Jesus revealed Himself in multiple visions to Paul the Apostle, who wrote most of the New Testament letters.

Jesus said that Heaven and Earth would pass away, but His Words will never pass away.

Matthew 24:35 (KJV)
35 **Heaven and earth shall pass away, but my words shall not pass**
away.

Jesus also said He would not judge us on Judgment Day, but the Words He spoke would judge us. Jesus taught that He only spoke what His Heavenly Father commanded Him to speak.

John 12:47-49 (KJV)
47 And if any man hear my words, and believe not, I judge him not:
for I came not to judge the world, but to save the world. 48 **He that**
rejecteth me, and receiveth not my words, hath one that judgeth him:

the word that I have spoken, the same shall judge him in the last
day. 49 For I have not spoken of myself; but the Father which sent
me, he gave me a commandment, what I should say, and what I
should speak.

When Jesus gave *The Great Commission* to His Apostles before He left the
Earth to be with the Father, He instructed His Apostles to teach people to
observe all He commanded them.

Matthew 28:18-20 (KJV)
18 And Jesus came and spake unto them, saying, All power is given unto
*me in heaven and in earth. 19 Go ye therefore, **and teach all nations,***
baptizing them in the name of the Father, and of the Son, and of the
*Holy Ghost: 20 **Teaching them to observe all things whatsoever I***
***have commanded you:** and, lo, I am with you always, even unto the*
end of the world. Amen.

New Testament Christians believe the Old Testament was written about
the coming Messiah. We know this Messiah to be the Lord Jesus Christ of
Nazareth. Jesus fulfilled the Law of Moses and all the Old Testament
prophesies. Jesus was crucified on Passover as the Lamb of God who takes
away the sins of the world. Passover is one of the major feast days in the
Law of Moses and is observed by many Christians and Jews still today.

Now that I have established the facts of all the prophesies Jesus fulfilled,
here are some other key facts about the Holy Scriptures. The Bible was
written as a Book of redemption, and not a historical or scientific book.
That being said, the Bible is one hundred percent historically and
scientifically accurate. Even to this day, archeologists are still finding
evidence to prove the accuracy of the Bible.

You can also visit the land of Israel and see all the historical places in the
Scriptures where Biblical events took place over thousands of years. You

can also visit many of the tombs of people written about in the Scriptures. These tombs prove the Bible is accurate and that all the events on its pages are factual.

The Bible is the infallible Word of God, which means it does not contain any errors because it was God-breathed. The Word of God is also true, evidenced by the heavenliness of its doctrines and its power to change lives. Just by reading the Bible, someone can be challenged and changed. No other Book accurately details the unseen heavenly realm, but the Bible. Without the Bible, humanity would be in the dark about what happens in the unseen realm and after someone dies. We know from the Bible you either go to Heaven or go to hell based upon what you did with Jesus Christ and His Words.

A very important point I want to make about faith is that Jesus said no one could come to Him unless they were drawn to Him by the Father.

John 6:44-45 (KJV)
*44 **No man can come to me, except the Father which hath sent me draw him:** and I will raise him up at the last day. 45 It is written in the prophets, And they shall be all taught of God. **Every man therefore that hath heard, and hath learned of the Father, cometh unto me.***

Jesus said the Father must allow someone to come to Christ and believe in Him. I could go on and on about the Bible being inspired by God, but I know from the Scriptures that some people will still doubt, no matter how many facts are revealed to them. At some point, a true believer will have an encounter or an eye-opening experience with God Himself, which will cause them to believe in God. God will allow their eyes to be opened to see Jesus as the prophesied Messiah and that the Bible is the very Word of God.

Without a revelation from God, people will live in doubt and attack God and His Word. I am not here to convince anyone about the validity of God's Word, but to strengthen the faith of those who already believe. I am also writing this book to help those genuinely seeking God who want solid answers to help grow their faith. Jesus Himself Divinely inspires faith in His followers. Jesus is the *Author* and *Finisher* of our faith. Jesus uses the Word of God by the leading of the Holy Spirit to establish and grow our faith in Him.

> *Hebrews 12:2 (KJV)*
> *2 Looking unto Jesus the author and finisher of our faith; who for the joy that was set before him endured the cross, despising the shame, and is set down at the right hand of the throne of God.*

God has sent men of God into every generation since the time of Christ to preach the Word of God to grow faith in people's hearts. The Word of God is like a seed to be received in a good heart. Faith grows out of the Word of God being sown and tended to correctly on a good heart.

> *Luke 8:15 (KJV)*
> *15 But that on the good ground are they, which in an honest and good heart, having heard the word, keep it, and bring forth fruit with patience.*

God has given us His Holy Scriptures so we can learn more about Him when we are ready. All true faith in God stems from what is written and revealed in God's Holy Word. The Word of God was given to us to make us wise unto salvation. The facts, truths, and Divine revelations found in its pages will truly change hearts when believed and adhered to.

The Word of God is the only Book that can be trusted to understand God and what He requires of humankind. Many people have written many books to explain the origins and meaning of this life, but without the Word of God, they end up with false teachings. The Christian Bible holds the truth of who God is, where we came from, why we are here, and what happens after we die. The eternal truths in the Word of God make up the Christian belief system, which is their faith. Faith represents what someone believes. Beliefs stem mostly from what someone has been taught by other people or formulated in their mind by what they have read from books.

The Bible teaches that when the Word of God is preached by someone sent by God, it brings faith.

> *Romans 10:14-17 (KJV)*
> *14 How then shall they call on him in whom they have not believed? and how shall they believe in him of whom they have not heard?* ***and how shall they hear without a preacher? 15 And how shall they preach, except they be sent?*** *as it is written, How beautiful are the feet of them that preach the gospel of peace, and bring glad tidings of good things! 16 But they have not all obeyed the gospel. For Esaias saith, Lord, who hath believed our report? 17* ***So then faith cometh by hearing, and hearing by the word of God.***

At some point in every person's life, they will have to decide on what they believe about the Christian Bible because it reveals many important facts that Jesus and God spoke by the Holy Spirit that will determine their eternal salvation. Your belief system will also determine the quality of life you can live on Earth before you die. God gave us the Bible to be a guide and manual to lead us to Him and salvation.

In conclusion, all faith comes from God and His Word. God's Word contains the foundation of all New Testament Christian beliefs. Within the pages of the Bible, we learn about where we came from, why we are here, and where we are going. If we did not have the Bible, we would be blind to the unseen world. The Bible was given as a gift from God so we can know all we are to believe about God and His salvation found in Jesus Christ.

> *Psalm 119:103 (KJV)*
> *103 How sweet are thy words unto my taste! yea, sweeter than honey to my mouth!*

The B I B L E can be defined as:

B asic

I nstructions

B efore

L eaving

E arth

CHAPTER 2

Precious Promises

N ow that I have established the Christian Bible as God's inspired, infallible Word, let's get into the next crucial foundation of authentic *Biblical Faith.* The promises of God, found within the pages of the Bible, play a big part in the foundation of our faith. The Bible is filled with promises from God that we can put our faith in. So, our faith starts with believing the Bible is the inspired Word of God. Then, our faith is further established by the revelations of the promises revealed within the pages of the Scriptures.

The Holy Bible is estimated to contain over 7,487 promises made by God to humankind. Some promises God has promised in His Word are:

- He will forgive our sins if we repent
- Give us the Holy Spirit
- Heal our bodies
- Provide for our physical needs

- Bless us with supernatural provision
- Answer our prayers
- Be with us in our time of need
- Give us victory over the devil
- Angelic protection
- Comfort us
- Save us from going to hell
- Grant us eternal salvation and entrance into Heaven
- Give us good gifts
- and many other promises

These promises from God are called *Precious Promises* in the Bible. The word *precious* means high value or worth, very expensive, costly, and rare. The *Promises of God* are exceedingly great and of high value, like a rare and precious gemstone.

> *2 Peter 1:3-4 (KJV)*
> *3 According as his divine power hath given unto us all things that pertain unto life and godliness, through the knowledge of him that hath called us to glory and virtue: 4 **Whereby are given unto us exceeding great and precious promises:** that by these ye might be partakers of the divine nature, having escaped the corruption that is in the world through lust.*

After Adam and Eve fell in the Garden of Eden and after the flood of Noah, God came to a man named Abram to establish His promises with him. These promises were made in the form of a Covenant God established with Abram, which is known as the **Abrahamic Covenant**. All ancient covenants came with promises to be performed if both parties kept their end of the covenant. Animal sacrifices were always involved in the making of these covenants, which is why they were also called Blood Covenants. Blood Covenants are soul-binding verbal agreements made between two parties which involve blessings and cursings spoken between each party based upon if one breaks or keeps the Blood Covenant.

God appeared to Abraham multiple times during His life to cut a Blood Covenant with him. This Blood Covenant was based on faith, and Abraham is known as the Father of Faith for the Jews and Christians. God also gave the sign of circumcision as a token of the Covenant. God was very serious about this Covenant and establishing His promises to Abraham. When God made this Covenant with Abraham, He was committed to keeping His end of the bargain and fulfilling all that was laid out in this Covenant. It is important to note that the Abrahamic Covenant preceded the Mosaic Covenant and is still in effect today.

God will **NEVER** break His side of the Blood Covenant. God bound Himself to this Covenant so we could have strong confidence that God will keep His Word, where we can place our faith like an anchor to our soul.

> *Psalm 89:34 (KJV)*
> *34 My covenant will I not break, nor alter the thing that is gone out of my lips.*

Let's read in the Scriptures where God established the Abrahamic Covenant, which contained the promises of God. When making an ancient Blood Covenant, both the parties would pass between the sacrificed animal that was cut in half. In the making of the Abrahamic Blood Covenant, God alone passed between the sacrifices.

Genesis 12:1-3 (KJV)

1 Now the Lord had said unto Abram, Get thee out of thy country, and from thy kindred, and from thy father's house, unto a land that I will shew thee: **2 And I will make of thee a great nation, and I will bless thee, and make thy name great; and thou shalt be a blessing: 3 And I will bless them that bless thee, and curse him that curseth thee: and in thee shall all families of the earth be blessed.**

Genesis 15:7-21 (KJV)

7 And he said unto him, I am the Lord that brought thee out of Ur of the Chaldees, to give thee this land to inherit it. 8 And he said, Lord God, whereby shall I know that I shall inherit it? **9 And he said unto him, Take me an heifer of three years old, and a she goat of three years old, and a ram of three years old, and a turtledove, and a young pigeon. 10 And he took unto him all these, and divided them in the midst, and laid each piece one against another: but the birds divided he not.** *11 And when the fowls came down upon the carcases, Abram drove them away. 12 And when the sun was going down, a deep sleep fell upon Abram; and, lo, an horror of great darkness fell upon him. 13 And he said unto Abram, Know of a surety that thy seed shall be a stranger in a land that is not theirs, and shall serve them; and they shall afflict them four hundred years; 14 And also that nation, whom they shall serve, will I judge: and afterward shall they come out with great substance. 15 And thou shalt go to thy fathers in peace; thou shalt be buried in a good old age. 16 But in the fourth generation they shall come hither again: for the iniquity of the Amorites is not yet full. 17* **And it came to pass, that, when the sun went down, and it was dark, behold a smoking furnace, and a burning lamp that passed between those pieces. 18 In the same day the Lord made a covenant with Abram,** *saying, Unto thy seed have I given this land, from the river of Egypt unto the great river, the river Euphrates: 19 The Kenites, and the Kenizzites, and the Kadmonites, 20 And the Hittites, and the Perizzites, and the Rephaims, 21 And the Amorites, and the Canaanites, and the Girgashites, and the Jebusites.*

In the Book of Genesis, God tested Abraham by instructing him to offer his son as a sacrifice. Abraham passed this test, and God reconfirmed His Covenant to bless him and his Seed. This story is also a prophetic portrait of what God the Father would do in sacrificing His *Only Begotten Son*. Let's read this profound story from the Scriptures in Genesis, Chapter 22.

Genesis 22:1-18 (KJV)
1 And it came to pass after these things, that God did tempt Abraham, and said unto him, Abraham: and he said, Behold, here I am. 2 And he said, Take now thy son, thine only son Isaac, whom thou lovest, and get thee into the land of Moriah; and offer him there for a burnt offering upon one of the mountains which I will tell thee of. 3 And Abraham rose up early in the morning, and saddled his ass, and took two of his young men with him, and Isaac his son, and clave the wood for the burnt offering, and rose up, and went unto the place of which God had told him. 4 Then on the third day Abraham lifted up his eyes, and saw the place afar off. 5 And Abraham said unto his young men, Abide ye here with the ass; and I and the lad will go yonder and worship, and come again to you. 6 And Abraham took the wood of the burnt offering, and laid it upon Isaac his son; and he took the fire in his hand, and a knife; and they went both of them together. 7 And Isaac spake unto Abraham his father, and said, My father: and he said, Here am I, my son. And he said, Behold the fire and the wood: but where is the lamb for a burnt offering? 8 And Abraham said, My son, God will provide himself a lamb for a burnt offering: so they went both of them together. 9 And they came to the place which God had told him of; and Abraham built an altar there, and laid the wood in order, and bound Isaac his son, and laid him on the altar upon the wood. 10 And Abraham stretched forth his hand, and took the knife to slay his son. 11 And the angel of the Lord called unto him out of heaven, and said, Abraham, Abraham: and he said, Here am I. 12 And he said, Lay not thine hand upon the lad, neither do thou any thing unto him: for now I know that thou fearest God, seeing thou hast not withheld thy son, thine only son

from me. 13 And Abraham lifted up his eyes, and looked, and behold behind him a ram caught in a thicket by his horns: and Abraham went and took the ram, and offered him up for a burnt offering in the stead of his son. 14 And Abraham called the name of that place Jehovahjireh: as it is said to this day, In the mount of the Lord it shall be seen. 15 And the angel of the Lord called unto Abraham out of heaven the second time, 16 And said, By myself have I sworn, saith the Lord, for because thou hast done this thing, and hast not withheld thy son, thine only son: 17 That in blessing I will bless thee, and in multiplying I will multiply thy seed as the stars of the heaven, and as the sand which is upon the sea shore; and thy seed shall possess the gate of his enemies; 18 And in thy seed shall all the nations of the earth be blessed; because thou hast obeyed my voice.

The Abrahamic Blood Covenant is where all the promises start with God, besides the promise God made with Noah not to flood the earth again. After the flood, God promised Noah that He would not flood the world again; the rainbow is a token of this promise. The problem God faced was that humankind had fallen from grace and could not go to heaven after the fall of Adam. The Abrahamic Covenant was God's secret plan to get Jesus on the earth so He could redeem humankind through His death, burial, and resurrection and make a New Covenant. The Blood of Jesus ratified the New Covenant.

God knew He would have to send His Son Jesus to die on the cross and be resurrected to save humanity. Before this occurred, He needed a man to initiate a covenant between God and man, whereby He could send Jesus to the earth through Abraham's bloodline. The promise He made to Abraham was that He would bless His *SEED*. We know this *SEED* was Jesus Christ. God had to establish a godly lineage whereby Jesus could come as the second Adam. The first Adam failed to be a true leader of

God's creation by eating the Tree of Knowledge of Good and Evil. Because of this, God sent Jesus to redeem humankind back to Him.

Galatians 3:16 (KJV)
*16 Now to Abraham and his seed were the promises made. He saith not, And to seeds, as of many; **but as of one, And to thy seed, which is Christ.***

Jesus was conceived by the Virgin Mary, who God's Holy Spirit Divinely impregnated, thus making God His Father. God had to bypass Jesus having a human father, so He could come as the second Adam and be allowed to obey God where the first Adam failed. When the first Adam failed and sinned against God, it gave the devil authority over the earth. Anyone born from Adam's lineage would remain in the devil's domain, even after they died.

Jesus was given the right to be the second Adam by being born through the lineage of Abraham, with whom God made a Blood Covenant. By Jesus being born of a virgin through Mary, He was given the authority as the second Adam to reclaim the rights over the earth and then He reclaimed the keys to hell and death when He was crucified. When Jesus was unjustly crucified on the cross, died, and rose again, He could reclaim the authority that satan took from the first Adam.

Hebrews 2:14-15 (KJV)
*14 Forasmuch then as the children are partakers of flesh and blood, he also himself likewise took part of the same; **that through death he might destroy him that had the power of death, that is, the devil;** 15 And deliver them who through fear of death were all their lifetime subject to bondage.*

Revelation 1:18 (KJV)
*18 I am he that liveth, and was dead; and, behold, **I am alive for evermore, Amen; and have the keys of hell and of death.***

We know from the Scriptures that when God told Abraham the world would be blessed in him, He was referring to the Gospel that Jesus Christ would preach. The Gospel is the *Good News* of the Kingdom of God coming to earth. The preaching of the Kingdom of God was the promise made to Abraham that God would bless the whole earth. Those who hear, repent, believe, and receive the *Good News* of the Gospel inherit the promises God made to Abraham.

Galatians 3:7-9 (KJV)
*7 Know ye therefore that they which are of faith, the same are the children of Abraham. 8 **And the scripture, foreseeing that God would justify the heathen through faith, preached before the Gospel unto Abraham, saying, In thee shall all nations be blessed.** 9 So then they which be of faith are blessed with faithful Abraham.*

If we have faith like Abraham, we can be blessed as he was. Our faith is in Jesus Christ, who is the *SEED* of Abraham. If we believe God raised Jesus from the dead and confess with our mouths that Jesus is Lord, we are saved.

Romans 10:8-11 (KJV)
*8 But what saith it? The word is nigh thee, even in thy mouth, and in thy heart: that is, the word of faith, which we preach; 9 **That if thou shalt confess with thy mouth the Lord Jesus, and shalt believe in thine heart that God hath raised him from the dead, thou shalt be saved. 10 For with the heart man believeth unto righteousness; and with the mouth confession is made unto salvation.** 11 For the scripture saith, Whosoever believeth on him shall not be ashamed.*

It is also important to note that when Jesus preached the Gospel of the Kingdom, this had everything to do with people getting healed, delivered, and receiving miracles. Receiving healing, deliverance, answers to prayers, or any miracle is the fulfillment of receiving the promise made to Abraham. Performing miracles through faith is how God would *bless* the whole earth. Let's look at some Scriptures to prove this point.

> *Matthew 4:23 (KJV)*
> *23 And Jesus went about all Galilee, teaching in their synagogues, **and preaching the Gospel of the kingdom, and healing all manner of sickness and all manner of disease among the people.***

> *Matthew 9:35 (KJV)*
> *35 And Jesus went about all the cities and villages, **teaching in their synagogues, and preaching the Gospel of the kingdom, and healing** every sickness and every disease among the people.*

Jesus also commanded His disciples to preach the Kingdom of God and perform the same miracles He did.

> *Matthew 10:7-8 (KJV)*
> *7 And as ye go, preach, saying, The kingdom of heaven is at hand. 8 Heal the sick, cleanse the lepers, raise the dead, cast out devils: freely ye have received, freely give.*

Healing the sick and deliverance is a big part of preaching the Gospel and the Great Commission.

> *Mark 16:15-18 (KJV)*
> *15 And he said unto them, **Go ye into all the world, and preach the gospel to every creature.** 16 He that believeth and is baptized shall be saved; but he that believeth not shall be damned. 17 **And these signs shall follow them that believe; In my name shall they cast out devils; they shall speak with new tongues; 18 They shall take up serpents;***

and if they drink any deadly thing, it shall not hurt them; they shall lay hands on the sick, and they shall recover.

The preaching of the Gospel fulfilled the Abrahamic Covenant of promise that the whole world would be blessed by his *SEED*. The Blessing of Abraham came in the form of miracles, signs, and wonders through the anointed ministry of Jesus Christ. All the promises of God found in the Scriptures, are God helping people in their time of need. God gives promises in His Word so we can believe He will help us by performing miracles and answer our prayers.

Jesus is the answer and fulfillment of all the promises of God in the Bible. When Jesus died and rose again from the dead, thus defeating the devil, He delivered us from any curse we might face. Jesus redeemed us from the curse of the law. The curse of the law is about all the curses found in Deuteronomy, Chapter 28, and Leviticus, Chapter 26.

Galatians 3:13-14 (KJV)
13 Christ hath redeemed us from the curse of the law, being made a curse for us: for it is written, Cursed is every one that hangeth on a tree: 14 That the blessing of Abraham might come on the Gentiles through Jesus Christ; that we might receive the promise of the Spirit through faith.

God in Christ promises to redeem you from any curse. Another way to define redeem is to say; He paid the price by going to the cross, so you don't have to be cursed anymore. This is an amazing promise from God. The Bible says that *ALL* the promises of God are *Yes* and *Amen* in Him. This means you can claim any promise in the Bible because of what Jesus did in His death, burial, and resurrection.

2 Corinthians 1:20 (KJV)
20 For all the promises of God in him are yea, and in him Amen,
unto the glory of God by us.

The Law of Moses was implemented as the world waited for the Promised *SEED* of Abraham to come. When Jesus died on the cross and rose again, He established the New Covenant. The New Covenant has better promises than the Law of Moses and fulfilled the Covenant that God first made with Abraham.

Hebrews 8:6 (KJV)
*6 But now hath he obtained a more excellent ministry, **by how much also he is the mediator of a better covenant, which was established upon better promises.***

If you believe in Jesus Christ, you can have access to *ALL* the promises of God found in the Holy Scriptures. This is where the incredible journey and secret to faith begins. Faith is all that is required to inherit *ALL* the promises of God. This is why your faith is so important. If you will believe God and what He says, *ALL* the promises of God are *Yes* and *Amen* to you, in Christ Jesus.

Putting this all together, your faith begins in the Word of God. The Holy Word of God reveals the promises of God found in Christ Jesus through the New Covenant. If you believe in God and His Word, you will inherit and receive all the promises of God. This is a wonderful revelation, and when you understand this truth from the Word of God and step out in faith, you will see God fulfill all His promises found in His Word.

Now, I need to reveal another aspect and secret to faith that is vital in receiving the promises of God found in His Word. A promise is only as good as the character and ability of the one making the promise. What I mean by this is if someone makes a promise and is a liar, what good is their promise? Or, if someone makes a promise but doesn't have the power or ability to fulfill the promise, what good is the promise? If either of these is the case, you cannot trust them to fulfill their promise.

If we are to trust and believe God for a promise, we must know for certain that God is not a liar. This is where your faith comes in. The Bible tells us that God is not a man that He should lie.

> *Numbers 23:19 (KJV)*
> *19 **God is not a man, that he should lie;** neither the son of man, that he should repent: hath he said, and shall he not do it? or hath he spoken, and shall he not make it good?*

The Bible also reveals that it is impossible for God to lie.

> *Hebrews 6:18a (KJV)*
> *18 **That by two immutable things, in which it was impossible for God to lie…***

Jesus said He is the *Way*, the *Truth*, and the *Life*. The essence of God's character is that He cannot and will not lie. He is the TRUTH. He establishes all TRUTH. No created being could ever trust the God of all Creation if He were a liar. God is not a liar.

> *John 14:6 (KJV)*
> *6 Jesus saith unto him, I am the way, **the truth,** and the life: no man cometh unto the Father, but by me.*

The Holy Spirit is called the Spirit of Truth.

> *John 15:26 (KJV)*
> *26 But when the Comforter is come, whom I will send unto you from the Father, **even the Spirit of truth,** which proceedeth from the Father, he shall testify of me:*

All lies stem from the father of lies, which is the devil.

> *John 8:44 (KJV)*
> *44 Ye are of your father the devil, and the lusts of your father ye will do. He was a murderer from the beginning, **and abode not in the truth, because there is no truth in him. When he speaketh a lie, he speaketh of his own: for he is a liar, and the father of it.***

One of the devil's biggest lies is to get people to believe God is not good. If you don't believe God is good and cannot lie, how could you ever put your full faith and trust in Him? For your faith to be solid in God, you must know and trust that God is inherently good and cannot lie. Your faith has to rest secure in the goodness and holiness of God. The Bible says that God is light, and in Him, there is no darkness; there is nothing evil in Him.

> *James 1:16-17 (KJV)*
> *16 Do not err, my beloved brethren. 17 Every good gift and every perfect gift is from above, and cometh down from **the Father of lights, with whom is no variableness, neither shadow of turning.***

The devil, the father of all lies, tries to deceive people of this fact and get them to doubt God and His goodness. He will say things like if God were good, why are their suffering children, or why did this person die? All evil came into this world because of the fall of Adam and the devil. There is no evil or problems in heaven; if we believe God, we can have heaven on earth. So, if you are in a situation where the devil is trying to get you to believe one of his lies, know you do not know all the facts. God is beyond good, and no matter what is going on, it will always work out for your good if you love Him and are called according to His purpose.

Romans 8:28 (KJV)
28 And we know that all things work together for good to them that love God, to them who are the called according to his purpose.

The next fact that has to be established to strengthen your faith is if God *can* fulfill what He promises. When I say *can*, I mean, does He have the *ability* to perform miracles? Let's start with the fact that we are dealing with a God who spoke everything into existence with His spoken Word.

Genesis 1:1-5 (KJV)
*1 In the beginning God created the heaven and the earth. 2 And the earth was without form, and void; and darkness was upon the face of the deep. And the Spirit of God moved upon the face of the waters. 3 **And God said, Let there be light: and there was light.** 4 And God saw the light, that it was good: and God divided the light from the darkness. 5 And God called the light Day, and the darkness he called Night. And the evening and the morning were the first day.*

The Bible says nothing shall be impossible with God, and nothing is too hard for the Lord.

Genesis 18:14a (KJV)
14 Is any thing too hard for the Lord?...

Jeremiah 32:27 (KJV)
*27 Behold, I am the Lord, the God of all flesh: **is there any thing too hard for me?***

Luke 1:37 (KJV)
*37 **For with God nothing shall be impossible.***

Let me explain in the simplest terms why nothing is impossible or too hard for the Lord. When talking about God, He can create or turn one thing into another with just His spoken Words. God can turn rocks into bread with His spoken Word. The devil knows this and tempted Jesus to use His power instead of obeying His Heavenly Father.

> *Luke 4:2-4 (KJV)*
> *2 Being forty days tempted of the devil. And in those days he did eat nothing: and when they were ended, he afterward hungered. 3 And the devil said unto him, **If thou be the Son of God, command this stone that it be made bread.** 4 And Jesus answered him, saying, It is written, That man shall not live by bread alone, but by every word of God.*

When God revealed Himself to Moses, He told him to put his hand in his bosom and take it out. When he took it out, his hand was leprous. Then, when God told him to put it back in his bosom and take it out, it was normal.

> *Exodus 4:6-7 (KJV)*
> *6 And the Lord said furthermore unto him, **Put now thine hand into thy bosom. And he put his hand into his bosom: and when he took it out, behold, his hand was leprous as snow. 7 And he said, Put thine hand into thy bosom again. And he put his hand into his bosom again; and plucked it out of his bosom, and, behold, it was turned again as his other flesh.***

We, as humans, see this world as solid, and we have to move and make things with our hands. The world, however, to God, is virtual. What I mean by virtual is God can do anything with His creation and manipulate it in any way He wants to with His spoken Word. God controls all of creation at a molecular level with His Words. This is why nothing is impossible to God because He has the power to do anything He wants with what He created by speaking to it. Miracles are as easy as God speaking a Word. He can make anything appear, disappear, and be transformed at His command. The Word of His power upholds all things.

Hebrews 1:3 (KJV)
*3 Who being the brightness of his glory, and the express image of his person, **and upholding all things by the word of his power,** when he had by himself purged our sins, sat down on the right hand of the Majesty on high:*

Once you fully understand God's power and ability, your faith will be increased. God can do ANYTHING!!! So, if you believe and have faith in Him, nothing will be impossible for you, either.

Matthew 17:20 (KJV)
*20 And Jesus said unto them, Because of your unbelief: for verily I say unto you, If ye have faith as a grain of mustard seed, ye shall say unto this mountain, Remove hence to yonder place; and it shall remove; **and nothing shall be impossible unto you.***

God has made *Precious Promises* and has the character and power to fulfill whatever He promised. Your faith will increase when you discover these two truths. Those who take God at His Word can be granted the privilege of God answering their prayers and performing miracles. These secret truths found in God's Word give hope and assurance that God will fulfill all His promises made to us in His Word.

King Solomon proclaimed that there had not failed one Word of all that God promised.

1 Kings 8:56 (KJV)
*56 Blessed be the Lord, that hath given rest unto his people Israel, **according to all that he promised: there hath not failed one word of all his good promise, which he promised by the hand of Moses his servant.***

Before Joshua went to be with the Lord, he declared the same truth.

Joshua 23:14 (KJV)
*14 And, behold, this day I am going the way of all the earth: and ye know in all your hearts and in all your souls, **that not one thing hath failed of all the good things which the Lord your God spake concerning you; all are come to pass unto you, and not one thing hath failed thereof.***

When God made His promise to Abraham, He confirmed it with an oath. That by two immutable things that God cannot lie. The two immutable things are the Oath and He swore by Himself. Immutable means; immovable, unchangeable, and unalterable.

Hebrews 6:13-20 (KJV)
*13 For when God made promise to Abraham, because he could swear by no greater, he sware by himself, 14 Saying, Surely blessing I will bless thee, and multiplying I will multiply thee. 15 And so, after he had patiently endured, he obtained the promise. 16 For men verily swear by the greater: and an oath for confirmation is to them an end of all strife. 17 Wherein God, willing more abundantly to shew unto the **heirs of promise** the **immutability** of his counsel, confirmed it by an oath: 18 **That by two immutable things, in which it was impossible for God to lie, we might have a strong consolation, who have fled for refuge to lay hold upon the hope set before us:** 19 Which hope we have as an anchor of the soul, both sure and stedfast, and which entereth into that within the veil; 20 Whither the forerunner is for us entered, even Jesus, made an high priest for ever after the order of Melchisedec.*

In conclusion of this important chapter, let the assurance of your faith be anchored in the Word of God, the character of God, and the power of God when it comes to His *Precious Promises.* The God who promised is well able to deliver on all His promises found in His Word. You will stand on a firm foundation of faith when you understand these truths. Your faith must be grounded in these *Faith Secrets* to succeed in your walk with God.

God can do exceedingly abundantly above all that we can ask or think according to His power that works in us (Ephesians 3:20). Always remember that it takes *Precious Faith* to inherit *Precious Promises*.

2 Peter 1:1 (KJV)
*1 Simon Peter, a servant and an apostle of Jesus Christ, to them that have obtained like **precious faith** with us through the righteousness of God and our Saviour Jesus Christ:*

CHAPTER 3

Inheriting the Promises of God

Many people throughout history did not know how to possess the promises of God, and because of this, they have gone without, though they didn't need to. Questions can arise when a person comes to a revelation of the Bible being God's infallible Word and the *Precious Promises* found within its pages. How do I inherit and obtain these *Promises*? Do the Promises of God just show up in my life, or do I have to do something to inherit them? In this chapter, I will reveal *Faith Secrets* on inheriting and possessing the *Precious Promises* of God.

Jesus taught many mysteries and secrets about how to receive the Bible, which is the Word of God so that it will work in a person's life. Jesus taught these mysteries and secrets through parables while He was on Earth. A parable is a simple short story used to illustrate a spiritual truth. The parables of Jesus contain the secrets of how to inherit and possess the promises of God. To understand how to inherit promises from the Word of God, we will thoroughly dissect the most important parable Jesus taught; the *Sower Sows the Word.*

Jesus said that if you didn't know and understand the parable of the *Sower Sows the Word,* how would you understand any parable that He taught?

> *Mark 4:13 (KJV)*
> *13 And he said unto them, Know ye not this parable? and how then will ye know all parables?*

The parable of the *Sower Sows the Word* is the most important parable of all the parables that Jesus taught. This parable is so important that three of the four Gospels mention it. Let's read this simple yet powerful parable of the *Sower Sows the Word,* starting in Mark, Chapter 4.

> *Mark 4:3-8 (KJV)*
> *3 Hearken; **Behold, there went out a sower to sow:** 4 And it came to pass, as he sowed, some fell by the way side, and the fowls of the air came and devoured it up. 5 And some fell on stony ground, where it had not much earth; and immediately it sprang up, because it had no depth of earth: 6 But when the sun was up, it was scorched; and because it had no root, it withered away. 7 And some fell among thorns, and the thorns grew up, and choked it, and it yielded no fruit. 8 And other fell on good ground, and did yield fruit that sprang up and increased; and brought forth, some thirty, and some sixty, and some an hundred.*

Now let's read how Jesus privately expounded on the secret hidden mystery behind this parable to His disciples.

> *Mark 4:14-20 (KJV)*
> *14 **The sower soweth the word.** 15 **And these are they by the way side, where the word is sown;** but when they have heard, Satan cometh immediately, and taketh away the word that was sown in their hearts. 16 **And these are they likewise which are sown on stony ground;** who,*

when they have heard the word, immediately receive it with gladness; 17 And have no root in themselves, and so endure but for a time: afterward, when affliction or persecution ariseth for the word's sake, immediately they are offended. 18 And these are they which are sown among thorns; such as hear the word, 19 And the cares of this world, and the deceitfulness of riches, and the lusts of other things entering in, choke the word, and it becometh unfruitful. 20 And these are they which are sown on good ground; such as hear the word, and receive it, and bring forth fruit, some thirtyfold, some sixty, and some an hundred.

In this passage, the sower is sowing seeds to grow a crop. Jesus revealed in this parable that the seed being sown is the Word of God being preached by a preacher. This parable also reveals what can hinder a crop from being cultivated and brought to a 100-fold harvest. The secret mystery behind this parable is that not every seed grows into a harvest. There are secrets to cultivating God's Word to grow the seed into a harvest.

If the Word of God is likened to a seed in this parable, the question must be asked, what is a seed? A seed is a small embryo in a shell capable of germinating if planted in the ground to produce a new plant, tree, or food source. A seed is tiny, but has the capability of growing into something very large that can benefit humankind. The power of the seed is in its potential. If the seed is planted in the ground and dies, it has the potential to grow into something great and bring forth much fruit.

John 12:24 (KJV)
24 Verily, verily, I say unto you, Except a corn of wheat fall into the ground and die, it abideth alone: but if it die, it bringeth forth much fruit.

Jesus likened the Word of God to a seed, which means the Word of God could produce a harvest if planted correctly on good ground and cared for.

However, not everyone who has seeds ends up with a harvest, and not everyone who has the promises of God in seed form ends up with a harvest of God's Kingdom. So, when discussing a promise of God from the Scriptures, it must be understood as potential.

It is important to note that seeds will stay in seed form and never grow into anything if not planted. It is not until someone takes the seed and plants it in the ground that it will produce a harvest. The Bible says that faith comes by hearing and hearing by the Word of God. This passage is about someone being sent by God and preaching the Word of God. Faith is produced when someone hears the preaching of the Word of God by someone sent by God.

> *Romans 10:14-17 (KJV)*
> *14 How then shall they call on him in whom they have not believed? and how shall they believe in him of whom they have not heard? and how shall they hear without a preacher? 15 And how shall they preach, except they be sent? as it is written, How beautiful are the feet of them that preach the gospel of peace, and bring glad tidings of good things! 16 But they have not all obeyed the gospel. For Esaias saith, Lord, who hath believed our report? 17 So then faith cometh by hearing, and hearing by the word of God.*

The one sent by God preaches the written Word of God to people; this is how the Word of God is sown in their hearts, producing faith. People get faith in the preached Word of God and believe God for all of His promises written in the Holy Scriptures. A seed can sit on a shelf for thousands of years and never produce a harvest if it is never sown into the ground. The Bible has been around for thousands of years, but if one sent by God never preaches it, it will continue to sit on people's shelves, producing nothing.

Archaeologists found 35 seeds that were excavated from sites they were digging in that were over 2,000 years old. Seven of these seeds were planted, germinated, and produced trees. They named the oldest seed planted Methuselah, which grew into a Judean Date Palm Tree. None of the seeds germinated had any side effects, and all grew successfully. The Bible has been written in over 2,000 to 3,500 years and it still produces the same harvest as when it was first written. God's Word is incorruptible and lasts forever, but God needs someone to plant the Word on good ground and take care of it for it to produce a harvest.

The Bible reveals itself to be the *incorruptible* seed of God. The word *incorruptible* means that it doesn't decay and lasts forever.

1 Peter 1:23 (KJV)
*23 Being born again, **not of corruptible seed, but of incorruptible, by the word of God,** which liveth and abideth for ever.*

Now that you understand the secret of God's Word being likened to a seed, you can better understand the parable of the *Sower Sows the Word.* One key factor that determines a harvest is the actual preaching or sowing of the seed of God's Word. The other factor is the condition of the ground the seed is sown into. The condition of your heart or ground is just as important as the seed. When you put the seed into good ground, you can produce a harvest every time.

Unless you understand the laws governing seedtime and harvest, you will not know how to inherit the *Promises* of God. I am writing this book to help people understand how God, His Word, and His Kingdom work so they can reap a harvest of God's Word. Once you understand these secret mysteries, you will see a harvest of the promises of God in your life.

Remember, life works by the law of seedtime and harvest. What I mean by this is that just as much as seedtime and harvest works with God's Word, it also works with words from the devil. If you listen to the words of the devil, you will produce a harvest from his words. Whatever you sow, you will reap. Whether or not people know it, sowing and reaping occurs in everyone's life. I am teaching you how to sow to the Spirit by God's Word so you can reap a harvest from God's Word.

> *Galatians 6:7-9 (KJV)*
> *7 Be not deceived; God is not mocked: for whatsoever a man soweth, that shall he also reap. 8 For he that soweth to his flesh shall of the flesh reap corruption; but he that soweth to the Spirit shall of the Spirit reap life everlasting. 9 And let us not be weary in well doing: for in due season we shall reap, if we faint not.*

An important fact about a seed is that if you have a seed, then you have what the seed can grow into. So, if you have an apple seed, you could say you have an apple tree that can produce apples for you to eat regularly. You just need to have patience for the seed to produce a harvest. This is where many Christians and people miss it when it comes to the promises of God. When they pray to God, claiming one of His promises, they give up too soon if they don't see immediate results. What would you say to a farmer who gave up too early when he didn't see the seed he planted in the ground to produce a crop in one day or a week?

The key to inheriting the *Precious Promises* of God is not being slothful and to have faith and patience. Slothful means to be lazy, sluggish, idle, dull, and stupid. Every wise farmer knows it takes good ground, hard work, watering cultivation, and patience to receive a harvest after they plant a seed in the ground.

Hebrews 6:12 (KJV)
12 That ye be not slothful, but followers of them who through faith
and patience inherit the promises.

If we will patiently do the will of God and be like a farmer doing the work
it takes for a harvest, we will receive the promises of God.

Hebrews 10:36 (KJV)
36 For ye have need of patience, that, after ye have done the will of
God, ye might receive the promise.

You have the promise or promises if you have the seed or the Word of
God. You just have to learn how to plant it on good ground, have patience,
and take care of it to produce the harvest that you need. In the *Sower Sows*
the Word parable, Jesus revealed the secret of why some people don't
receive a harvest while others do. I will break down this parable found in
the Gospels of Matthew, Mark, and Luke to discover hidden secrets on
what is needed and not needed to produce a harvest of God's Word in
your life. Remember, our faith has everything to do with the Word of God
producing in our lives or not.

Just as important as it is to understand the secret power of the seed, it is
also important to understand the condition of the heart where the seed is
sown. In the parable of the *Sower Sows the Word,* Jesus revealed four
different hearts where the seed was sown. Seeds must be planted in good
soil and cultivated to receive a harvest. The seed is always the same, but
what a person does with the seed is up to them. We will now study the
four different hearts that determined the harvest they would receive in this
famous parable.

HEART #1

Here is the condition of heart number one in the parable of the Sower Sows the Word:

> *Matthew 13:4 (KJV) And when he sowed, some seeds fell by the way side, and the fowls came and devoured them up:*

> *Mark 4:4 (KJV) And it came to pass, as he sowed, some fell by the way side, and the fowls of the air came and devoured it up.*

> *Luke 8:5 (KJV) A sower went out to sow his seed: and as he sowed, some fell by the way side; and it was trodden down, and the fowls of the air devoured it.*

The first heart reveals the seed was sown on the wayside, and the birds came and ate the seed. The seed was not planted in good ground and was exposed to the birds.

Here is the understanding that Jesus taught about the first heart:

> *Matthew 13:19 (KJV) When any one heareth the word of the kingdom, and understandeth it not, then cometh the wicked one, and catcheth away that which was sown in his heart. This is he which received seed by the way side.*

> *Mark 4:15 (KJV) And these are they by the way side, where the word is sown; but when they have heard, Satan cometh immediately, and taketh away the word that was sown in their hearts.*

> *Luke 8:12 (KJV) Those by the way side are they that hear; then cometh the devil, and taketh away the word out of their hearts, lest they should believe and be saved.*

The first heart reveals someone who hears the Word of God or the Word of the Kingdom and doesn't understand it. The wicked one (satan) takes the Word immediately that was sown in their heart, lest they should believe and be saved. To get a harvest of God's Word, you must understand how His Kingdom works. The Bible says that God's people are destroyed for lack of knowledge. For your faith to work in obtaining a promise from God, you must understand the mysteries of the Kingdom of God. The first mystery you need to understand about the Word of God is that it operates like a seed. The devil steals any understanding this heart would receive from the Word of God.

HEART #2

Here is the condition of heart number two in the parable of the Sower Sows the Word:

Matthew 13:5-6 (KJV) Some fell upon stony places, where they had not much earth: and forthwith they sprung up, because they had no deepness of earth: 6 And when the sun was up, they were scorched; and because they had no root, they withered away.

Mark 4:5-6 (KJV) And some fell on stony ground, where it had not much earth; and immediately it sprang up, because it had no depth of earth: 6 But when the sun was up, it was scorched; and because it had no root, it withered away.

Luke 8:6 (KJV) And some fell upon a rock; and as soon as it was sprung up, it withered away, because it lacked moisture.

The second heart reveals the heart is like stony ground or a rock. The seed immediately springs up but doesn't have much earth and lacks moisture. This seed is scorched by the sun because it has no root, can't get moisture, and it withers away.

Here is the understanding that Jesus taught about the second heart:

Matthew 13:20-21 (KJV) But he that received the seed into stony places, the same is he that heareth the word, and anon with joy receiveth it; 21 Yet hath he not root in himself, but dureth for a while: for when tribulation or persecution ariseth because of the word, by and by he is offended.

Mark 4:16-17 (KJV) And these are they likewise which are sown on stony ground; who, when they have heard the word, immediately receive it with gladness; 17 And have no root in themselves, and so endure but for a time: afterward, when affliction or persecution ariseth for the word's sake, immediately they are offended.

Luke 8:13 (KJV) They on the rock are they, which, when they hear, receive the word with joy; and these have no root, which for a while believe, and in time of temptation fall away.

This person hears the Word, receives it with joy, but has no root in themself. They are immediately offended when tribulation, affliction, or persecution arises because of the Word. They believe for a while, and in times of temptation, they fall away. The Word of God cannot take root in this person's heart because they lack commitment. This heart gives up easily because it doesn't have faith and patience.

HEART #3

Here is the condition of heart number three in the parable of the Sower Sows the Word:

Matthew 13:7 (KJV) And some fell among thorns; and the thorns sprung up, and choked them:

Mark 4:7 (KJV) And some fell among thorns, and the thorns grew up, and choked it, and it yielded no fruit.

Luke 8:7 (KJV) And some fell among thorns; and the thorns sprang up with it, and choked it.

The third heart reveals a thorny heart – Thorns spring up, choke the Word, and it doesn't yield fruit. The seed is growing, but the weeds are allowed to choke out what is planted.

Here is the understanding that Jesus taught about the third heart:

> *Matthew 13:22 (KJV) He also that received seed among the thorns is he that heareth the word; and the care of this world, and the deceitfulness of riches, choke the word, and he becometh unfruitful.*
>
> *Mark 4:18-19 (KJV) And these are they which are sown among thorns; such as hear the word, 19 And the cares of this world, and the deceitfulness of riches, and the lusts of other things entering in, choke the word, and it becometh unfruitful.*
>
> *Luke 8:14 (KJV) And that which fell among thorns are they, which, when they have heard, go forth, and are choked with cares and riches and pleasures of this life, and bring no fruit to perfection.*

This person hears the Word, but because of the cares of this world, the deceitfulness of riches, the lust of other things entering in choke the Word, and they are unfruitful. They are choked with cares of this world, riches, and pleasures of this life, and bring no fruit to perfection. This heart lacks focus. This heart could have received a harvest of God's Word, but allowed distractions to come in and choke out the Word of God.

HEART #4

Here is the condition of heart number four in the parable of the Sower Sows the Word:

> *Matthew 13:8 (KJV) But other fell into good ground, and brought forth fruit, some an hundredfold, some sixtyfold, some thirtyfold.*

Mark 4:8 (KJV) And other fell on good ground, and did yield fruit that sprang up and increased; and brought forth, some thirty, and some sixty, and some an hundred.

Luke 8:8 (KJV) And other fell on good ground, and sprang up, and bare fruit an hundredfold. And when he had said these things, he cried, He that hath ears to hear, let him hear.

The fourth heart reveals good ground. This heart yields a harvest, but it is important to note that not everyone receives a 100-fold harvest. Some brought forth fruit 100, 60, and 30-fold. So even during harvesting, we must be careful to receive a full harvest.

Here is the understanding that Jesus taught about the fourth heart:

Matthew 13:23 (KJV) But he that received seed into the good ground is he that heareth the word, and understandeth it; which also beareth fruit, and bringeth forth, some an hundredfold, some sixty, some thirty.

Mark 4:20 (KJV) And these are they which are sown on good ground; such as hear the word, and receive it, and bring forth fruit, some thirtyfold, some sixty, and some an hundred.

Luke 8:15 (KJV) But that on the good ground are they, which in an honest and good heart, having heard the word, keep it, and bring forth fruit with patience.

Because this heart is honest and good, this person hears the Word, receives it, understands it, and keeps it. They bring forth fruit, some 100, some 60, and some 30-fold, with patience. This person understands the Word of God and is committed to the Word of God during trials and tribulations. They stay focused on the Word of God until they receive a harvest. This person understands it takes hard work and patience to receive a harvest of the promises of God's Word. They must also understand they must be careful to receive a full 100-fold harvest.

From this simple yet profound parable, we can see three major factors when people don't reap a harvest with the Word of God or receive a promise from God's Word.

1. Lack of Understanding
2. Lack of Commitment
3. Lack of Focus

Many people complain to God when they don't receive an answer to their prayers right away and give up. This is called doubt and unbelief. Doubt and unbelief will not take the responsibility to do what it takes to inherit the promises of God. If you are going to inherit God's promises, start thinking like a farmer. If you have the seed, you have the answer.

Having patience while waiting on the promise of God has everything to do with you keeping your heart free from doubt and unbelief. You also have to know the work it will take every day to cultivate a harvest from God's Word. The work you have to do is keep your faith alive through prayer, confession, praise, thanksgiving, and staying in the Word of God.

If you understand God's Word and stay committed and focused, you will always inherit God's promises. Take responsibility to do your part to receive a harvest. If you do the work, the harvest will come every time. Once the harvest comes, all you have to do is to reap the harvest.

Here is another parable that Jesus taught about sowing and reaping:

Mark 4:26-29 (KJV)
26 And he said, So is the kingdom of God, as if a man should cast seed into the ground; 27 And should sleep, and rise night and day, and the seed should spring and grow up, he knoweth not how. 28 For the earth bringeth forth fruit of herself; first the blade, then the ear, after

*that the full corn in the ear. 29 **But when the fruit is brought forth, immediately he putteth in the sickle, because the harvest is come.***

Jesus used the understanding of seedtime and harvest to teach His disciples the mysteries of the kingdom of God and how faith in God's Word works. If you take the time to understand how seeds work and what farmers must do to produce a harvest, you will understand how your faith works with God's Word and receive multiple harvests during your lifetime. It becomes easy to inherit the promises of God with your faith, once you understand how God's Kingdom works.

Jesus said if you had faith as a grain of a mustard seed, you would speak to a sycamine tree, and it would obey you.

> *Luke 17:5-6 (KJV)*
> *5 And the apostles said unto the Lord, Increase our faith. 6 And the Lord said, **If ye had faith as a grain of mustard seed,** ye might say unto this sycamine tree, Be thou plucked up by the root, and be thou planted in the sea; and it should obey you.*

Your faith will grow and increase like a mustard seed when you take care of the Word of God in your heart.

> *Mark 4:30-32 (KJV)*
> *30 And he said, Whereunto shall we liken the kingdom of God? or with what comparison shall we compare it? 31 It is **like a grain of mustard seed,** which, when it is sown in the earth, is less than all the seeds that be in the earth: 32 But when it is sown, it groweth up, and becometh greater than all herbs, and shooteth out great branches; so that the fowls of the air may lodge under the shadow of it.*

The prophet Isaiah revealed 700 years before Christ came on the Earth that God's thoughts were not our thoughts, and His ways were not our ways. God reveals His thoughts and ways to us by sending out His Word like water to water the Earth, causing it to bring forth and bud, giving seed to the sower and bread to the eater. When God sends out His Word, it does not return to Him void, but accomplishes what He pleases and prospers in the thing He sends it to do. We just need to understand that His Word works like a seed that is sown into the earth.

Isaiah 55:8-11 (KJV)
*8 For my thoughts are not your thoughts, neither are your ways my ways, saith the Lord. 9 For as the heavens are higher than the earth, so are my ways higher than your ways, and my thoughts than your thoughts. 10 For as the rain cometh down, and the snow from heaven, and returneth not thither, **but watereth the earth, and maketh it bring forth and bud, that it may give seed to the sower, and bread to the eater: 11 So shall my word be that goeth forth out of my mouth: it shall not return unto me void, but it shall accomplish that which I please, and it shall prosper in the thing whereto I sent it.***

I want to pose this question to you: Why did God set it up where we have to wait like a seed planted in the ground to receive a harvest or to inherit a promise? The answer is simple. God set it up this way to weed out unbelievers. True faith understands it must stay committed and focused on God's Word until it receives a harvest. God uses the process of seedtime and harvest to weed out people who don't have faith, because we cannot please God without faith. The reason we cannot please God without faith is because God is a God of faith and uses His own faith to rule His Kingdom.

Hebrews 11:6 (KJV)
*6 **But without faith it is impossible to please him:** for he that cometh to God must believe that he is, and that he is a rewarder of them that diligently seek him.*

In conclusion, the *Precious Promises* of God's Word come in seed form. Therefore, it is critical that we understand the power of the seed and what it takes to produce a harvest if we are going to inherit the *Promises* of God. God's Word will work every time, just like a seed works, whenever it is planted on good soil, watered, and kept from weeds. The *Promises* of God are exceedingly great and precious, and our faith and patience allow us to receive all God has for us from His Word. We must take responsibility, do something with God's Word, and not expect God to do everything to receive a harvest. All of God's *Promises* are in seed form, and if we will walk by faith, do the work, claim His Word, and be patient, we will inherit all His ***Precious Promises***.

CHAPTER 4

This Means War

Everyone is engaged in a spiritual battle, but many people don't know it. The devil declared war against you before you were born. The devil is fighting to stop people from believing in the *New Covenant* and inheriting the *Precious Promises* of God. The devil will do everything he can to prevent people from receiving all God has for them. One way the devil steals from people is to blind their minds from understanding all that God has for them found in the Word of God. We must learn how to fight the good fight of faith if we are going to inherit the promises of God. In this chapter, I will reveal how you can fight and win the battle of faith in God's Word and defeat the devil.

It was revealed in the last chapter, in the parable of the *Sower Sows the Word*, that the devil steals the Word preached in people's hearts when they don't understand God's Word. When the sower sowed his seeds, the birds came and quickly ate the seeds that fell by the wayside. Jesus used this as an analogy of the devil stealing the Word of God out of people's hearts.

The devil stole the Word from their hearts because they didn't understand the Word preached to them.

Matthew 13:3-4 (KJV)
*3 And he spake many things unto them in parables, saying, Behold, a sower went forth to sow; 4 **And when he sowed, some seeds fell by the way side, and the fowls came and devoured them up:***

Matthew 13:18-19 (KJV)
*18 Hear ye therefore the parable of the sower. 19 **When any one heareth the word of the kingdom, and understandeth it not, then cometh the wicked one, and catcheth away that which was sown in his heart. This is he which received seed by the way side.***

The Bible says that the god of this world; the devil, blinds the minds of people that don't believe, lest the light of the glorious Gospel of Christ should shine on them.

2 Corinthians 4:3-4 (KJV)
*3 But if our gospel be hid, it is hid to them that are lost: 4 **In whom the god of this world hath blinded the minds of them which believe not, lest the light of the glorious gospel of Christ,** who is the image of God, should shine unto them.*

Jesus also spoke another parable about an enemy sowing tares with wheat to harm a crop. The tares that Jesus described in this parable are also known as the darnel seed and it resembles wheat in the beginning stages of its growth. However, after it starts to grow, it becomes clear that it is a poisonous weed. The wheat grows longer, bigger, and stronger than the tares at harvest time. There are tiny black seeds inside the tares, and if eaten can cause dizziness and make you nauseous. If tare seeds from the harvest are mixed with the wheat when ground, this intermixed flour will ruin the bread.

Matthew 13:24-30 (KJV)
24 Another parable put he forth unto them, saying, The kingdom of heaven is likened unto a man which sowed good seed in his field: 25 **But while men slept, his enemy came and sowed tares among the wheat, and went his way.** *26 But when the blade was sprung up, and brought forth fruit, then appeared the tares also. 27 So the servants of the householder came and said unto him, Sir, didst not thou sow good seed in thy field? from whence then hath it tares? 28* **He said unto them, An enemy hath done this.** *The servants said unto him, Wilt thou then that we go and gather them up? 29 But he said, Nay; lest while ye gather up the tares, ye root up also the wheat with them. 30 Let both grow together until the harvest: and in the time of harvest I will say to the reapers, Gather ye together first the tares, and bind them in bundles to burn them: but gather the wheat into my barn.*

We must be very aware that there is an enemy of God in this world who hates God and the children of God. The devil comes in with lies and fights against people. God gave us the truth of His Word to fight the devil's lies. This is why the Word of God is not only likened to a seed but also to a sword.

Ephesians 6:17 (KJV)
17 And take the helmet of salvation, **and the sword of the Spirit, which is the word of God:**

Hebrews 4:12 (KJV)
12 **For the word of God is quick, and powerful, and sharper than any twoedged sword,** *piercing even to the dividing asunder of soul and spirit, and of the joints and marrow, and is a discerner of the thoughts and intents of the heart.*

As believers, we must learn to take the sword of God's Word by faith and fight the devil from stealing from us. The devil is not only a liar, but also a thief. The devil will do everything he can to steal God's Word from being sown in your heart and producing a harvest. If you don't fight him with God's Word, he will not only steal from you, but will kill and destroy you. Jesus, however, who is the Word of God, has come that you might have life.

> *John 10:10 (KJV)*
> *10 The thief cometh not, but for to steal, and to kill, and to destroy: I am come that they might have life, and that they might have it more abundantly.*

The Bible commands us to fight the good fight of faith, which we do with the sword of God's Word.

> *1 Timothy 6:12 (KJV)*
> *12 Fight the good fight of faith, lay hold on eternal life, whereunto thou art also called, and hast professed a good profession before many witnesses.*

A shield symbolizes our faith in the Bible. The Word of God is the sword you fight with, and our faith is a shield that protects us from the fiery darts of the wicked one.

> *Ephesians 6:16 (KJV)*
> *16 Above all, taking the shield of faith, wherewith ye shall be able to quench all the fiery darts of the wicked.*

What are the fiery darts of the wicked one or the devil? The fiery darts are the thoughts, lies, and feelings shot at you from the devil, contrary to the Word of God. The devil likes to lie to people and tell them God's Word is untrue. The Bible teaches us that in this war, we must cast down imaginations and every high thing that exalts itself against the knowledge of God. We must also bring every thought captive to the obedience of Christ.

2 Corinthians 10:3-6 (KJV)
3 For though we walk in the flesh, we do not war after the flesh: 4 (For the weapons of our warfare are not carnal, but mighty through God to the pulling down of strong holds;) 5 Casting down imaginations, and every high thing that exalteth itself against the knowledge of God, and bringing into captivity every thought to the obedience of Christ; 6 And having in a readiness to revenge all disobedience, when your obedience is fulfilled.

The Word of God reveals the thoughts and ways of God, and the devil comes to steal God's thoughts and keep people from understanding God's ways. The devil understands that once you know God's true thoughts and understand His ways, he will be defeated in your life. The Bible also says that a lack of knowledge destroys God's people.

Hosea 4:6 (KJV)
6 My people are destroyed for lack of knowledge: because thou hast rejected knowledge, I will also reject thee, that thou shalt be no priest to me: seeing thou hast forgotten the law of thy God, I will also forget thy children.

You must understand God and His ways to fight the good fight of faith. People's eyes are closed because of a lack of commitment to Christ and obedience to His Word. Only those who fully surrender their whole life to God, His Kingdom, and following Christ will have their eyes opened to understand the mysteries of God. The devil is afraid of sold-out Christians.

When the disciples asked Jesus about the *Sower Sows the Word* parable, He told them their eyes and ears were blessed. The Apostle's eyes were opened to understand the parables of Jesus because they had forsaken everything to follow Christ. Peter, James, and John left their career as fishermen to follow Christ. Matthew left being a tax collector. All the disciples left something behind them and made a full commitment to Christ; thus, their eyes and ears were opened to see the Gospel.

> *Mark 4:10-13 (KJV)*
> *10 And when he was alone, they that were about him with the twelve asked of him the parable. 11 **And he said unto them, Unto you it is given to know the mystery of the kingdom of God: but unto them that are without, all these things are done in parables: 12 That seeing they may see, and not perceive; and hearing they may hear, and not understand; lest at any time they should be converted,** and their sins should be forgiven them. 13 And he said unto them, Know ye not this parable? and how then will ye know all parables?*

God hides the mysteries of His Kingdom and secrets found in His Word behind commitment levels. If someone does not make a strong commitment to Christ, their eyes will remain blinded to the truth of God's Word. So, yes, the devil steals the Word of God sown in their heart, but he can only steal from and blind those who are not fully committed to Christ. True Christians make a total commitment to God and Jesus being their Lord. When you truly make Jesus your Lord, He will open your eyes to comprehend the Scriptures.

Jesus opened the eyes of His committed Apostles to understand the Scriptures after He rose from the dead.

> *Luke 24:44-47 (KJV)*
> *44 And he said unto them, These are the words which I spake unto you, while I was yet with you, that all things must be fulfilled, which were written in the law of Moses, and in the prophets, and in the psalms, concerning me. 45 **Then opened he their understanding, that they might understand the scriptures,** 46 And said unto them, Thus it is written, and thus it behooved Christ to suffer, and to rise from the dead*

the third day: 47 And that repentance and remission of sins should be preached in his name among all nations, beginning at Jerusalem.

The enemy cannot steal God's Word from Christians who have given their whole life to Christ. Through the Holy Spirit, Christ Himself will teach you the truth of God's Word, and once you have this truth, you are prepared to fight the lies of the devil. It is God's will that the eyes of your understanding are enlightened, so you may know the hope of your calling.

Ephesians 1:15-23 (KJV)
15 Wherefore I also, after I heard of your faith in the Lord Jesus, and love unto all the saints, 16 Cease not to give thanks for you, making mention of you in my prayers; ***17 That the God of our Lord Jesus Christ, the Father of glory, may give unto you the spirit of wisdom and revelation in the knowledge of him: 18 The eyes of your understanding being enlightened; that ye may know what is the hope of his calling, and what the riches of the glory of his inheritance in the saints, 19 And what is the exceeding greatness of his power to us-ward who believe, according to the working of his mighty power, 20 Which he wrought in Christ, when he raised him from the dead, and set him at his own right hand in the heavenly places, 21 Far above all principality, and power, and might, and dominion, and every name that is named, not only in this world, but also in that which is to come: 22 And hath put all things under his feet, and gave him to be the head over all things to the church, 23 Which is his body, the fulness of him that filleth all in all.***

You must know the truth of God's Word to defeat the devil. You will be made free as you grow in wisdom and knowledge of God's Word.

John 8:32 (KJV)
32 And ye shall know the truth, and the truth shall make you free.

Once you know the truth of God's Word, you wield it like a sword and defeat all the devil's lies. You take God's Word in your mouth and fight the devil's words. This is called the war of words. Again, the only way you will gain access to the truth of God's Word and have Christ open your understanding to comprehend the Scriptures is by fully committing to Jesus being your Lord.

The first attack that the devil made on humankind was in the Garden of Eden with Eve over what God said about the Tree of Knowledge of Good and Evil. The devil deceived Eve over the simplicity of God's command to not eat from the Tree of Knowledge of Good and Evil.

2 Corinthians 11:3 (KJV)
3 But I fear, lest by any means, as the serpent beguiled Eve through his subtilty, so your minds should be corrupted from the simplicity that is in Christ.

Let's read the story of where the devil first deceived Eve to gain insight into how he works.

Genesis 3:1-7 (KJV)
*1 Now the serpent was more subtil than any beast of the field which the Lord God had made. And he said unto the woman, Yea, hath God said, Ye shall not eat of every tree of the garden? 2 And the woman said unto the serpent, We may eat of the fruit of the trees of the garden: 3 But of the fruit of the tree which is in the midst of the garden, God hath said, Ye shall not eat of it, neither shall ye touch it, lest ye die. 4 **And the serpent said unto the woman, Ye shall not surely die: 5 For God doth know that in the day ye eat thereof, then your eyes shall be opened, and ye shall be as gods, knowing good and evil.** 6 And when the woman saw that the tree was good for food, and that it was pleasant to the eyes, and a tree to be desired to make one wise, she took of the fruit thereof, and did eat, and gave also unto her husband with her; and he*

did eat. 7 And the eyes of them both were opened, and they knew that they were naked; and they sewed fig leaves together, and made themselves aprons.

This first attack of the devil was to get Eve to disobey God's simple command to not eat of the Tree of Knowledge of Good and Evil. The devil baited Eve by saying that her eyes would be opened to be like God to know good and evil. The devil also deceived Eve to think that God was keeping something from her and that she would become wise if she ate of this tree. She, instead, became a fool by listening to the devil and eating from the Tree of Knowledge of Good and Evil.

We must trust God with all our hearts when it comes to obeying all the commands of Christ and not let the devil deceive us into thinking God is holding something back from us. You will plunge into spiritual darkness if you disobey God and His Word. We must always keep our faith in God and His Word. Never let the devil steal from you by trying to get you to disobey God's Word.

When the devil tempted Jesus in the wilderness, Jesus used the written Word of God to defeat him. Jesus used the truth of God's Word to defeat the lies of the devil.

Matthew 4:1-11 (KJV)

*1 Then was Jesus led up of the Spirit into the wilderness to be tempted of the devil. 2 And when he had fasted forty days and forty nights, he was afterward an hungred. 3 And when the tempter came to him, he said, If thou be the Son of God, command that these stones be made bread. 4 But he answered and said, **It is written,** Man shall not live by bread alone, but by every word that proceedeth out of the mouth of God. 5 Then the devil taketh him up into the holy city, and setteth him on a pinnacle of the temple, 6 And saith unto him, If thou be the Son of God, cast thyself down: for it is written, He shall give his angels charge* *concerning thee: and in their hands they shall bear thee up, lest at any time thou dash thy foot against a stone. 7 Jesus said unto him, **It is written again**, Thou shalt not tempt the Lord thy God. 8 Again, the devil taketh him up into an exceeding high mountain, and sheweth him all the kingdoms of the world, and the glory of them; 9 And saith unto him, All these things will I give thee, if thou wilt fall down and worship me. 10 Then saith Jesus unto him, Get thee hence, Satan: **for it is written,** Thou shalt worship the Lord thy God, and him only shalt thou serve. 11 Then the devil leaveth him, and, behold, angels came and ministered unto him.*

Our good fight of faith comes into play by believing what God revealed in His Word. We take the truth of God's Word and fight the enemy's lies using the shield of faith to fend off all the lies he shoots at us in our minds and emotions. This is how you defeat the devil. The devil will come against you like a roaring lion, but you must stand your ground and resist him with your faith.

1 Peter 5:8-9 (KJV)
*8 **Be sober, be vigilant; because your adversary the devil, as a roaring lion, walketh about, seeking whom he may devour:** 9 **Whom resist stedfast in the faith,** knowing that the same afflictions are accomplished in your brethren that are in the world.*

We are called to be strong and put on all the armor of God to war against the devil and his evil hosts.

Ephesians 6:10-17 (KJV)
*10 Finally, my brethren, be strong in the Lord, and in the power of his might. 11 **Put on the whole armour of God, that ye may be able to stand against the wiles of the devil.** 12 For we wrestle not against flesh and blood, but against principalities, against powers, against the rulers of the darkness of this world, against spiritual wickedness in high places. 13 **Wherefore take unto you the whole armour of God,** that ye may*

be able to withstand in the evil day, and having done all, to stand. 14 Stand therefore, having your loins girt about with truth, and having on the breastplate of righteousness; 15 And your feet shod with the preparation of the gospel of peace; 16 Above all, taking the shield of faith, wherewith ye shall be able to quench all the fiery darts of the wicked. 17 And take the helmet of salvation, and the sword of the Spirit, which is the word of God:

New Testament Christians must realize they were enlisted in a war when they were saved and must learn to endure hardness as a good soldier of Jesus Christ.

2 Timothy 2:3 (KJV)
3 Thou therefore endure hardness, as a good soldier of Jesus Christ.

We must also not entangle ourselves with the affairs of this life to please Him, who has chosen us to be a soldier.

2 Timothy 2:4 (KJV)
4 No man that warreth entangleth himself with the affairs of this life; that he may please him who hath chosen him to be a soldier.

The war you are in is over your faith. The devil will fight you tooth and nail over the truth of God's Word. Jesus came with the truth of His Word and the *Good News* of the Gospel to set people free from the devil. If you make an all-in commitment to Christ, God will open your eyes by teaching you His Word and arm you to defeat the devil.

When satan attacked Job and stole his children, wealth, and health from him, Job stood strong and did not falsely accuse God. Satan attacked Job to see if he would curse God if satan took everything from him. Job kept his faith in God, although he was attacked in every way possible.

Job 2:1-10 (KJV)
1 Again there was a day when the sons of God came to present themselves before the Lord, and Satan came also among them to present himself before the Lord. 2 And the Lord said unto Satan, From whence comest thou? And Satan answered the Lord, and said, From going to and fro in the earth, and from walking up and down in it. 3 And the Lord said unto Satan, Hast thou considered my servant Job, that there is none like him in the earth, a perfect and an upright man, one that feareth God, and escheweth evil? **and still he holdeth fast his integrity, although thou movedst me against him, to destroy him without cause.** *4 And Satan answered the Lord, and said, Skin for skin, yea, all that a man hath will he give for his life. 5 But* **put forth thine hand now, and touch his bone and his flesh, and he will curse thee to thy face.** *6 And the Lord said unto Satan, Behold, he is in thine hand; but save his life. 7 So went Satan forth from the presence of the Lord, and smote Job with sore boils from the sole of his foot unto his crown. 8 And he took him a potsherd to scrape himself withal; and he sat down among the ashes. 9 Then said his wife unto him, Dost thou still retain thine integrity? curse God, and die. 10 But he said unto her, Thou speakest as one of the foolish women speaketh. What? shall we receive good at the hand of God, and shall we not receive evil?* **In all this did not Job sin with his lips.**

In all of Job's attacks, he kept the faith. At the end of the Book of Job, God appeared to Job and gave him more insight. God used this test and the attacks of the devil to teach Job. In the end, God gave Job double for his trouble, and he learned a great lesson.

Job 42:12-13 (KJV)
12 **So the Lord blessed the latter end of Job more than his beginning:** *for he had fourteen thousand sheep, and six thousand camels, and a thousand yoke of oxen, and a thousand she asses. 13 He had also seven sons and three daughters.*

Job endured and kept his faith in God through the whole attack of the enemy and was victorious. The Lord was very pitiful and showed Job tender mercy.

James 5:11 (KJV)
11 Behold, we count them happy which endure. Ye have heard of the patience of Job, and have seen the end of the Lord; that the Lord is very pitiful, and of tender mercy.

Another person who came under heavy attack from the enemy about their faith was Peter before Jesus went to the cross. Jesus warned Peter that the devil wanted to sift him like wheat, but Jesus had prayed for him that his faith would not fail. Jesus said that after he was converted from this attack, for him to strengthen his brothers.

Luke 22:31-32 (KJV)
31 And the Lord said, Simon, Simon, behold, Satan hath desired to have you, that he may sift you as wheat: 32 But I have prayed for thee, that thy faith fail not: and when thou art converted, strengthen thy brethren.

The devil attacked Peter when Christ was going through the trial of the Cross. Peter thought his faith was solid in Christ, but it had never been tested. When Peter was tested with a fiery trial, he denied knowing Jesus. Peter thought he was ready to go to prison and die for Christ, but his faith and commitment level were not there yet.

Luke 22:33 (KJV)
33 And he said unto him, Lord, I am ready to go with thee, both into prison, and to death.

Jesus knew Peter would go through a sifting of his faith, but He prayed that when Peter recovered from this attack, he would return and strengthen his brethren. We know that after Jesus rose from the dead, He restored Peter and prophesied that Peter would die on a cross. After Jesus rose from the dead and appeared to the Apostles, He asked Peter three times if he loved Him. It is interesting to note that Peter denied he knew Christ three times.

John 21:15-19 (KJV)
*15 So when they had dined, Jesus saith to Simon Peter, Simon, son of Jonas, lovest thou me more than these? He saith unto him, Yea, Lord; thou knowest that I love thee. He saith unto him, Feed my lambs. 16 He saith to him again the second time, Simon, son of Jonas, lovest thou me? He saith unto him, Yea, Lord; thou knowest that I love thee. He saith unto him, Feed my sheep. 17 He saith unto him the third time, Simon, son of Jonas, lovest thou me? Peter was grieved because he said unto him the third time, Lovest thou me? And he said unto him, Lord, thou knowest all things; thou knowest that I love thee. Jesus saith unto him, Feed my sheep. 18 **Verily, verily, I say unto thee, When thou wast young, thou girdest thyself, and walkedst whither thou wouldest: but when thou shalt be old, thou shalt stretch forth thy hands, and another shall gird thee, and carry thee whither thou wouldest not. 19 This spake he, signifying by what death he should glorify God.** And when he had spoken this, he saith unto him, Follow me.*

We know from history and the Scriptures that Peter was restored to his faith in Christ and became a prominent leader in the early Church. We also know from history that Peter was crucified on a cross upside down because of his faith in Christ. Peter had fully converted to a strong and undeniable faith in Christ. All true Christians will go through one test or another regarding their faith in Christ. God wants to know if you are willing to die for what you believe, and when faced with death, you will not deny Him.

The devil will come to test your faith; if you are weak in faith or lack understanding of God and His Word, you will fall away. There is no such thing as untested faith. True faith will always come out on top through every test, and this is why we can count it all joy when we are being tested, knowing that we are being perfected.

James 1:3-4 (KJV)
3 Knowing this, that the trying of your faith worketh patience. 4 But let patience have her perfect work, that ye may be perfect and entire, wanting nothing.

The Apostle Peter wrote in one of his letters about the trial of our faith. Peter, of all people, knew what it was like to be tried by fire. Let's read what he had to say about the trial of your faith.

1 Peter 1:6-9 (KJV)
*6 Wherein ye greatly rejoice, though now for a season, if need be, ye are in heaviness through manifold temptations: 7 **That the trial of your faith, being much more precious than of gold that perisheth, though it be tried with fire, might be found unto praise and honour and glory at the appearing of Jesus Christ:** 8 Whom having not seen, ye love; in whom, though now ye see him not, yet believing, ye rejoice with joy unspeakable and full of glory: 9 **Receiving the end of your faith, even the salvation of your souls.***

We have an enemy of our soul who will challenge and test your faith. The devil first comes to steal your understanding from God's Word, and when he fails, he will come to test to see if you really believe what you believe. In the middle of your greatest trial or test, he is trying to see if you will doubt God and give up on your faith. Those who love and genuinely believe in God will pass every test.

In conclusion, there is a real enemy called the devil, and you may not see him, but he is there to test your faith. God uses the devil to see who has faith and who does not. In the end, if you have faith, you will defeat the devil and take back everything he tries to steal from you. The most important thing is that you keep the faith and never doubt God or falsely accuse God of not being good when you are going through a battle. If you win the battle, your faith will be found to praise and honor God. You will defeat the devil as you hold fast to the truth of God's Word by using it like a sword and take the shield of faith to quench all the fiery darts of the wicked one. Stand strong in the Lord, and your faith will overcome all attacks from the enemy.

CHAPTER 5

Everlasting New Covenant

If you are going to understand God and the faith that pleases Him, you have to know what a covenant is. God used what man knew about ancient blood covenants to reveal what He would do in both the Old and New Covenants. The Bible consists of what we call the Old Testament and the New Testament. Another word for Testament is Covenant, and you cannot understand the Bible if you don't know what it means to make a covenant. Once you understand covenants, your faith will be strengthened. In this chapter, I will dig deeper into ancient man-made covenants and how this applies to God's Covenants.

God is a *Covenant Maker, Covenant Keeper, Covenant Revealer,* and *Covenant Enabler.* Whenever God looks at humanity, He thinks of everything according to covenant. God sees people either keeping His Covenant, breaking His Covenant, or not in His Covenant. The New Covenant plays an important role in your faith and inheriting the *Promises* of God. When you understand what it means to be in Covenant with God, your faith will soar to new heights.

The word covenant in the Bible means cutting, treaty, alliance, agreement, or a compact (by passing between pieces of a sacrifice). People who lived during ancient times made blood covenants, which was an agreement to be allies. A blood covenant is a legally binding sacred agreement with serious responsibilities between two or more parties to perform promises to each other. If the covenant was faithfully committed to, it would bring blessings or curses if broken. Blood covenants were a series of rituals performed between two parties; whereby unbreakable agreements were made. These rituals involved a series of actions that were very important when making the blood covenant. All these actions represented something important in the cutting of a covenant.

Here is an example of what an ancient blood covenant ceremonial ritual would look like:

ANCIENT BLOOD COVENANT CEREMONIAL RITUALS

1. Terms of the Covenant – Both parties stood before a witness who heard the terms of the covenant proclaimed, which included blessings if the terms were kept and curses if the terms were broken.

2. Cut the Covenant – An animal or animals were cut in half, and both parties would walk between the two halves of the animal(s). The walking between the dead animal(s) and over the dead animal(s) blood represented that they must die and spill their own blood if they broke the covenant, just like the sacrificed animal(s) spilled its blood.

3. **Name Changed** – In cutting the covenant, each party either changed their name or took part of the other party's name and incorporated it into their own.

4. **Sign of the Covenant** – They made a recognizable cut and scar on their bodies, usually the hand, and mingled the cut with each other's blood. Their scar was a visual reminder of the covenant they had made whenever they looked at it or others saw the scar.

5. **Memorial Meal** – They ate a meal together, which included a loaf of bread broken in half, and they drank wine as a symbol of the blood.

6. **Exchanged Something of Value** – They exchanged coats, robes, garments, belts, armor, or weapons.

7. **Marker Placed** – They placed a heap of rocks or planted a tree where the covenant was cut to remember the covenant between the two parties.

COVENANTS HAD FOUR BASIC PARTS:

1. **Promises** – A Declaration of Blessings received if the covenant is kept.

2. **Terms** – Vows (Responsibilities, Expectations, and Curses if not kept).

3. **Blood** – Two-fold Symbolism (Life to you if you kept it and death if you broke it).

4. **Seal** – A Mark or Symbol on the body.

Once you understand how these ancient covenants were cut, the Old Testament and the New Testament take on more meaning. As you read the Book of Genesis, the different requirements God expected of Abraham make more sense. When God visited Abraham, He established His Covenant in a way that Abraham and the people of the earth could relate to regarding covenant-making. Understanding the cutting of ancient covenants will also help you understand the New Covenant that was made with the blood of Jesus.

Ancient covenants were a big deal and not to be taken lightly. Anyone who made a covenant was very committed about keeping the terms of the covenant. They understood this type of blood covenant was a lifetime contract that meant blessings if they kept it, or curses of death if they broke it. This is the blood covenant God first made with Abraham and then made in Christ. A covenant with God is an everlasting unbreakable contract with heavy consequences for anyone who breaks it. When you become a Christian by making Jesus your Lord, you enter into the Everlasting New Covenant.

Now, I will reveal from the Old Testament Scriptures an example of this type of ancient covenant-making being made between God and Abraham. Jacob also entered the Abrahamic Covenant as his inheritance, and King David made a covenant with Jonathan after defeating Goliath.

ABRAHAMIC COVENANT

1. Terms of the Covenant – God first established the terms of the covenant by making promises to Abram.

Genesis 12:1-3 (KJV)
1 Now the Lord had said unto Abram, Get thee out of thy country,
and from thy kindred, and from thy father's house, unto a land that
*I will shew thee: 2 **And I will make of thee a great nation, and I***
will bless thee, and make thy name great; and thou shalt be a
blessing: 3 And I will bless them that bless thee, and curse him
that curseth thee: and in thee shall all families of the earth be
blessed.

2. Cut the Covenant – God Himself passed through the dead animals
    that Abram sacrificed as a smoking furnace and a burning lamp when
    making the Abrahamic Covenant.

    Genesis 15:8-17 (KJV)
    8 And he said, Lord God, whereby shall I know that I shall inherit
    it? 9 And he said unto him, Take me an heifer of three years old,
    and a she goat of three years old, and a ram of three years old, and
    a turtledove, and a young pigeon. 10 And he took unto him all these,
    and divided them in the midst, and laid each piece one against
    another: but the birds divided he not. 11 And when the fowls came
    down upon the carcases, Abram drove them away. 12 And when the
    sun was going down, a deep sleep fell upon Abram; and, lo, an horror
    of great darkness fell upon him. 13 And he said unto Abram, Know
    of a surety that thy seed shall be a stranger in a land that is not theirs,
    and shall serve them; and they shall afflict them four hundred years;
    14 And also that nation, whom they shall serve, will I judge: and
    afterward shall they come out with great substance. 15 And thou
    shalt go to thy fathers in peace; thou shalt be buried in a good old
    age. 16 But in the fourth generation they shall come hither again:
    *for the iniquity of the Amorites is not yet full. 17 **And it came to***
    pass, that, when the sun went down, and it was dark, behold a
    smoking furnace, and a burning lamp that passed between those
    pieces.

3. **Name Changed** – God changed Abram's name to Abraham as a part of the covenant He made with him. Abram means exalted father, and Abraham means father of many. God changed Abram's name to Abraham because a part of His Covenant with him was to make Abraham a father of multitudes.

    > *Genesis 17:1-7 (KJV)*
    > *1 And when Abram was ninety years old and nine, the Lord appeared to Abram, and said unto him, I am the Almighty God; walk before me, and be thou perfect. 2 And I will make my covenant between me and thee, and will multiply thee exceedingly. 3 And Abram fell on his face: and God talked with him, saying, 4 As for me, behold, my covenant is with thee, and thou shalt be a father of many nations. 5 **Neither shall thy name any more be called Abram, but thy name shall be Abraham; for a father of many nations have I made thee.** 6 And I will make thee exceeding fruitful, and I will make nations of thee, and kings shall come out of thee. 7 And I will establish my covenant between me and thee and thy seed after thee in their generations for an everlasting covenant, to be a God unto thee, and to thy seed after thee.*

4. **Sign of the Covenant** – God instituted circumcision as a sign of the Covenant between Him, Abraham, and Abraham's descendants. The cutting of the foreskin was a sign or token of the Abrahamic Covenant. Anyone who was not circumcised in Abraham's lineage was breaking God's covenant.

    > *Genesis 17:9-14 (KJV)*
    > *9 And God said unto Abraham, Thou shalt keep my covenant therefore, thou, and thy seed after thee in their generations. 10 **This is my covenant, which ye shall keep, between me and you and thy seed after thee; Every man child among you shall be circumcised. 11 And ye shall circumcise the flesh of your foreskin; and it shall**

*be a token of the covenant betwixt me and you. 12 And he that is eight days old shall be circumcised among you, every man child in your generations, he that is born in the house, or bought with money of any stranger, which is not of thy seed. 13 He that is born in thy house, and he that is bought with thy money, must needs be circumcised: **and my covenant shall be in your flesh for an everlasting covenant.** 14 And the uncircumcised man child whose flesh of his foreskin is not circumcised, that soul shall be cut off from his people; he hath broken my covenant.*

5. Memorial Meal – God visited Abraham in the form of three men, representing the Father, Son, and Holy Spirit. They ate a meal with Abraham and confirmed the Covenant He was making with him.

Genesis 18:1-8 (KJV)
*1 And the Lord appeared unto him in the plains of Mamre: and he sat in the tent door in the heat of the day; 2 **And he lift up his eyes and looked, and, lo, three men stood by him:** and when he saw them, he ran to meet them from the tent door, and bowed himself toward the ground, 3 And said, My Lord, if now I have found favour in thy sight, pass not away, I pray thee, from thy servant: 4 Let a little water, I pray you, be fetched, and wash your feet, and rest yourselves under the tree: 5 **And I will fetch a morsel of bread, and comfort ye your hearts; after that ye shall pass on: for therefore are ye come to your servant. And they said, So do, as thou hast said. 6 And Abraham hastened into the tent unto Sarah, and said, Make ready quickly three measures of fine meal, knead it, and make cakes upon the hearth. 7 And Abraham ran unto the herd, and fetcht a calf tender and good, and gave it unto a young man; and he hasted to dress it. 8 And he took butter, and milk, and the calf which he had dressed, and set it before them; and he stood by them under the tree, and they did eat.***

6. **Exchanged Something of Value** – We don't see this part of the covenant with God and Abraham, but you do see this when David made a covenant with Johnathan after he defeated Goliath. In the New Testament, we know God gives us His armor to wear (Ephesians 6:10-17).

> *1 Samuel 18:3-4 (KJV)*
> *3 Then Jonathan and David made a covenant, because he loved him as his own soul. 4 And Jonathan stripped himself of the robe that was upon him, and gave it to David, and his garments, even to his sword, and to his bow, and to his girdle.*

7. **Marker Placed** – When Jacob entered the Covenant God made with his grandfather Abraham, God visited him in a dream. In this dream, he saw a ladder reaching heaven, and the angels of God were ascending and descending upon a ladder. Jacob used the pillow he was sleeping on as a pillar, poured water upon it, and then made a vow to God. The rock became the marker he used as he entered the Abrahamic Covenant.

> *Genesis 28:10-22 (KJV)*
> *10 And Jacob went out from Beersheba, and went toward Haran. 11 And he lighted upon a certain place, and tarried there all night, because the sun was set; **and he took of the stones of that place, and put them for his pillows, and lay down in that place to sleep.** 12 And he dreamed, and behold a ladder set up on the earth, and the top of it reached to heaven: and behold the angels of God ascending and descending on it. 13 And, behold, the Lord stood above it, and said, I am the Lord God of Abraham thy father, and the God of Isaac: the land whereon thou liest, to thee will I give it, and to thy seed; 14 And thy seed shall be as the dust of the earth, and thou shalt spread abroad to the west, and to the east, and to the north, and to*

*the south: and in thee and in thy seed shall all the families of the earth be blessed. 15 And, behold, I am with thee, and will keep thee in all places whither thou goest, and will bring thee again into this land; for I will not leave thee, until I have done that which I have spoken to thee of. 16 And Jacob awaked out of his sleep, and he said, Surely the Lord is in this place; and I knew it not. 17 And he was afraid, and said, How dreadful is this place! this is none other but the house of God, and this is the gate of heaven. 18 **And Jacob rose up early in the morning, and took the stone that he had put for his pillows, and set it up for a pillar, and poured oil upon the top of it.** 19 And he called the name of that place Bethel: but the name of that city was called Luz at the first. 20 And Jacob vowed a vow, saying, If God will be with me, and will keep me in this way that I go, and will give me bread to eat, and raiment to put on, 21 So that I come again to my father's house in peace; then shall the Lord be my God: 22 **And this stone, which I have set for a pillar, shall be God's house:** and of all that thou shalt give me I will surely give the tenth unto thee.*

Now let's get into the **Everlasting New Covenant** Jesus made when He died, was buried, and rose again. The Lord Himself instituted the same rituals from ancient covenants when He made a New Covenant with all who would believe in Him.

EVERLASTING NEW COVENANT

1. Terms of the Covenant – The terms of the New Covenant are the very Words of Christ. We are commanded to obey all that Jesus taught. His very words will judge us on Judgment Day, whether we obeyed them or not.

Matthew 28:18-20 (KJV)
18 And Jesus came and spake unto them, saying, All power is given unto me in heaven and in earth. 19 Go ye therefore, and teach all nations, baptizing them in the name of the Father, and of the Son, and of the Holy Ghost: 20 **Teaching them to observe all things whatsoever I have commanded you:** *and, lo, I am with you always, even unto the end of the world. Amen.*

John 12:47-50 (KJV)
47 And if any man hear my words, and believe not, I judge him not: for I came not to judge the world, but to save the world. 48 **He that rejecteth me, and receiveth not my words, hath one that judgeth him: the word that I have spoken, the same shall judge him in the last day.** *49 For I have not spoken of myself;* **but the Father which sent me, he gave me a commandment, what I should say, and what I should speak.** *50 And I know that his commandment is life everlasting:* **whatsoever I speak therefore, even as the Father said unto me, so I speak.**

2. Cut The Covenant – The New Covenant was cut when Jesus spilled His Blood and died on the Cross. Jesus became the sacrifice that was represented in ancient covenants that both parties walked through. The New Covenant was made in the Blood of Jesus.

John 1:29 (KJV)
29 The next day John seeth Jesus coming unto him, and saith, **Behold the Lamb of God, which taketh away the sin of the world.**

Hebrews 12:24 (KJV)
24 **And to Jesus the mediator of the new covenant, and to the blood of sprinkling,** *that speaketh better things than that of Abel.*

Hebrews 13:20-21 (KJV)
20 **Now the God of peace, that brought again from the dead our Lord Jesus, that great shepherd of the sheep, through the blood of the everlasting covenant, 21** *Make you perfect in every good work*

to do his will, working in you that which is wellpleasing in his sight, through Jesus Christ; to whom be glory for ever and ever. Amen.

3. Name Changed – When Jesus died, was buried, and rose again, He was given a Name above all other names. It is His New Name, the **Lord Jesus Christ of Nazareth,** that we can pray and ask God for answers to our prayers. Overcoming Christians are also given a stone with a new name written on it that only they and God will know. God also puts the new name of God and the name of the New Jerusalem city on those who overcome and go to heaven.

Philippians 2:5-10 (KJV)
*5 Let this mind be in you, which was also in Christ Jesus: 6 Who, being in the form of God, thought it not robbery to be equal with God: 7 But made himself of no reputation, and took upon him the form of a servant, and was made in the likeness of men: 8 And being found in fashion as a man, he humbled himself, and became obedient unto death, even the death of the cross. 9 **Wherefore God also hath highly exalted him, and given him a name which is above every name: 10 That at the name of Jesus every knee should bow, of things in heaven, and things in earth, and things under the earth;***

Acts 2:36 (KJV)
*36 Therefore let all the house of Israel know assuredly, **that God hath made the same Jesus, whom ye have crucified, both Lord and Christ.***

John 16:23-24 (KJV)
*23 And in that day ye shall ask me nothing. Verily, verily, I say unto you, **Whatsoever ye shall ask the Father in my name, he will give it you. 24 Hitherto have ye asked nothing in my name:** ask, and ye shall receive, that your joy may be full.*

Revelation 2:17 (KJV)
*17 He that hath an ear, let him hear what the Spirit saith unto the churches; To him that overcometh will I give to eat of the hidden manna, **and will give him a white stone, and in the stone a new name written, which no man knoweth saving he that receiveth it.***

Revelation 3:12 (KJV)
*12 Him that overcometh will I make a pillar in the temple of my God, and he shall go no more out: **and I will write upon him the name of my God, and the name of the city of my God, which is new Jerusalem,** which cometh down out of heaven from my God: **and I will write upon him my new name.***

4. Sign of the Covenant – The holes in Jesus' hands from being Crucified and His pierced side are the sign of the New Covenant. Jesus still has the holes in His hand and the piercing in His side, even after He rose from the dead. The wounds Jesus took on the Cross will forever be the Sign and Token of the New Covenant.

John 20:24-27 (KJV)
*24 But Thomas, one of the twelve, called Didymus, was not with them when Jesus came. 25 The other disciples therefore said unto him, We have seen the Lord. But he said unto them, **Except I shall see in his hands the print of the nails, and put my finger into the print of the nails, and thrust my hand into his side, I will not believe.** 26 And after eight days again his disciples were within, and Thomas with them: then came Jesus, the doors being shut, and stood in the midst, and said, Peace be unto you. 27 Then saith he to Thomas, **Reach hither thy finger, and behold my hands; and reach hither thy hand, and thrust it into my side: and be not faithless, but believing.***

5. Memorial Meal – On the night before Jesus was arrested and went to the Cross, He ate the Passover meal with His disciples and instituted Communion. Communion was the breaking of bread and drinking of the vine with His disciples. The bread represented His body that was to be broken, and the cup of the vine represented His blood that was about to be spilled. Whenever we take Communion, we share a meal with God, remembering what Jesus did to ratify the **Everlasting New Covenant.** Jesus was also betrayed by one of His disciples on this night.

> *Luke 22:13-16 (KJV)*
> *13 And they went, and found as he had said unto them: **and they made ready the passover.** 14 And when the hour was come, he sat down, and the twelve apostles with him. 15 And he said unto them, **With desire I have desired to eat this passover with you before I suffer:** 16 For I say unto you, I will not any more eat thereof, until it be fulfilled in the kingdom of God.*

> *Mark 14:22-25 (KJV)*
> *22 **And as they did eat, Jesus took bread, and blessed, and brake it, and gave to them, and said, Take, eat: this is my body. 23 And he took the cup, and when he had given thanks, he gave it to them: and they all drank of it.** 24 And he said unto them, This is my blood of the new testament, which is shed for many. 25 Verily I say unto you, I will drink no more of the fruit of the vine, until that day that I drink it new in the kingdom of God.*

> *1 Corinthians 11:23-26 (KJV)*
> *23 For I have received of the Lord that which also I delivered unto you, **that the Lord Jesus the same night in which he was betrayed took bread: 24 And when he had given thanks, he brake it, and said, Take, eat: this is my body, which is broken for you: this do in remembrance of me. 25 After the same manner also he took the cup, when he had supped, saying, this cup is the new***

testament in my blood: this do ye, as oft as ye drink it, in remembrance of me. 26 For as often as ye eat this bread, and drink this cup, ye do shew the Lord's death till he come.

6. Exchanged Something of Value – God gives us His armor in the New Covenant, just like when Jonathan gave King David his armor when he made a covenant with him. New Testament believers are granted the privilege of wearing the whole armor of God to fight the devil. God's armor was first revealed in the Book of Isaiah.

Isaiah 59:16-18 (KJV)
*16 And he saw that there was no man, and wondered that there was no intercessor: therefore his arm brought salvation unto him; and his righteousness, it sustained him. 17 **For he put on righteousness as a breastplate, and an helmet of salvation upon his head; and he put on the garments of vengeance for clothing, and was clad with zeal as a cloak.** 18 According to their deeds, accordingly he will repay, fury to his adversaries, recompence to his enemies; to the islands he will repay recompence.*

Ephesians 6:10-17 (KJV)
*10 Finally, my brethren, be strong in the Lord, and in the power of his might. 11 **Put on the whole armour of God,** that ye may be able to stand against the wiles of the devil. 12 For we wrestle not against flesh and blood, but against principalities, against powers, against the rulers of the darkness of this world, against spiritual wickedness in high places. 13 **Wherefore take unto you the whole armour of God,** that ye may be able to withstand in the evil day, and having done all, to stand. 14 Stand therefore, having your loins girt about with truth, and having on the breastplate of righteousness; 15 And your feet shod with the preparation of the gospel of peace; 16 Above all, taking the shield of faith, wherewith ye shall be able to quench all the fiery darts of the wicked. 17 And take the helmet of salvation, and the sword of the Spirit, which is the word of God:*

Romans 13:12 (KJV)
*12 The night is far spent, the day is at hand: let us therefore cast off the works of darkness, **and let us put on the armour of light.***

7. Marker Placed – The very Cross of Christ is the spiritual marker placed to testify of the New Covenant we have in Christ Jesus. The Cross is a symbol of the death of Christ, and it is also a symbol of what Christians must do to be followers of Christ. Jesus commanded His followers to take up their Cross daily and deny themselves. The Cross of Christ is the only thing we should glory in as Christians.

    Matthew 16:24-26 (KJV)
    24 Then said Jesus unto his disciples, If any man will come after me, let him deny himself, and take up his cross, and follow me. 25 For whosoever will save his life shall lose it: and whosoever will lose his life for my sake shall find it. 26 For what is a man profited, if he shall gain the whole world, and lose his own soul? or what shall a man give in exchange for his soul?

    Galatians 6:14 (KJV)
    14 But God forbid that I should glory, save in the cross of our Lord Jesus Christ, by whom the world is crucified unto me, and I unto the world.

Remember, the Word of God and His Promises are based upon a Covenant. This is vital to understand because when you believe God for a miracle or answer to your prayer, God wants His children to know He legally bound Himself to a Covenant to fulfill His Word. When we come to God for salvation or any other problem, God wants us to have faith that He has no option but to fulfill His Word and keep the New Covenant.

I want to pose a jaw-dropping thought to you about covenants and God. When two people enter a covenant, there are either blessings if kept or cursings if the covenant is broken. In the Covenant of God, He placed a curse upon Himself if He broke His Covenant or Word. God bound Himself to keep His Word to us with a Covenant Promise. This means if God broke the Covenant He made with us, He would have to be eternally judged by His own Laws.

However, the beauty of all this is that God cannot lie and will never break His end of the Covenant. Jesus died on the Cross, not because God broke the covenant but because man broke covenant with God. Jesus had to die on the Cross because humankind broke their end of the bargain with God. But when it comes to God, He is the faithful God that keeps His Covenant.

> *Deuteronomy 7:9 (KJV)*
> *9 Know therefore that the Lord thy God, he is God, the faithful God, which keepeth covenant and mercy with them that love him and keep his commandments to a thousand generations;*
>
> *Psalm 89:34 (KJV)*
> *34 My covenant will I not break, nor alter the thing that is gone out of my lips.*

When you discover what covenants are and that God made one with us in Christ Jesus, your faith will never be the same. A revelation of the soul-binding power of a covenant will change you forever. Your faith can rest strongly on the fact that God will keep His Covenant Word to us. The *Precious Promises* granted to us in the New Covenant are sure and steadfast. The New Covenant made in Christ is established upon *Better Promises* than the Old Covenant made with Moses.

Hebrews 8:6 (KJV)
*6 But now hath he obtained a more excellent ministry, **by how much also he is the mediator of a better covenant, which was established upon better promises.***

The Bible also promises that God will show His Covenant to those that fear Him. God's Covenant is a secret and not revealed to everyone. If you are reading this book, God has chosen to reveal His secret Covenant to you.

Psalm 25:14 (KJV)
14 The secret of the Lord is with them that fear him; and he will shew them his covenant.

Another important fact to remember about the New Covenant is that it is everlasting. The **Everlasting New Covenant** that God made in Christ is the final Covenant He will ever make with humankind. The Covenant God made in the blood of Jesus will last for all eternity. When you enter the **Everlasting New Covenant**, your faith can rest assured that God will not break His Word to you. You can stand on this **Everlasting Covenant** and know that God will fulfill His promises to you.

Genesis 17:7 (KJV)
*7 And I will establish my covenant between me and thee and thy seed after thee in their generations for an **everlasting covenant**, to be a God unto thee, and to thy seed after thee.*

Isaiah 55:3 (KJV)
*3 Incline your ear, and come unto me: hear, and your soul shall live; and I will make an **everlasting covenant** with you, even the sure mercies of David.*

Isaiah 61:8 (KJV)
8 For I the Lord love judgment, I hate robbery for burnt offering;
*and I will direct their work in truth, and I will make an **everlasting***
***covenant** with them.*

Hebrews 13:20-21 (KJV)
20 Now the God of peace, that brought again from the dead our
Lord Jesus, that great shepherd of the sheep, through the blood of the
***everlasting covenant**, 21 Make you perfect in every good work to do*
his will, working in you that which is wellpleasing in his sight,
through Jesus Christ; to whom be glory for ever and ever. Amen.

Our faith rests in the assurance that it is impossible for God to lie and break His Covenant.

Numbers 23:19 (KJV)
*19 **God is not a man, that he should lie;** neither the son of man,*
*that he should repent: **hath he said, and shall he not do it? or hath***
he spoken, and shall he not make it good?

In conclusion, our Mighty God is a Covenant-making and Covenant-keeping God. God wanted man to trust Him fully, so He bound Himself with a Blood Covenant. Your faith will forever be changed when you understand what a Covenant means and how God made one with us. God didn't have to cut a Covenant with us through Jesus, but He did, and now we can fully trust Him. We can come to God, in full assurance of faith, that He will do everything He *Promised* in His Word that He said He would do. God has done everything for us; all we have to do is have faith in the Covenant making God.

CHAPTER 6

Whatsoever is Not of Faith is Sin

Previously, I went into great detail about ancient covenant-making and the New Covenant in Christ. God cut the New Covenant when Christ went to the Cross, died, and rose again. God has done everything on His end to keep the New Covenant. Now, we must ask ourselves, what is our responsibility, and what must we do to keep the New Covenant? All covenants are based upon two people holding their end of the agreement. In this chapter, I will teach what God requires in the New Covenant and what He considers sin.

We know someone is saved and enters the New Covenant by believing in their heart that God raised Jesus from the dead and confessing Him as Lord.

Romans 10:8-13 (KJV)
*8 But what saith it? The word is nigh thee, even in thy mouth, and in thy heart: that is, the word of faith, which we preach; 9 **That if thou shalt confess with thy mouth the Lord Jesus, and shalt believe in***

thine heart that God hath raised him from the dead, thou shalt be saved. 10 For with the heart man believeth unto righteousness; and with the mouth confession is made unto salvation. 11 For the scripture saith, Whosoever believeth on him shall not be ashamed. 12 For there is no difference between the Jew and the Greek: for the same Lord over all is rich unto all that call upon him. 13 For whosoever shall call upon the name of the Lord shall be saved.

I want to reveal a hidden secret in the word *confess* found in verse 9 of Romans Chapter 10. The word *confess* means covenant acknowledgment through a promise. This means a person uses their mouth to enter the New Covenant by making Jesus their Lord. The first part of salvation is believing that God raised Jesus from the dead, and the second is confessing Jesus as Lord.

When someone confesses Jesus being their Lord, they are making a covenant with their mouth to obey Jesus in all things. Jesus said, why do you call me Lord, Lord, and do not the things that I say? Your confession of making Jesus your Lord is a soul-binding covenant with your mouth to obey all the Words of the New Covenant spoken by Jesus.

Luke 6:46 (KJV)
46 And why call ye me, Lord, Lord, and do not the things which I say?

The only ones going to heaven are the ones who keep the New Covenant by obeying all the Words of Christ. True Christians continue doing God's will after they confess Jesus is their Lord. Confessing Jesus as Lord is not a get-out-of-jail-free card. Your confession of Jesus as your Lord means you will obey Him in all things.

Matthew 7:21-23 (KJV)
*21 Not every one that saith unto me, Lord, Lord, shall enter into the kingdom of heaven; but he that doeth the will of my Father which is in heaven. 22 Many will say to me in that day, Lord, Lord, have we not prophesied in thy name? and in thy name have cast out devils? and in thy name done many wonderful works? 23 **And then will I profess unto them, I never knew you: depart from me, ye that work iniquity.***

When Jesus said He never knew them, it was about them working iniquity. Jesus revealed a deep secret about true salvation and knowing God. A big part of how we know God is when we keep His Commandments and don't work iniquity. The work of iniquity is sinning, and those who continue in sin do not know God.

1 John 3:6-10 (KJV)
*6 **Whosoever abideth in him sinneth not: whosoever sinneth hath not seen him, neither known him.** 7 Little children, let no man deceive you: he that doeth righteousness is righteous, even as he is righteous. 8 He that committeth sin is of the devil; for the devil sinneth from the beginning. For this purpose the Son of God was manifested, that he might destroy the works of the devil. 9 **Whosoever is born of God doth not commit sin; for his seed remaineth in him: and he cannot sin, because he is born of God.** 10 In this the children of God are manifest, and the children of the devil: whosoever doeth not righteousness is not of God, neither he that loveth not his brother.*

Sin is the breaking of God's Commandments. Anyone who says they know God will not break His Commandments.

1 John 2:3-5 (KJV)
3 And hereby we do know that we know him, if we keep his commandments. 4 He that saith, I know him, and keepeth not his commandments, is a liar, and the truth is not in him. 5 But whoso

keepeth his word, in him verily is the love of God perfected: hereby know we that we are in him.

The way we know how someone knows God is by them keeping His Commandments. Another important truth about the New Covenant is revealed in the Book of Jeremiah, the prophet. In this Book, we can read where God prophesies about the New Covenant through Jeremiah. In this prophecy, we discover fundamental truths about the New Covenant found in Christ.

> *Jeremiah 31:31-34 (KJV)*
> *31 **Behold, the days come, saith the Lord, that I will make a new covenant with the house of Israel, and with the house of Judah:** 32 Not according to the covenant that I made with their fathers in the day that I took them by the hand to bring them out of the land of Egypt; which my covenant they brake, although I was an husband unto them, saith the Lord: 33 But this shall be the covenant that I will make with the house of Israel; After those days, saith the Lord, I will put my law in their inward parts, and write it in their hearts; and will be their God, and they shall be my people. 34 **And they shall teach no more every man his neighbour, and every man his brother, saying, Know the Lord: for they shall all know me, from the least of them unto the greatest of them,** saith the Lord: for I will forgive their iniquity, and I will remember their sin no more.*

In this passage, we find God saying they shall all know Me. This means that the people found in the New Covenant wouldn't need a priest or someone else to teach them the laws of God. The Laws of God would be written in their hearts, and this is how they would know God. In the New Covenant, the Laws of God are written in our hearts, which ties in with our conscience and our faith. Now we can understand more deeply when the Bible says whatsoever is not of faith is sin. Our faith is tied to our conscience and the Laws of God written in our hearts.

Romans 14:22-23 (KJV)
*22 Hast thou faith? have it to thyself before God. Happy is he that condemneth not himself in that thing which he alloweth. 23 And he that doubteth is damned if he eat, because he eateth not of faith: **for whatsoever is not of faith is sin.***

This passage of Scripture refers to someone not feeling good in their conscience about something they should eat or not eat. The Apostle Paul tells them they need to follow their own inward law and not eat something if they don't feel in their conscience they should. Then, he ties this in with their faith and says whatsoever is not of faith is sin. If something doesn't feel right in your conscience, don't do it. In other words, if you don't believe in your conscience, you should do this, or you shouldn't do that, follow your conscience. This is what the Bible calls living by faith.

Romans 14:1-5 (KJV)
*1 **Him that is weak in the faith receive ye, but not to doubtful disputations.** 2 For one believeth that he may eat all things: another, who is weak, eateth herbs. 3 Let not him that eateth despise him that eateth not; and let not him which eateth not judge him that eateth: for God hath received him. 4 Who art thou that judgest another man's servant? to his own master he standeth or falleth. Yea, he shall be holden up: for God is able to make him stand. 5 One man esteemeth one day above another: another esteemeth every day alike. **Let every man be fully persuaded in his own mind.***

During New Testament times, Christians lived in a pagan society where they were offering meats sacrificed to idols. Some Christians didn't feel right in their conscience about eating this food, whereas others believed it was okay. The Apostle Paul taught them to follow their conscience about whether they should eat the food sacrificed to idols or not. Let's read about this situation in 1 Corinthians 8.

1 Corinthians 8:1-13 (KJV)

*1 Now as touching things offered unto idols, we know that we all have knowledge. Knowledge puffeth up, but charity edifieth. 2 And if any man think that he knoweth any thing, he knoweth nothing yet as he ought to know. 3 But if any man love God, the same is known of him. 4 As concerning therefore the eating of those things that are offered in sacrifice unto idols, **we know that an idol is nothing in the world, and that there is none other God but one.** 5 For though there be that are called gods, whether in heaven or in earth, (as there be gods many, and lords many,) 6 But to us there is but one God, the Father, of whom are all things, and we in him; and one Lord Jesus Christ, by whom are all things, and we by him. 7 **Howbeit there is not in every man that knowledge: for some with conscience of the idol unto this hour eat it as a thing offered unto an idol; and their conscience being weak is defiled. 8 But meat commendeth us not to God: for neither, if we eat, are we the better; neither, if we eat not, are we the worse.** 9 But take heed lest by any means this liberty of yours become a stumblingblock to them that are weak. 10 For if any man see thee which hast knowledge sit at meat in the idol's temple, shall not the conscience of him which is weak be emboldened to eat those things which are offered to idols; 11 And through thy knowledge shall the weak brother perish, for whom Christ died? 12 But when ye sin so against the brethren, **and wound their weak conscience,** ye sin against Christ. 13 Wherefore, if meat make my brother to offend, I will eat no flesh while the world standeth, lest I make my brother to offend.*

The Apostle Paul taught the idol was nothing, but if someone felt they shouldn't eat something in their conscience, they shouldn't. He also taught strong Christians shouldn't offend the weak brother or sister's conscience by eating things sacrificed to idols in front of them. Eating food offered to idols in front of someone with a weak conscience could embolden them to go against their conscience. If they sin against their conscience, they violate the Laws of God written in their hearts.

The Bible teaches we must protect and obey our conscience because God will judge us on Judgment Day based upon our conscience. Therefore, your heart and conscience have the Laws of God written upon them, and you must always obey your conscience. Living by your conscience is living by faith. The Laws of God written in your heart are what you believe to be true, and you must follow your faith in what you believe to be true.

> *Romans 2:11-16 (KJV)*
> *11 For there is no respect of persons with God. 12 For as many as have sinned without law shall also perish without law: and as many as have sinned in the law shall be judged by the law; 13 (For not the hearers of the law are just before God, but the doers of the law shall be justified. 14 **For when the Gentiles, which have not the law, do by nature the things contained in the law, these, having not the law, are a law unto themselves: 15 Which shew the work of the law written in their hearts, their conscience also bearing witness, and their thoughts the mean while accusing or else excusing one another;) 16 In the day when God shall judge the secrets of men by Jesus Christ according to my gospel.***

A big part of the New Covenant is living by faith or living by the Laws of God written in your heart and confirmed by your conscience. Anyone who has ever sinned against their conscience knows how brutally their conscience can accuse you and beat you up. You don't need anyone else to accuse you because your conscience can beat you up more than any other person or religious leader ever could.

The Bible says if you continually sin against your conscience, you sear it with a hot iron.

> *Timothy 4:2 (KJV)*
> *2 Speaking lies in hypocrisy; **having their conscience seared with a hot iron;***

A seared conscience has been burned to where it no longer convicts you of right or wrong. Anyone who has seared their conscience to this level has become a reprobate. A reprobate is someone who has sinned against God and their conscience so much that they no longer know right and wrong. They will call right wrong and wrong right. This is a terrifying place to be.

Romans 1:26-32 (KJV)
*26 For this cause God gave them up unto vile affections: for even their women did change the natural use into that which is against nature: 27 And likewise also the men, leaving the natural use of the woman, burned in their lust one toward another; men with men working that which is unseemly, and receiving in themselves that recompence of their error which was meet. 28 **And even as they did not like to retain God in their knowledge, God gave them over to a reprobate mind, to do those things which are not convenient;** 29 Being filled with all unrighteousness, fornication, wickedness, covetousness, maliciousness; full of envy, murder, debate, deceit, malignity; whisperers, 30 Backbiters, haters of God, despiteful, proud, boasters, inventors of evil things, disobedient to parents, 31 Without understanding, covenantbreakers, without natural affection, implacable, unmerciful: 32 Who knowing the judgment of God, that they which commit such things are worthy of death, not only do the same, but have pleasure in them that do them.*

In the New Covenant, when someone becomes a true Christian, the blood of Jesus is sprinkled in their heart and He revives their evil conscience.

Hebrews 10:21-22 (KJV)
*21 And having an high priest over the house of God; 22 **Let us draw near with a true heart in full assurance of faith, having our hearts sprinkled from an evil conscience,** and our bodies washed with pure water.*

The blood of Jesus revives the sinner's conscience and writes the Laws of God in their heart. As soon as the blood of Jesus is applied to their heart and evil conscience, the repentant sinner no longer wants to sin; this is how they know they are saved. They now have a firm conviction about right and wrong. Their own heart tells them what is right and what is wrong. Or another way to say it is I live by what I believe to be right in my heart, and I don't do things I believe are wrong. This is knowing God for themselves and having the Laws of God written in their hearts.

Hebrews 8:8-13 (KJV)
8 For finding fault with them, he saith, Behold, the days come, saith the Lord, when I will make a new covenant with the house of Israel and with the house of Judah: 9 Not according to the covenant that I made with their fathers in the day when I took them by the hand to lead them out of the land of Egypt; because they continued not in my covenant, and I regarded them not, saith the Lord. 10 For this is the covenant that I will make with the house of Israel after those days, saith the Lord; **I will put my laws into their mind, and write them in their hearts: and I will be to them a God, and they shall be to me a people: 11 And they shall not teach every man his neighbour, and every man his brother, saying, Know the Lord: for all shall know me, from the least to the greatest.** *12 For I will be merciful to their unrighteousness, and their sins and their iniquities will I remember no more. 13 In that he saith, A new covenant, he hath made the first old. Now that which decayeth and waxeth old is ready to vanish away.*

It is important to understand that your conscience may not always be right, but it is never right to go against it. This is a powerful secret to understand. God writes Laws in people's hearts, but they don't always have all the Laws or ways of God written in them yet. The Christian life is one of growing from faith to faith and glory to glory. We will continually grow in our knowledge of God and His Word, so protecting our fellow believers' consciences is imperative while they develop. We also must protect our own conscience.

Living by faith means you don't sin willfully. Willful sin means you know not to do something because your conscience convicts you, but you still do it, anyway. Anyone who commits a willful sin breaks the New Covenant, and no more sacrifice remains for their sin.

> *Hebrews 10:26-27 (KJV)*
> *26 For if we sin wilfully after that we have received the knowledge of the truth, there remaineth no more sacrifice for sins, 27 But a certain fearful looking for of judgment and fiery indignation, which shall devour the adversaries.*

Even in the Old Testament Law of Moses, there was no sacrifice for those who sinned willfully. In the Law of Moses, this was called presumptuous sin. There is a difference between presumptuous sin and ignorant sin. Ignorant sin means someone sinned without knowing in their conscience that it was a sin. They later found out it was a sin and needed to repent by offering a sacrifice to God. Presumptuous sin is when someone knowingly knows something was a sin against the Law of Moses and still does it.

> *Numbers 15:24-31 (KJV)*
> *24 Then it shall be, if ought be committed by ignorance without the knowledge of the congregation, that all the congregation shall offer one young bullock for a burnt offering, for a sweet savour unto the Lord, with his meat offering, and his drink offering, according to the manner, and one kid of the goats for a sin offering. 25 And the priest shall make an atonement for all the congregation of the children of Israel, and it shall be forgiven them; for it is ignorance: and they shall bring their offering, a sacrifice made by fire unto the Lord, and their sin offering before the Lord, for their ignorance: 26 And it shall be forgiven all the congregation of the children of Israel, and the stranger that sojourneth*

*among them; **seeing all the people were in ignorance. 27 And if any soul sin through ignorance,** then he shall bring a she goat of the first year for a sin offering. 28 **And the priest shall make an atonement for the soul that sinneth ignorantly, when he sinneth by ignorance before the Lord, to make an atonement for him; and it shall be forgiven him.** 29 **Ye shall have one law for him that sinneth through ignorance,** both for him that is born among the children of Israel, and for the stranger that sojourneth among them. 30 **But the soul that doeth ought presumptuously, whether he be born in the land, or a stranger, the same reproacheth the Lord; and that soul shall be cut off from among his people.** 31 Because he hath despised the word of the Lord, and hath broken his commandment, that soul shall utterly be cut off; his iniquity shall be upon him.*

Anyone who sins willfully against their conscience and counts the blood of the New Covenant as an unholy thing opens themselves up to the judgment of God. This type of person has trodden under their feet the Son of God and does despite to the Spirit of grace. This person will be judged by God.

Hebrews 10:29-31 (KJV)
*29 **Of how much sorer punishment, suppose ye, shall he be thought worthy, who hath trodden under foot the Son of God, and hath counted the blood of the covenant, wherewith he was sanctified, an unholy thing, and hath done despite unto the Spirit of grace?** 30 For we know him that hath said, Vengeance belongeth unto me, I will recompense, saith the Lord. And again, **The Lord shall judge his people.** 31 It is a fearful thing to fall into the hands of the living God.*

The Scriptures teach that if someone falls away, they crucify the Son of God afresh and put Him to an open shame.

Hebrews 6:4-6 (KJV)
4 For it is impossible for those who were once enlightened, and have
tasted of the heavenly gift, and were made partakers of the Holy Ghost,
5 And have tasted the good word of God, and the powers of the world
to come, 6 If they shall fall away, to renew them again unto repentance;
seeing they crucify to themselves the Son of God afresh, and put him
to an open shame.

We must take this New Covenant as seriously as God takes it. When you enter the New Covenant, you are committing to make Jesus your Lord by obeying His Commands and your conscience. There are powerful promises to this New Covenant, but also curses if we break the Covenant with God. Your Covenant with God is the most powerful thing you have and must be adhered to with your most holy faith.

We should take Communion regularly to remind us of this great New Covenant in Christ. There is also a warning about taking Communion unworthily because we can bring a curse upon ourselves. There were Christians in the Church of Corinthian who died early for taking Communion in an unworthy way. We must judge ourselves before taking Communion because the Holy Communion represents the New Covenant.

1 Corinthians 11:23-31 (KJV)
23 For I have received of the Lord that which also I delivered unto you,
that the Lord Jesus the same night in which he was betrayed took bread:
24 And when he had given thanks, he brake it, and said, Take, eat:
*this is my body, which is broken for you: **this do in remembrance of***
***me.** 25 After the same manner also he took the cup, when he had*
supped, saying, this cup is the new testament in my blood: this do ye, as
*oft as ye drink it, **in remembrance of me.** 26 For as often as ye eat this*
bread, and drink this cup, ye do shew the Lord's death till he come. 27
Wherefore whosoever shall eat this bread, and drink this cup of the

*Lord, unworthily, shall be guilty of the body and blood of the Lord.
28 But let a man examine himself, and so let him eat of that bread, and
drink of that cup. 29 **For he that eateth and drinketh unworthily,
eateth and drinketh damnation to himself, not discerning the Lord's
body.** 30 For this cause many are weak and sickly among you, and many
sleep. 31 **For if we would judge ourselves, we should not be judged.***

Faithful ministers of the Gospel will always lead you into keeping your
Covenant with God by obeying all the Words of Christ and your
conscience. They will never lead you to themselves, or you must only listen
to them to be right with God. God wants to lead His people by His Voice
and His Holy Spirit within you. God leads His people by the inward Voice
of the Holy Spirit, and the Holy Spirit works with your conscience. Your
conscience works with the Laws of God that are written in your heart and
mind. You can know God by following your conscience and being led by
His Holy Spirit.

Those who live by obeying their conscience find great freedom in Christ.
No one can place heavy yokes of bondage upon them. They will be free to
live by the moral code of God's Laws written in their hearts. Living by
your conscience is as simple as not doing what you don't feel is right and
doing what you feel is right in your heart.

Once you are living by faith and not violating your conscience, you can
make requests to God in prayer, and He will answer you.

1 John 3:19-22 (KJV)
*19 And hereby we know that we are of the truth, and shall assure our
hearts before him. 20 For if our heart condemn us, God is greater than
our heart, and knoweth all things. 21 **Beloved, if our heart condemn
us not, then have we confidence toward God. 22 And whatsoever we
ask, we receive of him, because we keep his commandments, and do
those things that are pleasing in his sight.***

God has called you to live by faith, which means living by the moral code of God written upon your heart. This all begins when you confess Jesus as your Lord. Learning to live by faith is the best way to live.

Habakkuk 2:4 (KJV)
*4 Behold, his soul which is lifted up is not upright in him: **but the just** **shall live by his faith.***

In conclusion, God has set you free, and this freedom is found in living by faith in the New Covenant. God has granted you the opportunity to know Him for yourself. Once you fully understand the New Covenant, you will never be the same. Jesus came to free people through His Word and taught them to live by the moral code of God's Laws written on their hearts. Living in the New Covenant of God is the most important decision you will ever make. The decision is for you to make today!

CHAPTER 7

The Author and
Finisher of Our Faith

Jesus is the *Author* and the *Finisher* of our faith. Jesus is the one who initiates and brings to completion our faith. If it wasn't for Jesus, we wouldn't have any faith. Before Jesus was born on this earth, few men understood what it was to live by faith. Jesus introduced a new way of living by faith during His earthly ministry. He started with a handful of men and taught them what living by the new way of faith was. In this chapter, I will reveal from the Scriptures how Jesus not only *Authors* our faith but also *Finishes* our faith.

The statement about Jesus being the *Author* and *Finisher* of our faith comes from the Book of Hebrews.

Hebrews 12:2 (KJV)
2 Looking unto Jesus the author and finisher of our faith; who for
the joy that was set before him endured the cross, despising the shame,
and is set down at the right hand of the throne of God.

Author means originator, founder, initiator, Prince, and Captain. *Finisher* means completer, perfecter, consummator, and one who brings to final attainment. Jesus is the One who not only originates our faith, but He is the One who brings our faith to final victory. Before Jesus came and taught the Jewish people what it was to live by faith, they lived under the Law of Moses.

Galatians 3:23 (KJV)
23 But before faith came, we were kept under the law, shut up unto
the faith which should afterwards be revealed.

The Law of Moses was given as a schoolmaster to bring us to Christ. The Law of Moses was put in place until Jesus, the Messiah, would come and fulfill it. Jesus did away with the Law of Moses when He fulfilled it by living and then dying on the cross for the sins of the world.

Galatians 3:24-25 (KJV)
24 Wherefore the law was our schoolmaster to bring us unto Christ,
that we might be justified by faith. 25 But after that faith is come,
we are no longer under a schoolmaster.

In Matthew Chapter 5, Jesus declared in the great Sermon on the Mount that He came not to destroy the Law or the prophets, but to fulfill them. He said that until heaven and earth pass, one jot or one tittle shall in no wise pass from the Law, till it was all fulfilled. He also taught that whoever broke any of the commandments would be least in the Kingdom of Heaven, but whoever did and taught them would be great in the kingdom of heaven.

Matthew 5:17-19 (KJV)
*17 Think not that I am come to destroy the law, or the prophets: I am not come to destroy, **but to fulfil**. 18 For verily I say unto you, Till heaven and earth pass, one jot or one tittle shall in no wise pass from the law, **till all be fulfilled**. 19 Whosoever therefore shall break one of these least commandments, and shall teach men so, he shall be called the least in the kingdom of heaven: but whosoever shall do and teach them, the same shall be called great in the kingdom of heaven.*

When Jesus died on the cross, He cried out, **"IT IS FINISHED,"** which was about Him fulfilling all the Law of Moses. The death of Jesus dying on the cross completely paid for humankind to be saved if they believed in Him.

John 19:28-30 (KJV)
*28 After this, **Jesus knowing that all things were now accomplished, that the scripture might be fulfilled**, saith, I thirst. 29 Now there was set a vessel full of vinegar: and they filled a spunge with vinegar, and put it upon hyssop, and put it to his mouth. 30 When Jesus therefore had received the vinegar, he said, **It is finished**: and he bowed his head, and gave up the ghost.*

The moment Jesus died on the cross was when the whole Law of Moses was fulfilled. By Jesus fulfilling the Law of Moses, those who believed in Him could be declared forgiven and righteous before God. Jesus paid the price for all the sins of humankind when He died on the cross. After Jesus died on the cross and rose again, everything changed.

When Jesus died on the cross, the veil in the Temple tore in two, thus signifying that we now have access to God.

Mark 15:37-38 (KJV)
*37 And Jesus cried with a loud voice, and gave up the ghost. 38 **And the veil of the temple was rent in twain from the top to the bottom.***

Hebrews 10:19-22 (KJV)
*19 Having therefore, brethren, boldness to enter into the holiest by the blood of Jesus, 20 **By a new and living way, which he hath consecrated for us, through the veil, that is to say, his flesh;** 21 And having an high priest over the house of God; 22 Let us draw near with a true heart in full assurance of faith, having our hearts sprinkled from an evil conscience, and our bodies washed with pure water.*

Believers no longer needed the Temple, because their bodies became the Temple of God.

2 Corinthians 6:16 (KJV)
*16 And what agreement hath the temple of God with idols? **for ye are the temple of the living God;** as God hath said, I will dwell in them, and walk in them; and I will be their God, and they shall be my people.*

We also know from history that the Roman army entirely destroyed the Jewish Temple in Jerusalem in 70 AD according to the prophecy of Jesus.

Matthew 24:1-2 (KJV)
*1 And Jesus went out, and departed from the temple: and his disciples came to him for to shew him the buildings of the temple. 2 And Jesus said unto them, See ye not all these things? verily I say unto you, **There shall not be left here one stone upon another, that shall not be thrown down.***

The Temple was the central spiritual location where the Jews went to fulfill the Law. The Jewish people met with God in the Temple and made sacrifices according to the Law of Moses. The Jews were supposed to come to Jerusalem, where the Temple was, three times a year, to fulfill the Feasts of the Lord. However, with the destruction of the Jewish Temple, the Jews couldn't completely fulfill the Law, even if they wanted to. The Jews were also dispersed all over the world and were not able to come to Jerusalem to celebrate the Feasts of the Lord three times a year.

The life, ministry, death, burial, and resurrection of Jesus changed everything. In the Book of Acts, God allowed the Gentiles to be a part of the salvation of God that was previously only available to the Jews. God also changed the Law during this time from the Law of Moses to the Law of faith. Some Jews who were saved at that time said the Gentiles should keep the Law of Moses, but when the Church leaders put together a council, they determined that the Christian Gentiles were not required to keep the Law of Moses.

> *Acts 15:5 (KJV)*
> *5 But there rose up certain of the sect of the Pharisees which believed, saying, **That it was needful to circumcise them, and to command them to keep the law of Moses.***

> *Acts 15:24 (KJV)*
> *24 Forasmuch as we have heard, that certain which went out from us have troubled you with words, subverting your souls, saying, **Ye must be circumcised, and keep the law: to whom we gave no such commandment:***

The New Gentile Christians had entered the New Covenant and were not required to live by the Old Covenant made by Moses. Living by faith had to do with entering the New Covenant by obeying all the Words of Christ and obeying their conscience. I covered this in the last chapter: *Whatsoever is Not of Faith is Sin.*

Jesus authored a whole new way of living by faith. Now faith gets into people's consciences and how they believe God for miracles. When Jesus was on the earth and recognized people's faith, it was about believing in Him and His ability to work miracles. Jesus was continually teaching and talking to His disciples about faith. Jesus measured people where they were, according to their faith.

I want to focus on how Jesus *Authored* and *Finished* His Apostles' faith. It is fascinating in the Scriptures to see what Jesus did to develop His disciples' faith. We can learn how Jesus starts and finishes our faith by studying what He did with His Apostles.

Soon after Jesus chose His twelve Apostles, He got on a ship and headed to the other side of the Sea of Galilee. While on the ship, Jesus fell asleep on a pillow and a great storm arose and filled the boat with water. These boats were small, so Jesus must have been sleeping in the water. Finally, the Apostles, fearing for their lives, woke Jesus up. Let's read this story together and see what Jesus does and says about their faith.

> *Mark 4:35-41 (KJV)*
> *35 And the same day, when the even was come, he saith unto them, Let us pass over unto the other side. 36 And when they had sent away the multitude, they took him even as he was in the ship. And there were also with him other little ships. 37 And there arose a great storm of wind, and the waves beat into the ship, so that it was now full. 38 And he was in the hinder part of the ship, asleep on a pillow: and they awake him, and say unto him, Master, carest thou not that we perish? 39 And he arose, and rebuked the wind, and said unto the sea, Peace, be still. And the wind ceased, and there was a great calm. 40 **And he said unto them, Why are ye so fearful? how is it that ye have no faith?** 41 And they feared exceedingly, and said one to another, What manner of man is this, that even the wind and the sea obey him?*

In this situation, Jesus said to His disciples they had no faith, and He asked why they were so fearful. We can see that Jesus started to put faith in them when they saw Him rebuking the wind and speaking to the sea, and they obeyed Him. This was very early in the ministry of Jesus. He wanted to show His disciples that God was with Him and He could work miracles and save their lives. God allowed these disciples to be put in a life-threatening situation so He could reveal His power through His Son Jesus. Jesus used His faith to rebuke the wind and calm the sea.

Let's look at another story in the Bible where the Apostles are in a boat again. In this story, Jesus comes to them walking on water. The sea is boisterous, and when they see Jesus, they are afraid. This time, Peter asks if he can walk on the water to Jesus. Let's read what happens.

Matthew 14:24-33 (KJV)
24 But the ship was now in the midst of the sea, tossed with waves: for the wind was contrary. 25 And in the fourth watch of the night Jesus went unto them, walking on the sea. 26 And when the disciples saw him walking on the sea, they were troubled, saying, It is a spirit; and they cried out for fear. 27 But straightway Jesus spake unto them, saying, **Be of good cheer; it is I; be not afraid.** *28 And Peter answered him and said, Lord, if it be thou, bid me come unto thee on the water. 29 And he said, Come. And when Peter was come down out of the ship, he walked on the water, to go to Jesus. 30* **But when he saw the wind boisterous, he was afraid;** *and beginning to sink, he cried, saying, Lord, save me. 31 And immediately Jesus stretched forth his hand, and caught him, and said unto him,* **O thou of little faith, wherefore didst thou doubt?** *32 And when they were come into the ship, the wind ceased. 33 Then they that were in the ship came and worshipped him, saying, Of a truth thou art the Son of God.*

This Scripture shows the disciples are still afraid, but Peter now has the boldness to walk on water with Jesus. You can see that Peter's faith is developing more. However, Peter becomes frightened in the middle of the miracle of him walking on water in the storm and cries out to Jesus as he is sinking. But it is important to note that as Jesus helps Peter, he still walks on water back to the boat. The Apostle Peter's faith is growing while his fears are being dealt with.

The next development of faith for the apostles occurs when Jesus comes down off the Mount of Transfiguration. When Jesus approached the crowd, He was confronted that His Apostles could not cast a demon out of a child. When the Apostles later asked Jesus why they could not cast the demon out, He said it was because of their unbelief. Jesus also added that prayer and fasting were needed to cast this type of devil out.

Matthew 17:14-21 (KJV)
*14 And when they were come to the multitude, there came to him a certain man, kneeling down to him, and saying, 15 Lord, have mercy on my son: for he is lunatick, and sore vexed: for ofttimes he falleth into the fire, and oft into the water. 16 And I brought him to thy disciples, and they could not cure him. 17 **Then Jesus answered and said, O faithless and perverse generation, how long shall I be with you?** how long shall I suffer you? bring him hither to me. 18 And Jesus rebuked the devil; and he departed out of him: and the child was cured from that very hour. 19 Then came the disciples to Jesus apart, and said, **Why could not we cast him out? 20 And Jesus said unto them, Because of your unbelief: for verily I say unto you, If ye have faith as a grain of mustard seed, ye shall say unto this mountain, Remove hence to yonder place; and it shall remove; and nothing shall be impossible unto you.** 21 Howbeit this kind goeth not out but by prayer and fasting.*

Jesus continually taught His Apostles about faith and developed their faith in every circumstance. He taught them that if they had faith as a grain of a mustard seed, they could speak to a mountain, and it would move. The Apostles learned they could work miracles with faith-filled words, just like Jesus, who demonstrated His faith to them by working miracles with His spoken Words. Jesus revealed this truth more deeply when He complimented the faith of the Centurion.

Matthew 8:5-13 (KJV)

5 And when Jesus was entered into Capernaum, there came unto him a centurion, beseeching him, 6 And saying, Lord, my servant lieth at home sick of the palsy, grievously tormented. 7 And Jesus saith unto him, I will come and heal him. 8 The centurion answered and said, Lord, I am not worthy that thou shouldest come under my roof: but speak the word only, and my servant shall be healed. 9 For I am a man under authority, having soldiers under me: and I say to this man, Go, and he goeth; and to another, Come, and he cometh; and to my servant, Do this, and he doeth it. 10 When Jesus heard it, he marvelled, and said to them that followed, Verily I say unto you, I have not found so great faith, no, not in Israel. 11 And I say unto you, That many shall come from the east and west, and shall sit down with Abraham, and Isaac, and Jacob, in the kingdom of heaven. 12 But the children of the kingdom shall be cast out into outer darkness: there shall be weeping and gnashing of teeth. 13 And Jesus said unto the centurion, Go thy way; and as thou hast believed, so be it done unto thee. And his servant was healed in the selfsame hour.

The night before Jesus went to the cross, He shared The Last Supper with His disciples and worked on their faith. Jesus was working on them believing in Him and not just believing in God.

Here are some statements Jesus made on this night about believing in Him.

John 13:18-19 (KJV)

18 I speak not of you all: I know whom I have chosen: but that the scripture may be fulfilled, He that eateth bread with me hath lifted up his heel against me. 19 Now I tell you before it come, that, when it is come to pass, ye may believe that I am he.

John 14:1 (KJV)

1 Let not your heart be troubled: ye believe in God, believe also in me.

John 14:10-12 (KJV)
10 Believest thou not that I am in the Father, and the Father in me?
the words that I speak unto you I speak not of myself: but the Father
that dwelleth in me, he doeth the works. 11 Believe me that I am in
the Father, and the Father in me: or else believe me for the very
works' sake. 12 Verily, verily, I say unto you, He that believeth on
me, the works that I do shall he do also; and greater works than these
shall he do; because I go unto my Father.

John 14:28-29 (KJV)
28 Ye have heard how I said unto you, I go away, and come again unto
you. If ye loved me, ye would rejoice, because I said, I go unto the Father:
for my Father is greater than I. 29 And now I have told you before it
come to pass, that, when it is come to pass, ye might believe.

John 16:26-27 (KJV)
26 At that day ye shall ask in my name: and I say not unto you, that I
will pray the Father for you: 27 For the Father himself loveth you,
because ye have loved me, and have believed that I came out from
God.

John 16:28-31 (KJV)
28 I came forth from the Father, and am come into the world: again, I
leave the world, and go to the Father. 29 His disciples said unto him,
Lo, now speakest thou plainly, and speakest no proverb. 30 Now are we
sure that thou knowest all things, and needest not that any man should
ask thee: by this we believe that thou camest forth from God. 31 Jesus
answered them, Do ye now believe?

John 17:5-8 (KJV)
5 And now, O Father, glorify thou me with thine own self with the
glory which I had with thee before the world was. 6 I have manifested
thy name unto the men which thou gavest me out of the world: thine
they were, and thou gavest them me; and they have kept thy word. 7
Now they have known that all things whatsoever thou hast given me are
of thee. 8 For I have given unto them the words which thou gavest me;

*and they have received them, **and have known surely that I came out
from thee, and they have believed that thou didst send me.***

As you can see from these Scriptures, Jesus was working on His Apostles'
faith until His death on the cross. Their belief in Him and ability to work
miracles was paramount to Jesus. Jesus told them they would work
miracles and do greater works if they believed in Him.

John 14:12 (KJV)
*12 Verily, verily, I say unto you, He that believeth on me, the works
that I do shall he do also; and greater works than these shall he do;
because I go unto my Father.*

After Jesus rose from the dead, we can see that Jesus still needed to work
on the Apostle's faith. Jesus revealed Himself to a few women and men
after He rose from the dead, but the Apostles didn't believe them. Let's see
what Jesus had to say to them about them not believing those who saw
Him after His resurrection.

Mark 16:9-14 (KJV)
*9 Now when Jesus was risen early the first day of the week, he appeared
first to Mary Magdalene, out of whom he had cast seven devils. 10 And
she went and told them that had been with him, as they mourned and
wept. 11 And they, when they had heard that he was alive, and had
been seen of her, **believed not.** 12 After that he appeared in another
form unto two of them, as they walked, and went into the country. 13
And they went and told it unto the residue: **neither believed they them.**
14 Afterward he appeared unto the eleven as they sat at meat, and
upbraided them with their unbelief and hardness of heart, because
they believed not them which had seen him after he was risen.***

Jesus had to rebuke His Apostles for not believing the report that He had
risen from the dead. The Apostles would not believe until they saw Him.

Some doubted even when Jesus appeared to them after He rose from the dead.

Matthew 28:16-17 (KJV)
16 Then the eleven disciples went away into Galilee, into a mountain where Jesus had appointed them. 17 And when they saw him, they worshipped him: **but some doubted.**

The Apostle Thomas said he would not believe unless he put his fingers in the holes in Jesus' hands from being crucified and put his hand in Jesus' side where He was pierced. Because of this, Thomas was given the nickname throughout history, doubting Thomas.

John 20:24-29 (KJV)
24 But Thomas, one of the twelve, called Didymus, was not with them when Jesus came. 25 The other disciples therefore said unto him, We have seen the Lord. But he said unto them, **Except I shall see in his hands the print of the nails, and put my finger into the print of the nails, and thrust my hand into his side, I will not believe.** *26 And after eight days again his disciples were within, and Thomas with them: then came Jesus, the doors being shut, and stood in the midst, and said, Peace be unto you. 27 Then saith he to Thomas, Reach hither thy finger, and behold my hands; and reach hither thy hand, and thrust it into my side:* **and be not faithless, but believing.** *28 And Thomas answered and said unto him, My Lord and my God. 29 Jesus saith unto him,* **Thomas, because thou hast seen me, thou hast believed: blessed are they that have not seen, and yet have believed.**

It was important to Jesus that His Apostles believed the report from others that He had risen from the dead, because He was going to send them into the world to preach the Gospel of what they had seen and heard, so others would believe their report. When they went out and preached, the ones they were preaching to would need to believe their words without seeing the Risen Lord as they did.

Mark 16:15-20 (KJV)
*15 And he said unto them, Go ye into all the world, and preach the gospel to every creature. 16 He that **believeth** and is baptized shall be saved; but he that **believeth not** shall be damned. 17 **And these signs shall follow them that believe;** In my name shall they cast out devils; they shall speak with new tongues; 18 They shall take up serpents; and if they drink any deadly thing, it shall not hurt them; they shall lay hands on the sick, and they shall recover. 19 So then after the Lord had spoken unto them, he was received up into heaven, and sat on the right hand of God. 20 And they went forth, and preached every where, the Lord working with them, and confirming the word with signs following. Amen.*

Jesus is looking for people to believe in the preached Word of God from someone sent by God; this is where faith comes from. Faith comes by hearing and hearing the Word of God.

Romans 10:14-17 (KJV)
*14 **How then shall they call on him in whom they have not believed? and how shall they believe in him of whom they have not heard? and how shall they hear without a preacher?** 15 And how shall they preach, except they be sent? as it is written, How beautiful are the feet of them that preach the gospel of peace, and bring glad tidings of good things! 16 But they have not all obeyed the gospel. For Esaias saith, Lord, who hath believed our report? 17 **So then faith cometh by hearing, and hearing by the word of God.***

Jesus is still working on people's faith, even to this day. Although we don't see Jesus, we have His Words. We have the written Word of God, and when preached by a man of God, it brings faith. Jesus is the *Author* and *Finisher* of our faith. This faith has everything to do with believing the

Word of God that is preached without seeing. We must believe what God says to be true from His Word. The devil fights hard to blind people from seeing and believing all that God has done for them in Christ.

> *2 Corinthians 4:3-4 (KJV)*
> *3 But if our gospel be hid, it is hid to them that are lost: 4 In whom the god of this world hath blinded the minds of them which believe not, lest the light of the glorious gospel of Christ, who is the image of God, should shine unto them.*

We can see how important faith was and is to Jesus. Jesus brought a whole new way of living and speaking, which is all based upon faith. Jesus changed the world with His faith and worked many miracles for them that believed in Him and what He preached. He then sent His disciples to preach His Word to develop faith in those who heard all that Jesus said and did. We are all given the freedom of choice before God to believe or not believe the Word of God and the truth of the Gospel. If you choose to go down the path of faith, Jesus will not only *Author,* but He will *Finish* your faith.

A great analogy of Jesus *Authoring* and *Finishing* our faith can be found in the miraculous conception of Mary, the mother of Jesus. Jesus is the Word of God made flesh, and just like the Holy Spirit impregnated Mary with Jesus, the Word of God also impregnates us. When we are impregnated with the Word of God through the preaching of the Word of God, faith is sown in our hearts. This *Holy Faith* can only come from God, just like Jesus could only be sown into Mary's womb supernaturally by God's Holy Spirit.

Faith in God is supernatural and only grows supernaturally. After Jesus was born, He grew into a full-grown man, full of the very faith of God. Jesus demonstrated the essence and example of faith for all to see. Jesus used His faith to heal the sick, cast out demons, walk on water, calm storms, and work miracles never before seen. Christians are called to be just like Christ and use their faith to work miracles, as Jesus did. However, to become faith-filled like Christ, we must allow the Word of God to be birthed and grow inside of us. The Bible calls this Christ being formed in us.

Galatians 4:19 (KJV)
*19 My little children, **of whom I travail in birth again until Christ be formed in you,***

Jesus told His Apostles that whoever believed in Him would do greater works than He did. To get to this development in your faith, allow God to birth and grow His faith supernaturally within you. You cannot get to this level of faith on your own without the help of the Holy Spirit through the Word of God.

John 14:12 (KJV)
*12 Verily, verily, I say unto you, **He that believeth on me, the works that I do shall he do also; and greater works than these shall he do;** because I go unto my Father.*

In conclusion, Jesus works on everyone's faith when they come to Him. Jesus started working on a handful of disciples and developed their faith to be great and powerful. The disciples of Jesus advanced the Gospel and worked miracles with their faith. Their faith shook the world to where the whole Roman Empire was turned upside down. Jesus started a movement of faith in them that changed the world. God wants to do the same in our generation and find those who He can develop where they can move mountains and shake hell with their faith.

CHAPTER 8

The Ten Levels of Faith

God is measuring everyone according to their level of faith. When Jesus was on the earth, He continually pointed back to people's faith when He healed them. Jesus also told some people they had no faith, little faith, or great faith. It is clear to see Jesus was measuring everyone's faith. I will reveal in this chapter the Ten Levels of Faith and how God is measuring everyone's faith by these levels.

We know Jesus is the *Author* or *Originator* of our faith, which means everyone starts with no faith. Faith is something that has to be created inside someone. The Bible says that faith comes by hearing and hearing by the Word of God, which is in reference to someone hearing the Word of God preached. When someone hears the Gospel being preached, they can choose to believe or not believe. With this in mind, when Jesus started preaching the Gospel, He originated faith in the hearts of those who heard Him. Jesus was the first faith preacher.

God revealed to me the Ten Levels of Faith from the Scriptures by the Holy Spirit. Once my eyes were opened to these Ten Levels of Faith, I was instantly changed. I could measure myself and see where I was at. The truth that God measures people by their faith was hidden in plain sight but can be found throughout the Bible. Once you see this revelation, your eyes will also be opened, and you too can measure yourself by these ten levels. By measuring yourself, you can allow God to work on your faith. God gives us a measure of faith, but our responsibility is to allow Him to grow that measure.

Romans 12:3 (KJV)
3 For I say, through the grace given unto me, to every man that is among you, not to think of himself more highly than he ought to think; but to think soberly, according as God hath dealt to every man the measure of faith.

Here are The Ten Levels of Faith revealed in the Scriptures:

1. No Faith
2. Dead Faith
3. Weak Faith
4. Little Faith
5. Slow Faith
6. Faith
7. Great Faith
8. Strong Faith
9. Most Holy Faith
10. Perfect Faith

By studying each of these levels of faith, you can learn what Jesus saw or didn't see regarding people's faith. The Bible says that without faith, we cannot please God. Therefore, if you want to please God, aim to have perfected faith. The reason you go through trials is for your faith to grow. God is looking to perfect your faith and make you strong in what you believe. Your faith is what will be found to give praise, honor, and glory to Jesus when He appears.

> *1 Peter 1:7-9 (KJV)*
> *7 **That the trial of your faith, being much more precious than of gold that perisheth**, though it be tried with fire, **might be found unto praise and honour and glory at the appearing of Jesus Christ:** 8 Whom having not seen, ye love; in whom, though now ye see him not, yet believing, ye rejoice with joy unspeakable and full of glory: 9 **Receiving the end of your faith**, even the salvation of your souls.*

THE TEN LEVELS OF FAITH

1. No Faith

A person with no faith lives in fear and doesn't believe that God is there to help them. Fear believes the worst possible thing will happen. Fear ultimately fears dying, which is the worst thing that can happen to someone. Faith has hope in God that a situation will still work out in their favor. When someone has no faith, they cannot see that God wants to help them in their time of need. We can see fear at work in the story of the Apostles being caught in a storm with Jesus on a ship on the Sea of Galilee.

> *Mark 4:35-41 (KJV)*
> *35 And the same day, when the even was come, he saith unto them, Let us pass over unto the other side. 36 And when they had sent away the multitude, they took him even as he was in the ship. And there*

*were also with him other little ships. 37 And there arose a great storm of wind, and the waves beat into the ship, so that it was now full. 38 And he was in the hinder part of the ship, asleep on a pillow: and they awake him, and say unto him, Master, carest thou not that we perish? 39 And he arose, and rebuked the wind, and said unto the sea, Peace, be still. And the wind ceased, and there was a great calm. 40 **And he said unto them, Why are ye so fearful? how is it that ye have no faith?** 41 And they feared exceedingly, and said one to another, What manner of man is this, that even the wind and the sea obey him?*

God was not pleased with the children of Israel who came out of Egypt, when they refused to believe Him after all the miracles they saw. God did one miracle after another, but the children of Israel refused to believe God whenever they went through a test. God was unhappy with that generation and said they had no faith.

Deuteronomy 32:20 (KJV)
*20 And he said, I will hide my face from them, I will see what their end shall be: for they are a very froward generation, **children in whom is no faith.***

2. Dead Faith

A person with dead faith says they believe in God but have no works to back their beliefs. If we say we believe God, we must have actions to support what we believe, or our faith is called dead, according to the Bible. Anyone with genuine faith will back what they believe by an act of prayer, speaking to a mountain, or obeying God in something He commands them to do. Works must back faith; otherwise, it is dead.

James 2:14-26 (KJV)
14 What doth it profit, my brethren, though a man say he hath faith, and have not works? can faith save him? 15 If a brother or

*sister be naked, and destitute of daily food, 16 And one of you say unto them, Depart in peace, be ye warmed and filled; notwithstanding ye give them not those things which are needful to the body; what doth it profit? 17 **Even so faith, if it hath not works, is dead, being alone.** 18 Yea, a man may say, Thou hast faith, and I have works: shew me thy faith without thy works, and I will shew thee my faith by my works. 19 Thou believest that there is one God; thou doest well: the devils also believe, and tremble. 20 **But wilt thou know, O vain man, that faith without works is dead?** 21 Was not Abraham our father justified by works, when he had offered Isaac his son upon the altar? 22 Seest thou how faith wrought with his works, and by works was faith made perfect? 23 And the scripture was fulfilled which saith, Abraham believed God, and it was imputed unto him for righteousness: and he was called the Friend of God. 24 **Ye see then how that by works a man is justified, and not by faith only.** 25 Likewise also was not Rahab the harlot justified by works, when she had received the messengers, and had sent them out another way? 26 For as the body without the spirit is dead, **so faith without works is dead also.***

3. Weak Faith

A person who has weak faith is double-minded. They believe in some ways, but their mind is also filled with doubts. They believe, yet they don't believe. This person is like a wave of the sea tossed to and fro by the wind. There is nothing stable in their faith in believing God for a miracle. There was nothing weak in Abraham's faith when He believed God for him to have a son in his old age.

Romans 4:17-19 (KJV)
17 (As it is written, I have made thee a father of many nations,) before him whom he believed, even God, who quickeneth the dead, and calleth those things which be not as though they were. 18 Who against hope believed in hope, that he might become the father of

*many nations, according to that which was spoken, So shall thy seed be. 19 **And being not weak in faith,** he considered not his own body now dead, when he was about an hundred years old, neither yet the deadness of Sarah's womb:*

We are not to argue with those who are weak in faith.

Romans 14:1 (KJV)
1 Him that is weak in the faith receive ye, but not to doubtful disputations.

4. Little Faith

A person with little faith believes, but barely believes. Jesus called people out for having little faith during His ministry. Little faith means they lack confidence and are unwilling to believe something. This person's mind is filled with worry, and they don't fully trust the Lord and His promises. They start to believe God, but they are afraid when their faith is challenged. Genuine faith is free from fear because it knows God will take care of them and fulfill His Word.

Matthew 6:30 (KJV)
*30 Wherefore, if God so clothe the grass of the field, which to day is, and to morrow is cast into the oven, shall he not much more clothe you, **O ye of little faith?***

When Peter walked on water and began to sink, Jesus said he had little faith and asked why he doubted.

Matthew 14:25-31 (KJV)
25 And in the fourth watch of the night Jesus went unto them, walking on the sea. 26 And when the disciples saw him walking on the sea, they were troubled, saying, It is a spirit; and they cried out for fear. 27 But straightway Jesus spake unto them, saying, Be of good cheer; it is I; be not afraid. 28 And Peter answered him and

*said, Lord, if it be thou, bid me come unto thee on the water. 29 And he said, Come. And when Peter was come down out of the ship, he walked on the water, to go to Jesus. 30 **But when he saw the wind boisterous, he was afraid;** and beginning to sink, he cried, saying, Lord, save me. 31 And immediately Jesus stretched forth his hand, and caught him, and said unto him, **O thou of little faith, wherefore didst thou doubt?***

5. Slow Faith

Jesus told His Disciples that they were slow to believe what was written in the Scriptures after He rose from the dead. This is when someone believes but is very slow and takes their time with their faith. We must be quick to believe all that God has said. We must also be quick to respond when the Gospel is preached.

Luke 24:25-27 (KJV)
*25 Then he said unto them, **O fools, and slow of heart to believe all that the prophets have spoken:** 26 Ought not Christ to have suffered these things, and to enter into his glory? 27 And beginning at Moses and all the prophets, he expounded unto them in all the scriptures the things concerning himself.*

The Bible says Today is the Day of Salvation. We can't hold off tomorrow or another time to respond in faith to God and His Gospel. The children of Israel wandered in the wilderness because they didn't believe God when they were commanded to go into the Promised Land. That day was called the day of provocation. Provocation means exasperation. The children of Israel exasperated the Lord with their unbelief. The children of Israel tried to enter the Promise Land the next day, but the Lord was not with them.

Hebrews 3:15-19 (KJV)
*15 While it is said, **To day if ye will hear his voice, harden not your hearts, as in the provocation.** 16 For some, when they had heard, did provoke: howbeit not all that came out of Egypt by Moses. 17 But with whom was he grieved forty years? was it not with them that had sinned, whose carcases fell in the wilderness? 18 And to whom sware he that they should not enter into his rest, but to them that believed not? 19 **So we see that they could not enter in because of unbelief.***

6. Faith

The Bible says that without faith, it is impossible to please God. This person believes that God is and is a rewarder of them that diligently seek Him. God rewards those who have faith. This person is not filled with any fear, doubt, or unbelief.

Hebrews 11:6 (KJV)
*6 **But without faith it is impossible to please him: for he that cometh to God must believe that he is, and that he is a rewarder of them that diligently seek him.***

God is well pleased with those who have faith and rewards them by healing their body. Jesus always pointed to people's faith when He healed them. Miracles, signs, and wonders being performed in our midst are among the most powerful ways God rewards those with faith. This type of faith is free from all doubts about God and His ability to perform His *Precious Promises*.

Luke 18:35-43 (KJV)
35 And it came to pass, that as he was come nigh unto Jericho, a certain blind man sat by the way side begging: 36 And hearing the multitude pass by, he asked what it meant. 37 And they told him, that Jesus of Nazareth passeth by. 38 And he cried, saying, Jesus,

thou son of David, have mercy on me. 39 And they which went before rebuked him, that he should hold his peace: but he cried so much the more, Thou son of David, have mercy on me. 40 And Jesus stood, and commanded him to be brought unto him: and when he was come near, he asked him, 41 Saying, What wilt thou that I shall do unto thee? And he said, Lord, that I may receive my sight. 42 And Jesus said unto him, Receive thy sight: thy faith hath saved thee. 43 And immediately he received his sight, and followed him, glorifying God: and all the people, when they saw it, gave praise unto God.

Faith can come to God and get an answer to prayers when it is free from wavering.

James 1:5-7 (KJV)
*5 If any of you lack wisdom, let him ask of God, that giveth to all men liberally, and upbraideth not; and it shall be given him. 6 **But let him ask in faith, nothing wavering.** For he that wavereth is like a wave of the sea driven with the wind and tossed. 7 **For let not that man think that he shall receive any thing of the Lord.***

7. Great Faith

During the ministry of Jesus, He only mentioned two people as having great faith. The funny thing about this is that the two people He pointed out were Gentiles, not Jews. Both people astounded Jesus with their faith more than all the Jews and His disciples. Someone with great faith can cause even God to marvel.

The first Gentile to astound Jesus with their great faith was a Roman Centurion. The Centurion understood the power and authority of faith being spoken.

Matthew 8:5-13 (KJV)
5 And when Jesus was entered into Capernaum, there came unto him a centurion, beseeching him, 6 And saying, Lord, my servant lieth at home sick of the palsy, grievously tormented. 7 And Jesus saith unto him, I will come and heal him. 8 The centurion answered and said, Lord, I am not worthy that thou shouldest come under my roof: but speak the word only, and my servant shall be healed. 9 For I am a man under authority, having soldiers under me: and I say to this man, Go, and he goeth; and to another, Come, and he cometh; and to my servant, Do this, and he doeth it. 10 **When Jesus heard it, he marvelled, and said to them that followed, Verily I say unto you, I have not found so great faith, no, not in Israel.** *11 And I say unto you, That many shall come from the east and west, and shall sit down with Abraham, and Isaac, and Jacob, in the kingdom of heaven. 12 But the children of the kingdom shall be cast out into outer darkness: there shall be weeping and gnashing of teeth. 13 And Jesus said unto the centurion,* **Go thy way; and as thou hast believed, so be it done unto thee.** *And his servant was healed in the selfsame hour.*

The next person to astound Jesus with their great faith and cause Him to marvel was a Gentile woman who believed in God to deliver her daughter from a demon. Jesus pointed to her having great faith because she wouldn't give up. No matter what Jesus said, she kept coming back at Him with her persistent faith. Faith has everything to do with believing and never giving up.

Matthew 15:22-28 (KJV)
22 And, behold, a woman of Canaan came out of the same coasts, and cried unto him, saying, Have mercy on me, O Lord, thou son of David; my daughter is grievously vexed with a devil. 23 But he answered her not a word. And his disciples came and besought him, saying, Send her away; for she crieth after us. 24 But he answered and said, I am not sent but unto the lost sheep of the house of Israel.

*25 Then came she and worshipped him, saying, Lord, help me. 26 But he answered and said, It is not meet to take the children's bread, and to cast it to dogs. 27 And she said, Truth, Lord: yet the dogs eat of the crumbs which fall from their masters' table. 28 **Then Jesus answered and said unto her, O woman, great is thy faith: be it unto thee even as thou wilt.** And her daughter was made whole from that very hour.*

8. Strong Faith

Abraham is called the father of our faith for a good reason. Abraham was among the first people in ancient times to believe God. Even when tested, Abraham stood strong in his faith. When God promised him that he would have a child in his old age, he believed God. Abraham believed God and was strong in his faith and did not stagger at God's promises. Strong faith gives glory to God.

Romans 4:17-21 (KJV)
*17 (As it is written, I have made thee a father of many nations,) before him whom he believed, even God, who quickeneth the dead, and calleth those things which be not as though they were. 18 Who against hope believed in hope, that he might become the father of many nations, according to that which was spoken, So shall thy seed be. 19 And being not weak in faith, he considered not his own body now dead, when he was about an hundred years old, neither yet the deadness of Sarah's womb: 20 He staggered not at the promise of God through unbelief; **but was strong in faith**, giving glory to God; 21 And being fully persuaded that, what he had promised, he was able also to perform.*

9. Most Holy Faith

I added Most Holy Faith in the Ten Levels of faith because this is a person who is not only strong in their holy faith but is also powerful.

This person is not only filled with faith, but they are also filled with the power of the Holy Spirit and works miracles. Jesus and His Apostles were filled with faith and power.

> *Jude 1:20 (KJV)*
> *20 But ye, beloved, building up yourselves on your most holy faith, praying in the Holy Ghost,*

Stephen was a man not only filled with faith, but he was also filled with the Holy Spirit and worked miracles. Not everyone filled with faith works miracles. Someone filled with Holy Faith and the power of the Holy Spirit will work miracles.

> *Acts 6:8 (KJV)*
> *8 And Stephen, full of faith and power, did great wonders and miracles among the people.*

10. Perfect Faith

The Apostle Paul prayed for the Thessalonica Church that God might perfect that which was lacking in their faith. I put Perfect Faith as the last of the Ten Levels of Faith because I believe God will continually be perfecting our faith until we go to be with Him in Heaven. God gives us faith, but it needs to grow to full maturity and be perfected. Until you go to be with God in Heaven, God will continue to perfect your faith while on this earth.

> *1 Thessalonians 3:10 (KJV)*
> *10 Night and day praying exceedingly that we might see your face, and might perfect that which is lacking in your faith?*

God worked on Abraham's faith His whole life by putting him through tests. The biggest test Abraham faced was the offering of his son Isaac as a sacrifice. God perfected Abraham's faith throughout his life, as He will perfect your faith throughout your life.

James 2:21-22 (KJV)
*21 Was not Abraham our father justified by works, when he had offered Isaac his son upon the altar? 22 Seest thou how faith wrought with his works, **and by works was faith made perfect?***

The question must now be asked, how does one grow from a level one faith to a level ten faith? The answer is simple: repent of wrong thinking and think new thoughts. A person with fear, doubt and unbelief thinks much different from a person who has great, strong, and perfected faith. To grow in your faith, you must repent of thoughts of fear, doubt, and unbelief. God's thoughts of faith are much higher than our thoughts. Your thoughts make up who you are. Powerful people with great faith think strong thoughts of faith.

Isaiah 55:7-9 (KJV)
*7 **Let the wicked forsake his way, and the unrighteous man his thoughts:** and let him return unto the Lord, and he will have mercy upon him; and to our God, for he will abundantly pardon. 8 **For my thoughts are not your thoughts,** neither are your ways my ways, saith the Lord. 9 **For as the heavens are higher than the earth,** so are my ways higher than your ways, and my thoughts than your thoughts.*

Whenever God's Word is preached, it challenges the hearers with new ways of thinking and believing. Jesus challenged fear, doubt, and unbelief at every level when He preached. By receiving the message that Jesus preached and lived, you can grow to a level ten faith, but you will have to repent of all unbelief. Your faith must mix with the message of the Gospel when you hear it preached to grow to a level ten faith.

Hebrews 4:2 (KJV)
*2 **For unto us was the gospel preached,** as well as unto them: **but the word preached did not profit them, not being mixed with faith in them that heard it.***

God also uses fiery trials to drive out all fear, doubt, and unbelief with the goal of developing someone into a level ten faith.

1 Peter 1:6-7 (KJV)
*6 Wherein ye greatly rejoice, though now for a season, if need be, ye are in heaviness through manifold temptations: 7 **That the trial of your faith, being much more precious than of gold that perisheth, though it be tried with fire,** might be found unto praise and honour and glory at the appearing of Jesus Christ:*

James 1:2-4 (KJV)
*2 My brethren, **count it all joy when ye fall into divers temptations;** 3 Knowing this, **that the trying of your faith worketh patience.** 4 But let patience have her perfect work, **that ye may be perfect and entire, wanting nothing.***

The measure of faith that God gives to everyone is the size of a mustard seed. The mustard seed is tiny but has the potential to grow into something great.

Mark 4:30-32 (KJV)
*30 And he said, Whereunto shall we liken the kingdom of God? or with what comparison shall we compare it? 31 **It is like a grain of mustard seed,** which, when it is sown in the earth, is less than all the seeds that be in the earth: 32 But when it is sown, it groweth up, and becometh greater than all herbs, and shooteth out great branches; so that the fowls of the air may lodge under the shadow of it.*

Jesus taught that it only took faith the size of a mustard seed to move a mountain.

Matthew 17:20 (KJV)
*20 And Jesus said unto them, Because of your unbelief: for verily I say unto you, **If ye have faith as a grain of mustard seed, ye shall say unto this mountain, Remove hence to yonder place; and it shall remove; and nothing shall be impossible unto you.***

If someone doesn't have faith, they can't receive from God. When Jesus went back to His hometown of Nazareth, He couldn't do mighty miracles because of their unbelief. Jesus marveled at the unbelief He found in His hometown.

Mark 6:1-6 (KJV)
*1 And he went out from thence, and came into his own country; and his disciples follow him. 2 And when the sabbath day was come, he began to teach in the synagogue: and many hearing him were astonished, saying, From whence hath this man these things? and what wisdom is this which is given unto him, that even such mighty works are wrought by his hands? 3 Is not this the carpenter, the son of Mary, the brother of James, and Joses, and of Juda, and Simon? and are not his sisters here with us? **And they were offended at him.** 4 But Jesus, said unto them, A prophet is not without honour, but in his own country, and among his own kin, and in his own house. 5 And he could there do no mighty work, save that he laid his hands upon a few sick folk, and healed them. 6 **And he marvelled because of their unbelief.** And he went round about the villages, teaching.*

One question Jesus asked His disciples was, *"Where is your faith?"* God wants to know what level of faith you have.

Luke 8:25 (KJV)
*25 And he said unto them, **Where is your faith?** And they being afraid wondered, saying one to another, What manner of man is this! for he commandeth even the winds and water, and they obey him.*

Where is your faith? Or what level of faith do you have? Do you have no faith? Is your faith little? Or do you have great faith? Measuring faith with these Ten Levels can help you see where you are in your faith, and where you need to improve.

Once God gives someone a measure of faith, it is up to them what they decide to do with it. Some people do nothing with the faith God gave them. Others take the faith God gave them and produce a plenteous harvest. Either way, God wants to know where your faith is at, and what you are going to do with the faith He gave you.

In conclusion, our faith is very important to Jesus. Jesus is still measuring people's faith, even to this day. Without faith you cannot be saved, healed, delivered, or receive answers to your prayers from God. Jesus, the *Author* and *Finisher* of our faith, won't stop working on us until we have perfected faith. Your faith will grow as you grow in the knowledge of God and His Word and pass every faith test God sends your way. God is looking for those who will make Him marvel because of their great, strong, holy, and perfected faith.

CHAPTER 9

The Gifts of God

God has given the five-fold ministry of the apostles, prophets, evangelists, pastors, and teachers as gifts to the body of Christ. In addition, God has also given nine gifts of the Spirit for everyone to be blessed by. God uses the gifts of the Spirit and the five-fold ministries to manifest the *Precious Promises* of God to those who believe. In this chapter, I will reveal how these gifts are raised up, and why God calls them gifts.

The word *gift* means blessing, undeserved benefit, favor, and a present given without a payment due. A *gift* is something of value voluntarily transferred from one person to another without expecting payment or anything in return. A *gift* can also mean someone endowed with the power or ability to help others. *Gifts* are free, with no strings attached to the person receiving the *gift*.

The Bible teaches that when Jesus died and rose again, He gave gifts to men. These gifts came as the five-fold ministry of apostles, prophets, evangelists, pastors, and teachers.

> *Ephesians 4:7-12 (KJV)*
> *7 **But unto every one of us is given grace according to the measure of the gift of Christ.** 8 Wherefore he saith, When he ascended up on high, he led captivity captive, **and gave gifts unto men.** 9 (Now that he ascended, what is it but that he also descended first into the lower parts of the earth? 10 He that descended is the same also that ascended up far above all heavens, that he might fill all things.) 11 **And he gave some, apostles; and some, prophets; and some, evangelists; and some, pastors and teachers;** 12 For the perfecting of the saints, for the work of the ministry, for the edifying of the body of Christ:*

Jesus started His ministry by raising up His twelve apostles, but when He ascended to the Father, He also ordained the rest of the five-fold ministry. At this time, Jesus was doing away with the Law and the Old Priesthood connected to the Law of Moses. The new five-fold ministers would be the new priesthood, along with the rest of the body of Christ. This new priesthood would minister the New Covenant to believers.

Christ was made the High Priest after the order of Melchisedec in the New Covenant.

> *Hebrews 7:11-12 (KJV)*
> *11 If therefore perfection were by the Levitical priesthood, (for under it the people received the law,) **what further need was there that another priest should rise after the order of Melchisedec,** and not be called after the order of Aaron? 12 For the priesthood being changed, there is made of necessity a change also of the law.*

God raised up the five-fold ministry of Jesus to be a blessing to the body of Christ. These men were to bless the body of Christ by spiritual guidance, teaching and preaching the Word of God, and the working of miracles. The working of miracles was one of the nine gifts of the Spirit. The nine gifts of the Spirit were also to be imparted to others in the body of Christ, who were not a five-fold minister. The five-fold minister was used by God's Spirit to not only operate in one of the nine gifts of the Spirit, but to work with God and help orchestrate the manifestation of the gifts of the Holy Spirit to the body of Christ.

1 Corinthians 12:4-11 (KJV)
4 Now there are diversities of gifts, but the same Spirit. 5 And there are differences of administrations, but the same Lord. 6 And there are diversities of operations, but it is the same God which worketh all in all. 7 But the manifestation of the Spirit is given to every man to profit withal. 8 For to one is given by the Spirit the word of wisdom; to another the word of knowledge by the same Spirit; 9 To another faith by the same Spirit; to another the gifts of healing by the same Spirit; 10 To another the working of miracles; to another prophecy; to another discerning of spirits; to another divers kinds of tongues; to another the interpretation of tongues: 11 But all these worketh that one and the selfsame Spirit, dividing to every man severally as he will.

I want to point out that when God raises up a true five-fold ministry, the gifts of the Spirit will be involved. It is called an anointing when someone is operating in the gifts of the Spirit. When a five-fold ministry is raised up from God, operating in the anointing it is a sight to behold. Many people are blessed with this gift while they operate in the gifts of the Spirit. Jesus operated in an astounding anointing where blind eyes were opened, the dead were raised, and many more mighty miracles occurred.

Acts 2:22 (KJV)
22 Ye men of Israel, hear these words; Jesus of Nazareth, a man approved of God among you by miracles and wonders and signs, which God did by him in the midst of you, as ye yourselves also know:

Acts 10:38 (KJV)
38 How God anointed Jesus of Nazareth with the Holy Ghost and with power: who went about doing good, and healing all that were oppressed of the devil; for God was with him.

The Apostles followed in the footsteps of Jesus and performed mighty miracles in the Book of Acts.

Acts 2:43 (KJV)
43 And fear came upon every soul: and many wonders and signs were done by the apostles.

Acts 4:33 (KJV)
33 And with great power gave the apostles witness of the resurrection of the Lord Jesus: and great grace was upon them all.

Another powerful man raised up in the Book of Acts was Stephen. He wasn't an apostle, but he worked miracles.

Acts 6:8 (KJV)
8 And Stephen, full of faith and power, did great wonders and miracles among the people.

There was also a man named Philip, who was raised up in the early Church that worked signs and wonders.

Acts 8:5-8 (KJV)
5 Then Philip went down to the city of Samaria, and preached Christ unto them. 6 And the people with one accord gave heed unto those things which Philip spake, hearing and seeing the miracles which he did. 7 For unclean spirits, crying with loud voice, came out of many that were possessed with them: and many taken with palsies, and that were lame, were healed. 8 And there was great joy in that city.

God used these men to bring healing and deliverance to many, and when these gifts were raised up, it was a blessing to many. Jesus commanded them that they had received freely and were to give freely. This is about them not expecting money from the ones they were ministering to because God's gifts are free.

Matthew 10:7-8 (KJV)
7 And as ye go, preach, saying, The kingdom of heaven is at hand. 8 ***Heal the sick, cleanse the lepers, raise the dead, cast out devils: freely ye have received, freely give.***

I want to highlight that when Jesus or one of the five-fold ministries flowed in the gifts of the Spirit, it appeared like a miracle happened immediately. I am bringing up this point because I have been teaching that the Kingdom of God is like a seed, and it takes time to receive a harvest. This is the normal process when we pray and believe God for an answer to our prayers.

A deeper understanding about a gift or gifts of God being raised up is when God raises up a person to operate in a powerful anointing; they can be likened to a tree or plant bearing fruit. Jesus continually used seeds, fruit, and harvesting in His teaching to help His disciples better understand how the Kingdom of God worked.

The night before Jesus was to be crucified, He told His Apostles that they could only bear fruit if they abided in Him. He also said they would be His disciples if they bore much fruit. The fruit Jesus was talking about was regarding miracles and doing the work of the ministry.

John 15:1-8 (KJV)
1 I am the true vine, and my Father is the husbandman. 2 ***Every branch in me that beareth not fruit he taketh away: and every branch that beareth fruit, he purgeth it, that it may bring forth more fruit.*** *3 Now ye are clean through the word which I have spoken unto you. 4* ***Abide in me, and I in you. As the branch cannot bear fruit***

*of itself, except it abide in the vine; no more can ye, except ye abide in me. 5 I am the vine, ye are the branches: **He that abideth in me, and I in him, the same bringeth forth much fruit:** for without me ye can do nothing. 6 If a man abide not in me, he is cast forth as a branch, and is withered; and men gather them, and cast them into the fire, and they are burned. 7 If ye abide in me, and my words abide in you, ye shall ask what ye will, and it shall be done unto you. 8 **Herein is my Father glorified, that ye bear much fruit; so shall ye be my disciples.***

Jesus likened a mustard seed growing and becoming a magnificent tree as an example of the Kingdom of God. He said the mustard seed was the smallest among seeds but would grow so big the birds would lodge in its branches. The analogy of birds lodging in the mustard tree branches is about a person being a blessing to many through the anointing and gifts of the Holy Spirit.

Matthew 13:31-32 (KJV)
*31 Another parable put he forth unto them, saying, **The kingdom of heaven is like to a grain of mustard seed,** which a man took, and sowed in his field: 32 Which indeed is the least of all seeds: but when it is grown, it is the greatest among herbs, and becometh a tree, **so that the birds of the air come and lodge in the branches thereof.***

Plants grow and produce fruit quicker, but a fruit tree can take three to six years before it bears fruit. There are many places in the Scriptures where God likens a man of God to a tree bearing fruit.

Jeremiah 17:7-8 (KJV)
*7 Blessed is the man that trusteth in the Lord, and whose hope the Lord is. 8 **For he shall be as a tree planted by the waters,** and that spreadeth out her roots by the river, and shall not see when heat cometh, but her leaf shall be green; and shall not be careful in the year of drought, **neither shall cease from yielding fruit.***

Psalm 1:1-3 (KJV)
*1 Blessed is the man that walketh not in the counsel of the ungodly, nor standeth in the way of sinners, nor sitteth in the seat of the scornful. 2 But his delight is in the law of the Lord; and in his law doth he meditate day and night. 3 **And he shall be like a tree planted by the rivers of water, that bringeth forth his fruit in his season;** his leaf also shall not wither; and whatsoever he doeth shall prosper.*

I am teaching to emphasize this point because many people believe the miracles of Jesus happened immediately, but they did not. You have to factor in that Jesus didn't start His ministry until He was thirty years old. Why didn't He heal anyone before He began His ministry? We know He was the Son of God His entire life. Jesus grew into His ministry just like everyone else has to grow into their ministry, which takes time.

We also know that John the Baptist came before Jesus and prepared the people for the ministry of Jesus. John preached repentance and baptism. All the people that Jesus healed heard John the Baptist's preaching and repented; therefore, they could receive their healing from Jesus. John the Baptist also used the analogy of trees and people bringing forth fruit.

Luke 3:3-9 (KJV)
*3 And he came into all the country about Jordan, preaching the baptism of repentance for the remission of sins; 4 As it is written in the book of the words of Esaias the prophet, saying, The voice of one crying in the wilderness, **Prepare ye the way of the Lord, make his paths straight.** 5 Every valley shall be filled, and every mountain and hill shall be brought low; and the crooked shall be made straight, and the rough ways shall be made smooth; 6 And all flesh shall see the salvation of God. 7 Then said he to the multitude that came forth to be baptized of him, O generation of vipers, who hath warned you to flee from the wrath to come? 8 **Bring forth therefore fruits worthy of repentance, and begin not to say within yourselves,** We have Abraham to our father: for I say*

*unto you, That God is able of these stones to raise up children unto Abraham. 9 **And now also the axe is laid unto the root of the trees: every tree therefore which bringeth not forth good fruit is hewn down, and cast into the fire.***

It takes time for a five-fold ministry or someone with a gift of the Spirit to be raised up. Nothing happens overnight in God's Kingdom. This is why it is important to understand the *Laws of Seedtime and Harvest* and what it takes to grow a fruit tree. A deeper understanding of farming will go a long way in understanding God's anointing and bearing fruit in His Kingdom. Also, don't forget God started everything off at the beginning of creation by placing man in a Garden.

Genesis 2:8 (KJV)
8 And the Lord God planted a garden eastward in Eden; and there he put the man whom he had formed.

Jesus told His Apostles that they were entering the labors of others and they would reap where other men sowed.

John 4:34-38 (KJV)
*34 Jesus saith unto them, My meat is to do the will of him that sent me, and to finish his work. 35 Say not ye, There are yet four months, and then cometh harvest? behold, I say unto you, Lift up your eyes, and look on the fields; for they are white already to harvest. 36 And he that reapeth receiveth wages, and gathereth fruit unto life eternal: that both he that soweth and he that reapeth may rejoice together. 37 And herein is that saying true, **One soweth, and another reapeth.** 38 I sent you to reap that whereon ye bestowed no labour: other men laboured, and ye are entered into their labours.***

Jesus told His Apostles that the harvest was plenteous, but the laborers were few. There were many people ready to be saved and healed, but there weren't enough people raised up with gifts of the Spirit to help them. God is looking for people He can raise up with an anointing to reap the harvest of souls and bring them healing.

Matthew 9:36-38 (KJV)
36 But when he saw the multitudes, he was moved with compassion on them, because they fainted, and were scattered abroad, as sheep having no shepherd. 37 Then saith he unto his disciples, **The harvest truly is plenteous, but the labourers are few; 38 Pray ye therefore the Lord of the harvest, that he will send forth labourers into his harvest.**

God takes His time when raising up a five-fold minister with a heavy anointing. As the man of God grows like a tree, his roots are going deep into the earth, so he will be strong and able to withstand any storm. The roots also extract water from the ground to make the fruit they bear more luscious and delicious. The water represents the Holy Spirit. The man of God pulls the water from hearing and doing the Word of God. A man who stays faithful to God, His Word, and His Holy Spirit will be raised up in due time.

When this person is raised up, it will look like miracles are happening immediately. The reality is it took years for the anointed person to bear fruit. They are considered a gift because anyone who receives from their ministry can be blessed immediately by the Holy Spirit through them. The people they bless can pull a miracle or receive from God from them as easily as pulling fruit from a tree.

Now, I will teach you how a person walking in the anointing operates in distributing the gifts of the Spirit. Here are three ways the gifts of God are distributed:

1. Done For You
2. Done With You
3. Do It Yourself

DISTRIBUTION OF GIFTS

1. Done For You

What I mean by done for you is that when the anointing is in operation, the person operating in the anointing works a miracle for the person. The person needing the miracle might be dead or unable to use their faith. The man of God steps in and uses their faith to work a miracle. This is called *Done-For-You*. The five-fold minister or the one operating in the anointing works a miracle for the one needing a miracle with *their* faith. The miracle is *Done-For* the one needing the miracle by the faith of the minister.

We can see the truth of a *Done-For-You* miracle in the story of Lazarus being raised from the dead. Jesus used His faith to bring about a miracle for Lazarus. Jesus also told Martha that if she believed, she would see the glory of God. This was about Lazarus being raised from the dead. Jesus used His faith and Maratha's faith to raise Lazarus from the dead. Lazarus was dead and couldn't use his faith, so this miracle was done for him.

> *John 11:38-45 (KJV)*
> *38 Jesus therefore again groaning in himself cometh to the grave. It was a cave, and a stone lay upon it. 39 Jesus said, Take ye away the stone. Martha, the sister of him that was dead, saith unto him, Lord, by this time he stinketh: for he hath been dead four days. 40 Jesus saith unto her, **Said I not unto thee, that, if thou wouldest believe, thou shouldest see the glory of God?** 41 Then they took away the*

*stone from the place where the dead was laid. And Jesus lifted up his eyes, and said, Father, I thank thee that thou hast heard me. 42 And I knew that thou hearest me always: **but because of the people which stand by I said it, that they may believe that thou hast sent me.** 43 And when he thus had spoken, he cried with a loud voice, Lazarus, come forth. 44 And he that was dead came forth, bound hand and foot with graveclothes: and his face was bound about with a napkin. Jesus saith unto them, Loose him, and let him go. 45 **Then many of the Jews which came to Mary, and had seen the things which Jesus did, believed on him.***

Another example of a *Done-For-You* miracle was when Jesus healed Peter's mother-in-law of a fever.

Matthew 8:14-15 (KJV)
*14 And when Jesus was come into Peter's house, he saw his wife's mother laid, and sick of a fever. 15 **And he touched her hand, and the fever left her:** and she arose, and ministered unto them.*

A *Done-For-You* miracle is when Jesus or a man of God works a miracle for you, and you don't have to do anything. Instead, the man of God uses their faith to bring healing or a miracle.

2. Done With You

A *Done-With-You* miracle is performed when a person is required to do something in order to receive a miracle. Whatever is required of them to do, they will receive their miracle if they do it. The man of God will hear from the Holy Spirit through the anointing what the person must do to receive their healing. If the person obeys what the man of God tells them to do, they will receive their miracle from God. We can see this clearly when Elisha heard from God for the man with leprosy to have him dip in the Jordan seven times.

2 Kings 5:1-14 (KJV)

*1 Now Naaman, captain of the host of the king of Syria, was a great man with his master, and honourable, because by him the Lord had given deliverance unto Syria: he was also a mighty man in valour, but he was a leper. 2 And the Syrians had gone out by companies, and had brought away captive out of the land of Israel a little maid; and she waited on Naaman's wife. 3 And she said unto her mistress, Would God my lord were with the prophet that is in Samaria! for he would recover him of his leprosy. 4 And one went in, and told his lord, saying, Thus and thus said the maid that is of the land of Israel. 5 And the king of Syria said, Go to, go, and I will send a letter unto the king of Israel. And he departed, and took with him ten talents of silver, and six thousand pieces of gold, and ten changes of raiment. 6 And he brought the letter to the king of Israel, saying, Now when this letter is come unto thee, behold, I have therewith sent Naaman my servant to thee, that thou mayest recover him of his leprosy. 7 And it came to pass, when the king of Israel had read the letter, that he rent his clothes, and said, Am I God, to kill and to make alive, that this man doth send unto me to recover a man of his leprosy? wherefore consider, I pray you, and see how he seeketh a quarrel against me. 8 And it was so, when Elisha the man of God had heard that the king of Israel had rent his clothes, that he sent to the king, saying, Wherefore hast thou rent thy clothes? let him come now to me, and he shall know that there is a prophet in Israel. 9 So Naaman came with his horses and with his chariot, and stood at the door of the house of Elisha. 10 **And Elisha sent a messenger unto him, saying, Go and wash in Jordan seven times, and thy flesh shall come again to thee, and thou shalt be clean.** 11 But Naaman was wroth, and went away, and said, Behold, I thought, He will surely come out to me, and stand, and call on the name of the Lord his God, and strike his hand over the place, and recover the leper. 12 Are not Abana and Pharpar, rivers of Damascus, better than all the waters of Israel? may I not wash in them, and be clean? So he turned and went away in a rage. 13 And his servants came near, and spake* *unto him, and said, My father, if the prophet had bid thee do some great thing, wouldest thou not have done it? how much rather then, when he saith to thee, Wash, and be clean?* **14 Then went he down, and dipped himself seven times in Jordan, according to the saying of the man of God: and his flesh came again like unto the flesh of a little child, and he was clean.**

Another example of a *Done-With-You* miracle is when Jesus told the blind man to wash in the Siloam pool after He made clay from His spit and rubbed it in His eyes.

John 9:1-7 (KJV)
1 And as Jesus passed by, he saw a man which was blind from his birth. 2 And his disciples asked him, saying, Master, who did sin, this man, or his parents, that he was born blind? 3 Jesus answered, Neither hath this man sinned, nor his parents: but that the works of God should be made manifest in him. 4 I must work the works of him that sent me, while it is day: the night cometh, when no man can work. 5 As long as I am in the world, I am the light of the world. 6 When he had thus spoken, he spat on the ground, and made clay of the spittle, and he anointed the eyes of the blind man with the clay, 7 And said unto him, **Go, wash in the pool of Siloam, (which is by interpretation, Sent.) He went his way therefore, and washed, and came seeing.**

3. Do It Yourself

A *Do-It-Yourself* miracle is when you pray directly to God, believing for a miracle. We can receive miracles directly from God with our faith without a gift being in operation. You go boldly to the Throne of Grace and use your own faith in prayer to receive an answer to your prayer of a miracle.

Hebrews 4:16 (KJV)
16 Let us therefore come boldly unto the throne of grace, that we may obtain mercy, and find grace to help in time of need.

You might find yourself in a situation where no man of God is operating in a gift, but you still need help. You can go directly to God and receive an answer to your prayer using your own faith.

1 John 5:14-15 (KJV)
14 And this is the confidence that we have in him, that, if we ask any thing according to his will, he heareth us: 15 And if we know that he hear us, whatsoever we ask, we know that we have the petitions that we desired of him.

If you are going to do a *Do-It-Yourself* miracle, you must believe God and speak to the mountain with your own faith. If you have faith and doubt not, the mountain will move. The mountain represents anything standing in your way. You can work miracles with your own mouth by faith. Jesus said **whosoever** can have **whatsoever** if they use their faith to speak to a mountain.

Mark 11:22-24 (KJV)
*22 And Jesus answering saith unto them, **Have faith in God.** 23 For verily I say unto you, That **whosoever** shall say unto this mountain, Be thou removed, and be thou cast into the sea; and shall not doubt in his heart, but shall believe that those things which he saith shall come to pass; he shall have **whatsoever** he saith. 24 Therefore I say unto you, **What things soever** ye desire, when ye pray, believe that ye receive them, and ye shall have them.*

A *Do-It-Yourself* miracle usually takes some time. This is where you need to learn the principles of seedtime and harvest. It takes time to receive a harvest after you plant the seed. The Bible says it takes faith and patience to inherit the promises. *Do-It-Yourself* miracles take a lot of faith and work. The work comes in your daily confession and speaking to the mountain with thanksgiving after you know what you are praying for is in God's will.

Hebrews 6:12 (KJV)
12 That ye be not slothful, but followers of them who through faith and patience inherit the promises.

As I conclude this chapter, you can see a gift is a real blessing to the body of Christ. Yes, we can believe God directly with a *Do-It-Yourself* miracle, but receiving from a gift is so much easier. In the long run, God will continually develop your faith, but gifts in the body of Christ make it so much easier to receive from God. This is why you need to support and back any anointed man of God operating in the gifts of the Spirit. God knows people need help with their faith, and that is why He gave gifts to men.

CHAPTER 10

Miraculous Faith Pattern

God has revealed a *Miraculous Faith Pattern* in His Word to receive miracles from Him we can follow to find help in our time of need. Everyone will need God to perform a miracle for them at some point in their life. This world is cursed, and we are all helpless without the God of miracles. Everyone in this life will face a crisis so bad that they will need to call out to God. God knows we will all need Him at some point, which is why He has given us His Word that He will be there for us in our time of need, if we believe Him. In this chapter, I will reveal the *Miraculous Faith Pattern* and what it takes to receive a miracle from God.

There is a passage of Scripture found in Romans Chapter 4 that reveals the *Miraculous Faith Pattern* we must follow to receive a miracle from God. This passage of Scripture lays out how Abraham received a miracle from God. Let's read this passage of Scripture together, and I will reveal God's pattern for miracles.

Romans 4:17-21 (KJV)

17 (As it is written, I have made thee a father of many nations,) before him whom he believed, even God, who quickeneth the dead, and calleth those things which be not as though they were. 18 Who against hope believed in hope, that he might become the father of many nations, according to that which was spoken, So shall thy seed be. 19 And being not weak in faith, he considered not his own body now dead, when he was about an hundred years old, neither yet the deadness of Sarah's womb: 20 He staggered not at the promise of God through unbelief; but was strong in faith, giving glory to God; 21 And being fully persuaded that, what he had promised, he was able also to perform.

This passage of Scripture was clearly written with the Divine purpose of revealing what God is looking for to perform a miracle. You can take this passage of Scripture and see that Jesus used this pattern to perform miracles while He ministered on the earth. You can also find this *Miraculous Faith Pattern* in every miracle found in the Bible. Once you learn this pattern, you, too, can receive miracles from God. One day, God may even use you with this same pattern to work miracles for others.

Below is the 8-step *Miraculous Faith Pattern:*

1. Believe in the Covenant Promises of God Found in His Word

2. Call Those Things That Be Not as Though They Were

3. Hope Against Hope

4. Not Weak in Faith

5. Consider Not the Problem

6. Stagger Not at the Promises of God Through Unbelief

7. Strong in Faith

8. Fully Persuaded That What God Promised He is Able Also to Perform

Abraham is called the father of all who believe because he was one of the first people to have faith in God. Abraham revealed there were steps in how to believe God for a miracle. These faith steps can also be called the *Miraculous Faith Pattern*. God used Abraham's faith as an example of how to believe Him for miracles.

> **Romans 4:11-12 (KJV)**
> *11 And he received the sign of circumcision, a seal of the righteousness of the faith which he had yet being uncircumcised: **that he might be the father of all them that believe,** though they be not circumcised; that righteousness might be imputed unto them also: 12 And the father of circumcision to them who are not of the circumcision only, **but who also walk in the steps of that faith of our father Abraham,** which he had being yet uncircumcised.*

MIRACULOUS FAITH PATTERN

Now, let's see what God is looking for in someone's faith before He performs a miracle through this Divine *Miraculous Faith Pattern*.

1. Believe in the Covenant Promises of God Found in His Word

The foundation of all faith starts in God's Word, which reveals His Promises and His Covenant. Abraham lived in a time when no written Scriptures existed, so he had to rely on the voice of God. The Words of the Covenant that God spoke to Abraham were later written down, which are now included in our modern-day Bible. God made a Covenant with Abraham called the Abrahamic Covenant, or the

Blessing of Abraham. The rest of the Bible was written later, containing all the *Precious Promises* of God.

> *Romans 4:17 (KJV)*
> *17 (As it is written, I have made thee a father of many nations,) before him whom he believed, even God, who quickeneth the dead, and calleth those things which be not as though they were.*

Abraham only believed what God spoke to him. All faith is based on God's Word. We cannot go beyond what God has spoken, but we can firmly lay hold of anything God has said in His Word. So, when you are in the middle of a crisis and need a miracle, stand on God's Word and only God's Word. This is called taking God at His Word. You can also call this laying hold of God's Covenant. We can also stand on prophetic Words spoken over our lives that we know come from God and are backed by the Scriptures.

> *Isaiah 56:6 (KJV)*
> *6 Also the sons of the stranger, that join themselves to the Lord, to serve him, and to love the name of the Lord, to be his servants, every one that keepeth the sabbath from polluting it, **and taketh hold of my covenant;***

When the angel Gabriel told Mary she would be impregnated by the Holy Spirit and give birth to the Son of God, she said she believed God's Word.

> *Luke 1:35-38 (KJV)*
> *35 And the angel answered and said unto her, The Holy Ghost shall come upon thee, and the power of the Highest shall overshadow thee: therefore also that holy thing which shall be born of thee shall be called the Son of God. 36 And, behold, thy cousin Elisabeth, she hath also conceived a son in her old age: and this is the sixth month with her, who was called barren. 37 For with God nothing shall be*

impossible. 38 And Mary said, Behold the handmaid of the Lord;
be it unto me according to thy word. And the angel departed from
her.

When Apostle Paul was on a ship in the middle of a great storm, an angel came to him and said that everyone in the boat would be saved. Afterward, Apostle Paul told everyone to be of good cheer because he believed God and that it would be even as it was told him.

Acts 27:25 (KJV)
25 Wherefore, sirs, be of good cheer: for I believe God, that it
shall be even as it was told me.

God established His covenant with Abraham to bless the whole world. We also know that Jesus has redeemed us from the curse of the Law.

Galatians 3:13 (KJV)
13 Christ hath redeemed us from the curse of the law, being made
a curse for us: for it is written, Cursed is every one that hangeth on
a tree:

We also know that all the promises of God found in the Word of God are all *yes* and *amen* in Christ.

2 Corinthians 1:20 (KJV)
20 For all the promises of God in him are yea, and in him Amen,
unto the glory of God by us.

So, if you find yourself in any curse found in the Law (Deuteronomy 28; Leviticus 26), you can claim any promise in God's Word. As you believe and stand on God's Word, you are laying hold of His Covenant, and God will answer you in response to His Covenant Promises. God watches over His Word to perform it.

Jeremiah 1:12 (KJV)
*12 Then said the Lord unto me, Thou hast well seen: **for I will***
hasten my word to perform it.

We also know that God is ever mindful of His Covenant.

Psalm 111:5 (KJV)
*5 He hath given meat unto them that fear him: **he will ever be***
mindful of his covenant.

Whenever you need God's help, remember to stand on God's Covenant Word and promises, and He will answer you. However, God will only answer you based on His Covenant, but the beauty of God is He made provision for all our needs in the New Covenant. So, if you need a miracle, stand on God's Word and His Covenant Promises, because God will never break His Covenant.

Psalm 89:34 (KJV)
*34 **My covenant will I not break, nor alter the thing that is gone***
out of my lips.

2. Call Those Things That Be Not as Though They Were

All of God's promises must be spoken into existence. God calls things that be not as though they were. This means God speaks things into existence. God spoke Isaac into existence, and this is how Abraham and Sarah were able to have a child in their old age.

Romans 4:17 (KJV)
17 (As it is written, I have made thee a father of many nations,)
before him whom he believed, even God, who quickeneth the dead,
and calleth those things which be not as though they were.

Jesus said that we must also speak to things if we want to see a miracle. Jesus called this speaking to mountains. If you want to see a miracle,

God must speak to the problem, but He also revealed we have to speak to the problem. Jesus referred to problems as mountains. A mountain is anything standing in the way of you receiving a miracle.

> *Mark 11:22-24 (KJV)*
> *22 And Jesus answering saith unto them, Have faith in God. 23 For verily I say unto you, That whosoever shall say unto this mountain, Be thou removed, and be thou cast into the sea; and shall not doubt in his heart, but shall believe that those things which he saith shall come to pass; he shall have whatsoever he saith. 24 Therefore I say unto you, What things soever ye desire, when ye pray, believe that ye receive them, and ye shall have them.*

Someone has to speak to the mountain, or it will not move. Calling things that be not as though they were means you speak to the problem and tell it to be removed. Abraham was childless, so God spoke into his problem and caused a child to show up whom God named Isaac. God speaks to things and causes things to appear that are not there. He has also given us the authority to speak to mountains and make them move.

Jesus marveled at the Centurion's faith because he understood the power of the spoken Word. The Centurion knew if Jesus spoke the Word, his servant would be healed.

> *Matthew 8:5-10 (KJV)*
> *5 And when Jesus was entered into Capernaum, there came unto him a centurion, beseeching him, 6 And saying, Lord, my servant lieth at home sick of the palsy, grievously tormented. 7 And Jesus saith unto him, I will come and heal him. 8 The centurion answered and said, Lord, I am not worthy that thou shouldest come under my roof: but speak the word only, and my servant shall be healed. 9 For I am a man under authority, having soldiers under me: and I*

*say to this man, Go, and he goeth; and to another, Come, and he cometh; and to my servant, Do this, and he doeth it. 10 **When Jesus heard it, he marvelled, and said to them that followed, Verily I say unto you, I have not found so great faith, no, not in Israel.***

God created everything in the known universe by His spoken Word in the first six days of creation, and it is by His spoken Word that He gets things done. God has also called us to speak to the known universe, which is how we will see miracles happen. God's Word never returns to Him void but accomplishes what He pleases and prospers where He sends it. If you put God's Word in your mouth, it will not return void but accomplish what it was spoken to do.

Isaiah 55:11 (KJV)
11 So shall my word be that goeth forth out of my mouth: it shall not return unto me void, but it shall accomplish that which I please, and it shall prosper in the thing whereto I sent it.

3. Hope Against Hope

Someone hoping against hope believes God, no matter how bad the situation is. Abraham and Sarah were well past the years of having a child, and it was a hopeless situation for them to even think of having a child. God gave them hope against hope to believe Him for a child. Only God can give hope where there is no hope.

Romans 4:18 (KJV)
*18 **Who against hope believed in hope**, that he might become the father of many nations, according to that which was spoken, So shall thy seed be.*

Hope means to desire with expectation for something good to occur. Hope goes beyond wishful thinking and implies some expectation of possibly possessing or having something good occur. You don't yet have what you are hoping for, but you are hoping you will have it or see it come to pass. Hoping against hope means you have hope in God for a miracle, even though in the natural everything says it is not possible.

> *Romans 8:24-25 (KJV)*
> *24 For we are saved by hope: but hope that is seen is not hope: for what a man seeth, why doth he yet hope for? 25 But if we hope for that we see not, then do we with patience wait for it.*

The Bible says faith is the substance of things hoped for, the evidence of things not seen. Faith brings into existence what you are hoping for.

> *Hebrews 11:1 (KJV)*
> *1 Now faith is the substance of things hoped for, the evidence of things not seen.*

Jesus taught we must believe we have received what we are praying for. If you are hoping against hope, you must believe you have received what you are praying for.

> *Mark 11:24 (KJV)*
> *24 Therefore I say unto you, What things soever ye desire, when ye pray, believe that ye receive them, and ye shall have them.*

With Abraham, there was no hope of him having a child in his old age without God doing a miracle. When someone finds themselves in a hopeless situation, they can believe God for a miracle. The miracle could never occur without God, but with God, all things are possible. Because of God's promises and His power, we can hope against hope and believe God to cause miracles to occur. Our faith, combined with God's faith, allows us to receive miracles and not be hopeless like the rest of the world when they face a crisis.

When all seems lost, only God can fill someone with hope, because God can work miracles for those who believe in Him. If you have faith in God and hope against hope, God will come out of nowhere, work a miracle for you, and save the day through the power of His Holy Spirit.

Romans 15:13 (KJV)
13 Now the God of hope fill you with all joy and peace in believing, that ye may abound in hope, through the power of the Holy Ghost.

4. Not Weak in Faith

Someone weak in faith is full of fear, doubt, and unbelief, and they are not fully convinced that God will keep His Word. This person is like a wave of the sea being tossed around with all their anxiety. Abraham had no weakness in his faith in God. This means you couldn't find fear, doubt, or unbelief in Abraham when he believed God.

Romans 4:19 (KJV)
19 And being not weak in faith, he considered not his own body now dead, when he was about an hundred years old, neither yet the deadness of Sarah's womb:

If you want to receive anything from God, you cannot waver in what you believe. Anyone who wavers is weak in their faith and cannot receive anything from God. A person who wavers is full of fear, doubt, and unbelief. A person who wavers is also called double-minded in the Bible.

James 1:5-8 (KJV)
5 If any of you lack wisdom, let him ask of God, that giveth to all men liberally, and upbraideth not; and it shall be given him. 6 But let him ask in faith, nothing wavering. For he that wavereth is

*like a wave of the sea driven with the wind and tossed. 7 **For let not
that man think that he shall receive any thing of the Lord. 8 A
double minded man is unstable in all his ways.***

5. Consider Not the Problem

The Bible says that Abraham *Considered Not* his own body being dead
or the deadness of Sarah's womb. Being dead is a reference to his body,
and Sarah's body not being able to have kids anymore. God considers
things dead that are not functioning according to their original
intended purpose. Abraham didn't consider his body being dead and
the deadness of Sarah's womb as a problem.

> *Romans 4:19 (KJV)*
> *19 And being not weak in faith, **he considered not his own body
> now dead, when he was about an hundred years old, neither yet
> the deadness of Sarah's womb:***

Considering Not is one of the hardest things for people to do when
believing God for a miracle. People's minds focus too much on the
problem they are facing. However, if you have faith, you will force
your mind to think only about God and His promises. Those who
believe in God and have strong faith cross over into what is called the
peace of God that passes all understanding.

To have the peace of God come upon you, you must go to God with
believing and thankful prayer. When we come to God in faith, He
imparts His peace to us. His peace is imparted to us because He
confirms He will perform His Word. When the peace of God comes
upon someone, they can supernaturally not fear what they are facing,
but be filled with the wonderful thoughts of God and Him coming
through for them.

Philippians 4:6-7 (KJV)
6 Be careful for nothing; but in every thing by prayer and supplication with thanksgiving let your requests be made known unto God. 7 And the peace of God, which passeth all understanding, shall keep your hearts and minds through Christ Jesus.

Here are the signs of someone who is *Considering Not the Problem*:

1. They are unconcerned about the problem.
2. They blatantly and deliberately ignore the existence of something.
3. They refuse to think about something.
4. They pass over something without giving it due attention.

Abraham didn't consider his body being dead nor the deadness of Sarah's womb. King David didn't consider the size of Goliath before he killed him. Moses didn't consider the power and might of Egypt when delivering the children of Israel from the hand of Pharoah. Joshua didn't consider the height of the walls of Jericho before God knocked them down. Elijah didn't consider it hadn't rained in three years when he prayed for it to rain again. Elisha didn't consider the boy dead when raising him to life again. Jairus didn't consider his daughter being dead before Jesus raised her from the dead. The Centurion didn't consider his servant's sickness before Jesus healed him. Jesus didn't consider Lazarus dead for four days and stinking when He raised him from the dead.

6. Stagger Not at The Promises of God Through Unbelief

Abraham didn't stagger at the promises of God through unbelief. To stagger means to hesitate, waver, or move unsteadily, to show uncertainty about the right course of action, and to doubt. There was no staggering in Abraham's walk of faith when he believed God. When you don't stagger, you give glory to God.

> *Romans 4:20 (KJV)*
> *20 He staggered not at the promise of God through unbelief; but was strong in faith, giving glory to God;*

We are called to walk by faith and not by sight.

> *2 Corinthians 5:7 (KJV)*
> *7 (For we walk by faith, not by sight:)*

Staggering is a sign of someone not walking by faith. When you walk by faith and not by sight, you don't stagger in unbelief by what you see around you. You are able, by faith, to look into the unseen world and see what God is doing. By looking into the unseen world, by faith, you become strong in your faith, and this gives glory to God.

> *2 Corinthians 4:18 (KJV)*
> *18 While we look not at the things which are seen, but at the things which are not seen: for the things which are seen are temporal; but the things which are not seen are eternal.*

When someone walks by faith, without staggering, they are not moved by what they see or hear, but only by what they believe.

7. Strong in Faith

Abraham not only had faith, but he was strong in faith. There are different levels of faith. Some people have little or weak faith. Some people have no faith or dead faith, while others have faith. Abraham walked in strong faith.

Romans 4:20 (KJV)
*20 He staggered not at the promise of God through unbelief; **but was strong in faith**, giving glory to God;*

God has called all of us to not just have faith, but to be strong in our faith. Faith is like a muscle; the more you use it, the stronger the muscle becomes. As you grow in your walk of faith, you will be put into multiple situations where you must exercise your faith. Every time you exercise and use your faith, you will become stronger.

God has called you to be strong in the Lord and in the power of His might.

Ephesians 6:10 (KJV)
*10 **Finally, my brethren, be strong in the Lord, and in the power of his might.***

8. Fully Persuaded That What God Promised He is Able Also to Perform

To be fully persuaded means you have entirely given yourself over to a way of thinking and believing. Some people may think they can never get to this place in their faith, but that is not true. If you stay in God's Word and fight fear, doubt, and unbelief at every level, you can get to where Abraham was in his faith. Abraham was fully persuaded that God could perform what He promised.

Romans 4:21 (KJV)
*21 **And being fully persuaded that, what he had promised, he was able also to perform.***

When someone is fully persuaded that something is true, they cannot be convinced that there is any other way than what they believe. No evidence to the contrary will budge or affect them in what they believe. This is where you get to where you know that you know that you know what God says is true. To be fully persuaded means there is no more room for second-guessing and no more doubts.

God is not glorified by His children walking in fear, doubt, and unbelief. God has laid out a pattern in His Word for us to follow when walking by faith and believing Him for miracles. If Abraham followed this pattern, we also are able to follow this same pattern. Abraham is called the *Father of Faith*, and we are called to follow his example and walk in the same steps of faith that Abraham walked in.

Every person God has used throughout history was used because they had faith. When you look into their faith, you will find this 8-step *Miraculous Faith Pattern*. This 8-step pattern of faith can be seen in every miraculous story of the Bible. Men and women of the Bible glorified God with their faith and were fully persuaded that God was able to perform what He had promised.

This 8-step *Miraculous Faith Pattern* is powerful when fully understood. When this pattern is followed, you will receive miracles from God every time. This 8-step pattern can define faith. Jesus operated in this 8-step pattern of faith in His ministry. You cannot expect God to perform a miracle if this 8-step *Miraculous Faith Pattern* is not followed.

Here is another way of wording this 8-step *Miraculous Faith Pattern*:

1. Faith Stands on The Promises of God, Found in The Word of God.

2. Faith Speaks to Mountains, and Calls Things That Be Not as Though They Were.

3. Faith Hopes Against Hope.

4. Faith Is Not Weak.

5. Faith Doesn't Consider the Problem.

6. Faith Staggers Not at The Promise of God Through Unbelief.

7. Faith Is Strong in What It Believes and Gives Glory to God.

8. Faith Is Fully Persuaded That God Is Able to Perform What He Promised.

In conclusion, God has called us to walk by faith, live by faith, and be strong in our faith. God, in His mercy, has revealed a way for us to receive miracles from Him. The *Miraculous Faith Pattern* revealed in Romans 4:17-21 is the road map for all miracles. As you study the miracles of God in the Bible, you will see that everyone who received a miracle from God followed this same pattern. God is looking for faith, and the *Miraculous Faith Pattern* reveals what God is looking for to perform a miracle. As you study this pattern, you can see where you need to improve and where you can strengthen your faith. I pray this pattern helps you to understand how to receive miracles from God.

The Miraculous Faith Pattern Reveals What Faith is, What God is Looking For, and What Pleases God!

CHAPTER 11

Mountain Moving Faith

J esus taught His disciples that if they had faith and didn't doubt, they could speak to a mountain and make it move. Mountains represent anything standing in the way of God and His promises. One key to moving mountains is to speak to it in faith, with no doubt in your heart. There was also other secret keys Jesus taught that were critical in moving a mountain. In this chapter, I will teach you the secret keys to speaking to a mountain and making it move with your faith.

In the Scriptures, you will sometimes see the same story being told multiple times. Whenever this is the case, you will discover different secrets found in each version of the same story. Jesus spoke about how to speak by faith in Matthew, Mark, and Luke. Every time Jesus taught this truth, He revealed hidden key secrets from each passage on how to use your faith by speaking to things. Jesus used a mountain and a sycamine tree to represent problems we face, which can be impossible situations standing in our way that need to be moved.

The most famous section of Scripture where Jesus taught His disciples to speak to mountains and make them move is found in Mark Chapter 11. Jesus walked by a fig tree one day and cursed it when it had no figs for Him to eat because He was hungry. By the next day, the fig tree had dried up by the roots. When Peter saw how fast the fig tree dried up, he remembered Jesus had cursed it the day before. At this point, Jesus taught His Apostles the most profound truth about speaking to mountains and making them move with faith-filled words.

Here is the astounding story of Jesus teaching His Apostles how to speak to mountains with their faith, found in the Book of Mark:

> *Mark 11:20-26 (KJV)*
> *20 And in the morning, as they passed by, they saw the fig tree dried up from the roots. 21 And Peter calling to remembrance saith unto him, Master, behold, the fig tree which thou cursedst is withered away. 22 And Jesus answering saith unto them, Have faith in God. 23 For verily I say unto you, That whosoever shall say unto this mountain, Be thou removed, and be thou cast into the sea; and shall not doubt in his heart, but shall believe that those things which he saith shall come to pass; he shall have whatsoever he saith. 24 Therefore I say unto you, What things soever ye desire, when ye pray, believe that ye receive them, and ye shall have them. 25 And when ye stand praying, forgive, if ye have ought against any: that your Father also which is in heaven may forgive you your trespasses. 26 But if ye do not forgive, neither will your Father which is in heaven forgive your trespasses.*

Here are some key secrets found in this passage of Scripture about making mountains move by faith:

1. You must have faith in God to speak to a mountain.
2. Whosoever can speak to a mountain.
3. The mountain must be spoken to for it to obey you.

4. You must believe that what you say will come to pass.

5. You can have whatever you say if you have faith and no doubt in your heart.

6. You must believe that you received whatever you asked for in prayer.

7. When speaking to a mountain by faith, you must forgive anyone who sinned against you for your faith to work.

Now let's look at this same story of Jesus speaking to the fig tree, but this time in the Book of Matthew:

Matthew 21:18-22 (KJV)
18 Now in the morning as he returned into the city, he hungered. 19 And when he saw a fig tree in the way, he came to it, and found nothing thereon, but leaves only, and said unto it, Let no fruit grow on thee henceforward for ever. And presently the fig tree withered away. 20 And when the disciples saw it, they marvelled, saying, How soon is the fig tree withered away! 21 Jesus answered and said unto them, Verily I say unto you, If ye have faith, and doubt not, ye shall not only do this which is done to the fig tree, but also if ye shall say unto this mountain, Be thou removed, and be thou cast into the sea; it shall be done. 22 And all things, whatsoever ye shall ask in prayer, believing, ye shall receive.

Let's walk through this version of the fig tree being spoken to in the Book of Matthew and look for more hidden secret keys.

1. Faith can affect what it speaks to quickly.

2. Faith must not have any doubt.

3. The Apostles could speak to fig trees and mountains, and they would obey them just like they obeyed Jesus.

4. Mountains, which represent impossible situations, need to be spoken to by faith for them to move.

5. Whatever you ask in prayer, believe you will receive.

Now let's look at a third time Jesus taught His disciples that they could speak to a mountain and make it move with their faith. This time Jesus was coming down from the Mount of Transfiguration with Peter, James, and John, where they had just encountered the Father, Moses, and Elijah. The Father told Peter, James, and John that Jesus was His beloved Son and for them to hear Him.

When Jesus came down the mountain from this experience, He found His other Apostles in a situation where they could not cast the devil out of a lunatic boy. Jesus ended up casting this devil out and cured the boy using His faith to command the devil to leave. The Apostles who couldn't cast the devil out came to Jesus and asked why they couldn't cast the devil out. Jesus told them it was because of their unbelief and added that this kind doesn't come out without prayer and fasting.

Let's read this story together found in the Book of Matthew:

Matthew 17:14-21 (KJV)
14 And when they were come to the multitude, there came to him a certain man, kneeling down to him, and saying, 15 Lord, have mercy on my son: for he is lunatick, and sore vexed: for ofttimes he falleth into the fire, and oft into the water. 16 And I brought him to thy disciples, and they could not cure him. 17 Then Jesus answered and said, O faithless and perverse generation, how long shall I be with you? how long shall I suffer you? bring him hither to me. 18 And Jesus rebuked the devil; and he departed out of him: and the child was cured from that very hour. 19 Then came the disciples to Jesus apart, and said, Why could not we cast him out? 20 And Jesus said unto them, Because of your unbelief: for verily I say unto you, If ye have faith as a grain of mustard seed, ye shall say unto this mountain, Remove hence to yonder

place; and it shall remove; and nothing shall be impossible unto you. 21 Howbeit this kind goeth not out but by prayer and fasting.

Here are important facts and secret keys found in this version of speaking to mountains and making them move:

1. The devil had to be rebuked for him to leave.
2. Unbelief will stop your words from being effective.
3. Your faith only needs to be the size of a mustard seed for it to work.
4. You must tell the mountain precisely where you want it to go.
5. Mountains will obey faith-filled words.
6. If you have faith and no doubt, nothing will be impossible for you.
7. Some devils only come out with prayer and fasting, which means prayer and fasting helps your faith.

Another important passage of Scripture is in the Book of Luke, where Jesus taught His Apostles they could speak to something and make it move with their faith-filled words. One day, the Apostles asked Jesus to increase their faith. At this point, Jesus taught His Apostles that they could speak to a sycamine tree, which would obey them if they had faith the size of a mustard seed. At this same time, He also told them a parable about servants obeying their masters.

Luke 17:5-10 (KJV)
5 And the apostles said unto the Lord, Increase our faith. 6 And the Lord said, If ye had faith as a grain of mustard seed, ye might say unto this sycamine tree, Be thou plucked up by the root, and be thou planted in the sea; and it should obey you. 7 But which of you, having a servant plowing or feeding cattle, will say unto him by and by, when he is come from the field, Go and sit down to meat? 8 And will not rather say unto him, Make ready wherewith I may sup, and gird thyself, and serve me,

till I have eaten and drunken; and afterward thou shalt eat and drink? 9 Doth he thank that servant because he did the things that were commanded him? I trow not. 10 So likewise ye, when ye shall have done all those things which are commanded you, say, We are unprofitable servants: we have done that which was our duty to do.

Here are important facts and key secrets about faith found in this passage of Scripture:

1. Your faith only needs to be the size of a mustard seed for it to work.
2. The sycamine tree, which represents impossible situations, will obey your words.
3. Things like the sycamine tree will listen to your faith and obey your words like a servant obeys their master.
4. Things like sycamine trees have to obey your faith-filled words.

When you break down all these verses and put them together, you find amazing key secrets about your ability to speak to things by faith. Jesus taught that if we had faith and no doubt in our hearts, we could speak by faith and move mountains and sycamine trees. Jesus used a mountain and a sycamine tree as a metaphor for impossible situations standing in the way of God. Mountains also represent anything standing in the way of God and His promises.

Some people don't believe they can speak to things and make them obey, but you cannot deny that Jesus taught this truth. We also see Jesus practicing this truth throughout His whole ministry. The message of speaking to things by faith is found four times in the Gospels, clearly showing how vital this message is to Jesus. If something is mentioned once in the Bible, it is important, but mentioning it four times shows how extremely important this message is to God.

Here are the important key secrets we can see from all the passages from Matthew, Mark, and Luke that Jesus taught about speaking by faith tied together:

1. You must have faith to move a mountain/sycamine tree.
2. Your faith can be as small as a mustard seed.
3. You cannot doubt in your heart when speaking to a mountain.
4. You must believe your words will come to pass.
5. When praying, you must believe you have received what you are praying for.
6. Whatever you ask in prayer, believe you will receive.
7. You cannot have any unforgiveness in your heart for your faith to work.
8. You must speak directly to the mountain or sycamine tree, which represents impossible situations, with faith-filled words for them to move.
9. Mountains, sycamine trees, and anything you speak to will obey your faith-filled words like servants obeying their master.
10. Nothing is impossible for the person who believes.
11. Whosoever can have whatsoever if they speak by faith and do not doubt.

It is a Biblical fact and truth that you can speak to mountains and make them move with faith-filled words. The concept of speaking to mountains can also be found in the Old Testament. God commanded the prophet Zechariah to speak to a mountain.

Zechariah 4:6-7 (KJV)
*6 Then he answered and spake unto me, saying, This is the word of the Lord unto Zerubbabel, saying, Not by might, nor by power, but by my spirit, saith the Lord of hosts. 7 **Who art thou, O great mountain?** before Zerubbabel thou shalt become a plain: and he shall bring forth the headstone thereof with shoutings, crying, Grace, grace unto it.*

The prophet Zechariah was told to speak Grace, Grace to the mountain. Grace has to do with God's undeserved favor. Zechariah was told that it would be by the Spirit that would get things done and not by might nor power. This means it is only by the Spirit of God and through His grace, we can move mountains with our faith.

I now want to ask you a question. When you pray to God and expect Him to answer your prayer, how do you think God answers your prayer and performs what you ask Him to do? I am amazed how so many people don't know the answer to this question, but how vital it is to understand when it comes to prayer and speaking to mountains with our faith.

To answer this question, let's go back to how we move mountains with our faith. We must speak to the mountain to make it move with our faith. Let me pose to you that this is exactly what God does. When we pray to God, asking Him to perform a miracle, He has to speak to the situation with His faith to answer our prayer. So, we use our faith when speaking to the mountain to get God to use His faith. The mountain moves when God backs what we say with His faith. When God speaks, He does not doubt in His heart. Everything obeys His faith-filled Words. God has no doubt in His heart, and when He speaks to things with His faith, they obey Him. God uses His faith the same way He wants us to use our faith.

When Jesus, who is God, ministered on this earth, He spoke to mountains and made them move with His faith. The fig tree listened to the Words of

Jesus and dried up by the roots. We also know from the Scriptures it was Jesus that created the World in six days with faith-filled words.

Ephesians 3:9 (KJV)
*9 And to make all men see what is the fellowship of the mystery, which from the beginning of the world hath been hid in God, **who created all things by Jesus Christ:***

Colossians 1:16 (KJV)
*16 **For by him were all things created, that are in heaven, and that are in earth, visible and invisible, whether they be thrones, or dominions, or principalities, or powers: all things were created by him, and for him:***

The Bible also says that Jesus upholds all things by the Word of His power.

Hebrews 1:1-3 (KJV)
*1 God, who at sundry times and in divers manners spake in time past unto the fathers by the prophets, 2 Hath in these last days spoken unto us by his Son, whom he hath appointed heir of all things, **by whom also he made the worlds;** 3 Who being the brightness of his glory, and the express image of his person, **and upholding all things by the word of his power,** when he had by himself purged our sins, sat down on the right hand of the Majesty on high:*

When you bring this all together, God wants you to come to Him by faith in prayer, seeking an answer to your petition. Once you know it is God's will, He expects you to speak to the mountain by faith. Then, if you have faith and no doubt in your heart, God will use His faith-filled Words along with your faith-filled words and make the mountain obey you.

We were made in God's image, and God spoke everything into existence with His Words. Accepting this truth is difficult for some people to understand, but we were created to speak to things like God did when He created the worlds.

Hebrews 11:3 (KJV)
*3 **Through faith we understand that the worlds were framed by the word of God,** so that things which are seen were not made of things which do appear.*

When you look back at the story of Adam's fall in the Garden of Eden, you can see that he lost his ability to speak to things. Before Adam sinned, he tended to the Garden of Eden with his words. When Adam sinned by eating from the Tree of the Knowledge of Good and Evil, God cursed him with having to work by the sweat of his brow. This meant he would have to work in the hot sun with his hands. Adam was not cursed with work because work is not a curse. Work is not a curse because we know God worked with His mouth when creating all things in six days. When Adam fell, he lost his ability to speak to things, as God spoke to things.

Genesis 3:17-19 (KJV)
*17 And unto Adam he said, Because thou hast hearkened unto the voice of thy wife, and hast eaten of the tree, of which I commanded thee, saying, Thou shalt not eat of it: cursed is the ground for thy sake; in sorrow shalt thou eat of it all the days of thy life; 18 Thorns also and thistles shall it bring forth to thee; and thou shalt eat the herb of the field; 19 **In the sweat of thy face shalt thou eat bread,** till thou return unto the ground; for out of it wast thou taken: for dust thou art, and unto dust shalt thou return.*

So much was lost because of the fall of Adam. It wasn't until Jesus returned, He started teaching people they could work with their words again. Jesus spoke to trees, mountains, demons, storms, fevers, blind eyes, and dead bodies, and they all obeyed Him. Jesus also taught His disciples to start speaking to things and working with their words.

A Roman Centurion was one of the first men to recognize that Jesus could work with His Words. This Centurion knew Jesus could speak a Word and His servant would be healed. The Centurion understood the authority of the spoken word because he was a man under authority, and he had soldiers under him that obeyed his words. Jesus marveled at the Roman Centurion's faith and said He hadn't found faith like this in all of Israel. The Centurion recognized Jesus was operating under the authority of Heaven and had power with His Words.

> *Matthew 8:5-13 (KJV)*
> *5 And when Jesus was entered into Capernaum, there came unto him a centurion, beseeching him, 6 And saying, Lord, my servant lieth at home sick of the palsy, grievously tormented. 7 And Jesus saith unto him, I will come and heal him. 8 The centurion answered and said, Lord, I am not worthy that thou shouldest come under my roof: **but speak the word only, and my servant shall be healed. 9 For I am a man under authority, having soldiers under me: and I say to this man, Go, and he goeth; and to another, Come, and he cometh; and to my servant, Do this, and he doeth it. 10 When Jesus heard it, he marvelled,** and said to them that followed, **Verily I say unto you, I have not found so great faith, no, not in Israel.** 11 And I say unto you, That many shall come from the east and west, and shall sit down with Abraham, and Isaac, and Jacob, in the kingdom of heaven. 12 But the children of the kingdom shall be cast out into outer darkness: there shall be weeping and gnashing of teeth. 13 And Jesus said unto the centurion, Go thy way; and as thou hast believed, so be it done unto thee. And his servant was healed in the selfsame hour.*

Your life will never be the same when you understand and believe you can work by speaking with faith to mountains, and they will obey you. Nothing will be impossible if you learn to speak to mountains by faith. All things are possible to those who believe and speak what they believe. Things are waiting to listen to you and for you to tell them what you want them to do. As you speak by faith, God will back your faith with His faith, and together you will move mountains.

There is another important story to read to help us better understand the power of faith-filled words found in the Old Testament, where God commanded Moses to speak to a rock to bring forth water. The children of Israel needed water, and God commanded Moses to speak to the rock, and it would bring forth water. However, Moses disobeyed God, struck the rock twice with His rod, and didn't speak to the rock as commanded. The rock still brought forth water, but God punished Moses by saying he couldn't go into the *Promised Land* because of his disobedience in not speaking to the rock.

Let's read this story together, and then I will expound on why God told Moses he couldn't go into the *Promise Land* because of his disobedience:

Numbers 20:7-12 (KJV)

*7 And the Lord spake unto Moses, saying, 8 Take the rod, and gather thou the assembly together, thou, and Aaron thy brother, **and speak ye unto the rock before their eyes; and it shall give forth his water,** and thou shalt bring forth to them water out of the rock: so thou shalt give the congregation and their beasts drink. 9 And Moses took the rod from before the Lord, as he commanded him. 10 And Moses and Aaron gathered the congregation together before the rock, and he said unto them, Hear now, ye rebels; must we fetch you water out of this rock? 11 **And Moses lifted up his hand, and with his rod he smote the rock twice:** and the water came out abundantly, and the congregation drank, and their beasts also. 12 And the Lord spake unto Moses and Aaron, **Because ye believed me not, to sanctify me in the eyes of the children of Israel, therefore ye shall not bring this congregation into the land which I have given them.***

Whenever God told men in the Old Testament to do things, it was often to portray what He would do with Christ in the New Testament. For example, the Bible says the Law was a shadow of the image that was to come.

Hebrews 10:1 (KJV)
1 For the law having a shadow of good things to come, and not the very image of the things, can never with those sacrifices which they offered year by year continually make the comers thereunto perfect.

In the story of Moses hitting the rock, we see God wanted to use Moses speaking to the rock as a shadow of the image of Christ coming to speak to things with His faith-filled words. There are a number of revelations in this story, but the punishment God gave Moses for not speaking to the rock reveals a great secret. God punished Moses for not speaking to the rock by not allowing him to enter the *Promised Land*. The *Promise Land* represents all the *Precious Promises* of God found in His Word.

This story reveals that you would have to speak to things to inherit the promises of God. You will miss entering **YOUR** *Promise Land* if you don't learn to speak to things. The *Precious Promises* of God found in His Word are only inherited by those who learn to speak to mountains by faith. Using our faith to speak to impossible situations to inherit the promises of God was the great secret, along with other keys Jesus revealed to His Apostles.

In conclusion, God is looking for those who take Him at His Word and speak to mountains by faith. If you have faith and don't doubt in your heart, you will speak to things, and they will obey you, just like they obeyed Jesus. Jesus never said He was the only one who could speak to mountains. Jesus taught that *whosoever* could have *whatsoever* if they have faith in God and learn to speak to mountains. God has commissioned you to speak by faith and move mountains. Now is your time to move mountains with your faith-filled words and inherit *YOUR Promised Land!*

CHAPTER 12

The Prayer of Faith

There is a famous passage of Scripture found in the Book of James where God promises to heal the sick when *The Prayer of Faith* is offered. This passage of Scripture was written as a promise to anyone sick, and how to receive healing from Church Elders. There are secrets hidden in this passage of Scripture that are critical to understand when praying for the sick. In this chapter, I will reveal secrets about *The Prayer of Faith* and how people can receive healing from the Lord.

Let's start by reading this famous Scripture about *The Prayer of Faith* found in James Chapter 5, and then I will reveal hidden secrets found in this passage.

James 5:13-18 (KJV)
*13 Is any among you afflicted? let him pray. Is any merry? let him sing psalms. 14 Is any sick among you? let him call for the elders of the church; and let them pray over him, anointing him with oil in the name of the Lord: 15 **And the prayer of faith** shall save the sick, and the Lord*

shall raise him up; and if he have committed sins, they shall be forgiven him. 16 Confess your faults one to another, and pray one for another, that ye may be healed. The effectual fervent prayer of a righteous man availeth much. 17 Elias was a man subject to like passions as we are, and he prayed earnestly that it might not rain: and it rained not on the earth by the space of three years and six months. 18 And he prayed again, and the heaven gave rain, and the earth brought forth her fruit.

I want to point out the words pray/prayer is mentioned seven times in this passage. But it is important to note different words are being used in the Greek language for the words pray/prayer in this section of Scripture. When studying the Bible, it is critical to study the different words and definitions from the original language the Bible was written in to interpret different passages properly. In this passage, important revelations are lost when each Greek word being used for pray/prayer is not translated correctly.

Here is a breakdown of the definition of the Greek words for pray/prayer and how it is used each time in this passage.

1. Verse 13 — *let him* **pray.** The Greek word for **pray** is *proseúchomai.* Praying to God to obtain something good or averting evil.

2. Verse 14 — *let them call for the elders of the church and let them* **pray** *over him.* The Greek word for **pray** is *proseúchomai.* Praying to God to obtain something good or averting evil.

3. Verse 15 — *And the* **prayer** *of faith will save the sick.* The Greek word for **prayer** is *euchē.* A wish expressed as a petition to God,

or votive obligation, prayer, vow. The basic meaning of the Greek word *euchē* means a wish or vow.

4. **Verse 16** — *Confess your faults to one another and **pray** for one another.* The Greek word for ***pray*** is *euchomai*. To speak out and utter out loud a wish. It also means to pray or to vow to God.

5. **Verse 16** — *The effectual **prayer** of a righteous man availeth much.* The Greek word for ***prayer*** is *deēsis*. To make known one's particular need. A petition, prayer, request, or supplication for particular benefits.

6. **Verse 17** — *Elijah was a man subject to like passions as we are, and he **prayed** earnestly that it might not rain.* The Greek word for ***prayed*** comes from two combined words *proseúchomai: proseuchē.* To pray to God and offer prayer earnestly.

7. **Verse 18** — *And he **prayed** again, and the heaven gave rain.* The Greek word for ***prayed*** is *proseúchomai.* Praying to God to obtain something good or averting evil.

Within these six verses, we see different meanings in the Greek language being used for pray/prayer. Most of the definitions for the words pray/prayer have to do with making a petition to God. However, the word *prayer* used in *The Prayer of Faith* has to do with a wish and a vow to God. Adding a vow to the definition of the word *prayer* changes the whole equation of what we know and understand when it comes to *The Prayer of Faith*.

So, ask yourself, what is a vow? The word vow is defined as a spoken promise to do or not do a specified thing. A person making a vow verbally promises and binds their soul with a promise to do or not to do something. Vows are not to be taken lightly, and God hears every vow we make and holds us accountable to them. This is why wedding vows are so important. If you break a vow, you can bring a curse upon yourself.

Whenever you utter a vow out of your mouth to God, you must keep your word.

> *Numbers 30:2 (KJV)*
> *2 If a man vow a vow unto the Lord, or swear an oath to bind his soul with a bond; he shall not break his word, he shall do according to all that proceedeth out of his mouth.*

Now, let's return to the passage of Scripture found in James Chapter 5 and see what someone would vow to do or not to do. The vow is regarding someone who has sinned and needs healing. Before the sick person is healed through *The Prayer of Faith*, they must confess their sin. So, the vow must have something to do with sin.

Let's reread this passage, and I will add two more verses at the end that confirm that this passage is talking about sin and the vow having to do with sin.

> *James 5:13-20 (KJV)*
> *13 Is any among you afflicted? let him pray. Is any merry? let him sing psalms. 14 **Is any sick among you?** let him call for the elders of the church; and let them pray over him, anointing him with oil in the name of the Lord: 15 **And the prayer of faith shall save the sick,** and the Lord shall raise him up; **and if he have committed sins, they shall be forgiven him. 16 Confess your faults one to another, and pray one for another, that ye may be healed.** The effectual fervent prayer of a*

righteous man availeth much. *17 Elias was a man subject to like passions as we are, and he prayed earnestly that it might not rain: and it rained not on the earth by the space of three years and six months. 18 And he prayed again, and the heaven gave rain, and the earth brought forth her fruit. 19 Brethren, if any of you do err from the truth, and one convert him; 20* **Let him know, that he which converteth the sinner from the error of his way shall save a soul from death, and shall hide a multitude of sins.**

From this passage, we can see that someone is sick because of sin and needs to confess their faults before they can be prayed for with *The Prayer of Faith* from the church Elders. Sin must be confessed before the sick person can be healed. Confession of sins has to do with past sins, but the vow has to do with future sins. A person must confess past sins and vow to quit sinning in the future for *The Prayer of Faith* to work.

This truth of vowing to not sin in the future is found in a powerful story of when Jesus healed a man. After Jesus healed this man, He told him to *go and sin no more* lest a worst thing comes upon him. If sinning no more was not possible, Jesus would have never made the statement. So, the vow has to do with vowing to not sin anymore. The man had to make a vow to stop sinning, or a worse sickness would come on him.

John 5:13-14 (KJV)
13 And he that was healed wist not who it was: for Jesus had conveyed himself away, a multitude being in that place. 14 Afterward Jesus findeth him in the temple, and said unto him, Behold, thou art made whole: **sin no more, lest a worse thing come unto thee.**

In the Book of James, regarding *The Prayer of Faith,* we can see that the issue of sin has to be dealt with for the sick person to receive healing. This passage reveals that the sinner with the sickness needs to vow to quit sinning for God to heal them. Not all sickness results from someone sinning, but when sickness comes because of sin, the sin must be dealt with before the person can be healed. The person must first confess and repent of their past sin(s), but they must also vow to quit that specific sin in the future.

Understanding what Jesus taught about sin is essential to understand this passage better. Jesus taught that if a person sinned, they were a slave to sin. Jesus came to set people free from sin. When a person is set free from sin, they have the power to quit sinning and live a holy life before God. If it wasn't possible to live without sinning, Jesus never would have taught this. If you understand this truth, you can walk free from sin all the days of your life, because Jesus makes you free.

> *John 8:31-36 (KJV)*
> *31 Then said Jesus to those Jews which believed on him, If ye continue in my word, then are ye my disciples indeed; 32 **And ye shall know the truth, and the truth shall make you free**. 33 They answered him, We be Abraham's seed, and were never in bondage to any man: how sayest thou, Ye shall be made free? 34 Jesus answered them, Verily, verily, I say unto you, **Whosoever committeth sin is the servant of sin**. 35 And the servant abideth not in the house for ever: but the Son abideth ever. 36 **If the Son therefore shall make you free, ye shall be free indeed**.*

I am teaching this truth because many false teachers teach we can never stop sinning even after being made free by Christ. Someone could indeed choose to fall back into a sin or slip up, even after being set free, but it is important to understand that Jesus sets people free from sin. When you are set free from sin, you choose not to sin anymore and live a holy life by the power of the Holy Spirit. If you don't understand this truth, then you wouldn't think it was possible to make a vow to quit sinning.

The Book of Romans reinforces the truth of Christians being freed from sin. The Apostle Paul says we should not continue in sin so that grace may abound. Grace has to do with God's undeserved favor to forgive and save us from our sins. The grace of God is bestowed upon the repentant sinner when they accept Christ as their Savior. When the grace of God comes upon the repentant sinner, they are made free from sin.

> *Romans 6:1-7 (KJV)*
> *1 What shall we say then? **Shall we continue in sin, that grace may abound? 2 God forbid. How shall we, that are dead to sin, live any longer therein?** 3 Know ye not, that so many of us as were baptized into Jesus Christ were baptized into his death? 4 Therefore we are buried with him by baptism into death: that like as Christ was raised up from the dead by the glory of the Father, even so we also should walk in newness of life. 5 For if we have been planted together in the likeness of his death, we shall be also in the likeness of his resurrection: 6 Knowing this, that our old man is crucified with him, **that the body of sin might be destroyed, that henceforth we should not serve sin. 7 For he that is dead is freed from sin.***

When someone sins, their freedom is taken from them, and a sickness can come upon them. If you or someone you know is sick, and it is connected to their sinning, they need to confess and forsake their sin if they want to be made free and healed. Whoever confesses and forsakes their sins will be shown mercy from the Lord. Forsaking your sin involves making a vow to quit sinning. If someone only confesses their sin and doesn't vow to stop sinning, a worse sickness will come upon them. What good is it to be forgiven a sin by the Lord, to only continue in sin?

> *Proverbs 28:13 (KJV)*
> *13 **He that covereth his sins shall not prosper: but whoso confesseth and forsaketh them shall have mercy.***

Now, let's talk about how *The Prayer of Faith* is implemented to the sick person. It says in James 5:14-18 that the sick person is to call for the Church Elders to pray over them and to anoint them with oil in the Name of the Lord.

James 5:14-18 (KJV)
14 Is any sick among you? **let him call for the elders of the church; and let them pray over him,** *anointing him with oil in the name of the Lord: 15* **And the prayer of faith shall save the sick,** *and the Lord shall raise him up; and if he have committed sins, they shall be forgiven him. 16 Confess your faults one to another, and pray one for another, that ye may be healed. The effectual fervent prayer of a righteous man availeth much. 17 Elias was a man subject to like passions as we are, and he prayed earnestly that it might not rain: and it rained not on the earth by the space of three years and six months. 18 And he prayed again, and the heaven gave rain, and the earth brought forth her fruit.*

It is important to recognize that Elijah the prophet is mentioned when referencing the Church Elders praying for the sick. So, you have to ask yourself, what does the story of Elijah and him praying for rain have to do with praying *The Prayer of Faith* for the sick? This means there must be a hidden secret found in the story of Elijah, and if found, could help us better understand *The Prayer of Faith*.

Let's go to 1 Kings Chapter 16 and read what was going on with Elijah and the rain. During the time of Elijah, Ahab was the King of Israel married to his wicked wife, Jezebel. Ahab and Jezebel sinned against the Lord by worshipping and serving the false god named baal. They were both wicked rulers who were sinning and doing great evil before the Lord.

1 Kings 16:30-33 (KJV)
30 And Ahab the son of Omri did evil in the sight of the Lord above all that were before him. 31 And it came to pass, as if it had been a

light thing for him to walk in the sins of Jeroboam the son of Nebat, that he took to wife Jezebel the daughter of Ethbaal king of the Zidonians, and went and served Baal, and worshipped him. 32 And he reared up an altar for Baal in the house of Baal, which he had built in Samaria. 33 And Ahab made a grove; and Ahab did more to provoke the Lord God of Israel to anger than all the kings of Israel that were before him.

The Lord raised the righteous prophet Elijah to deal with these two wicked rulers. When Elijah first confronts Ahab, he tells him it won't rain except at his word. Elijah then goes into hiding while Ahab, Jezebel, and all of Israel enter a severe drought.

1 Kings 17:1 (KJV)
*1 And Elijah the Tishbite, who was of the inhabitants of Gilead, said unto Ahab, As the Lord God of Israel liveth, before whom I stand, **there shall not be dew nor rain these years, but according to my word.***

The Lord warned the children of Israel in the Law of Moses that if they sinned by serving other gods and worshipping them, He would stop the rain.

Deuteronomy 11:16-17 (KJV)
*16 **Take heed to yourselves, that your heart be not deceived, and ye turn aside, and serve other gods, and worship them;** 17 And then the Lord's wrath be kindled against you, **and he shut up the heaven, that there be no rain,** and that the land yield not her fruit; and lest ye perish quickly from off the good land which the Lord giveth you.*

Rain from Heaven is a blessing from God. The Old Testament Law taught that if we obey God and serve Him with all of our hearts, He will send rain on our land.

Deuteronomy 11:13-14 (KJV)
13 And it shall come to pass, if ye shall hearken diligently unto my commandments which I command you this day, to love the Lord your God, and to serve him with all your heart and with all your soul, 14 That I will give you the rain of your land in his due season, the first rain and the latter rain, that thou mayest gather in thy corn, and thy wine, and thine oil.

After three and a half years, Elijah emerges from hiding at the Word of the Lord to confront Ahab again. God told Elijah to show himself to Ahab and that He would send the rain again.

1 Kings 18:1-2 (KJV)
*1 And it came to pass after many days, that the word of the Lord came to Elijah in the third year, saying, **Go, shew thyself unto Ahab; and I will send rain upon the earth**. 2 And Elijah went to shew himself unto Ahab. And there was a sore famine in Samaria.*

A showdown occurs between Elijah and the false prophets of baal at this meeting with Ahab. This showdown happened on Mount Carmel in Israel, besides the Mediterranean Sea. Elijah challenged them that whoever the real God is would answer by fire. The false prophets of baal cried out to Baal most of the day, to no avail. When they are finished, Elijah sets up the altar of the Lord, sacrifices animals, and has four barrels of water poured on his sacrifice three times. Then, when Elijah prayed to his God, God answered by fire from heaven and consumed the burnt sacrifice, wood, stones, dust, and all the water. After the fire of God fell, Elijah had all the prophets of baal killed.

1 Kings 18:30-40 (KJV)
30 And Elijah said unto all the people, Come near unto me. And all the people came near unto him. And he repaired the altar of the Lord that was broken down. 31 And Elijah took twelve stones, according to

*the number of the tribes of the sons of Jacob, unto whom the word of the Lord came, saying, Israel shall be thy name: 32 And with the stones he built an altar in the name of the Lord: and he made a trench about the altar, as great as would contain two measures of seed. 33 And he put the wood in order, and cut the bullock in pieces, and laid him on the wood, and said, **Fill four barrels with water, and pour it on the burnt sacrifice, and on the wood. 34 And he said, Do it the second time. And they did it the second time. And he said, Do it the third time. And they did it the third time. 35 And the water ran round about the altar; and he filled the trench also with water.** 36 And it came to pass at the time of the offering of the evening sacrifice, that Elijah the prophet came near, and said, Lord God of Abraham, Isaac, and of Israel, let it be known this day that thou art God in Israel, and that I am thy servant, and that I have done all these things at thy word. 37 Hear me, O Lord, hear me, that this people may know that thou art the Lord God, and that thou hast turned their heart back again. 38 **Then the fire of the Lord fell, and consumed the burnt sacrifice, and the wood, and the stones, and the dust, and licked up the water that was in the trench.** 39 And when all the people saw it, they fell on their faces: and they said, The Lord, he is the God; the Lord, he is the God. 40 **And Elijah said unto them, Take the prophets of Baal; let not one of them escape. And they took them: and Elijah brought them down to the brook Kishon, and slew them there.***

After the fire fell from Heaven and Elijah killed the prophets of baal, he told Ahab he heard the sound of the abundance of rain.

1 Kings 18:41-42 (KJV)
*41 And Elijah said unto Ahab, Get thee up, eat and drink; **for there is a sound of abundance of rain.** 42 So Ahab went up to eat and to drink. And Elijah went up to the top of Carmel; and he cast himself down upon the earth, and put his face between his knees,*

Next, Elijah goes to the top of Carmel, casts himself to the ground, and starts praying with his face between his knees. While praying, Elijah tells his servant to look toward the sea. Elijah's servant returned, saying he didn't see anything. Elijah sent his servant seven times to the sea to tell him what he saw. It wasn't until the seventh time that he came back and said he saw a cloud the size of a man's hand. Elijah knew God heard his prayer, and he told Ahab to prepare his chariot and get down from the mountain, so the rain didn't stop him. The heavens then became black with clouds and wind, and there was a great rain.

> *1 Kings 18:42-45 (KJV)*
> *42 So Ahab went up to eat and to drink. And Elijah went up to the top of Carmel; and he cast himself down upon the earth, and put his face between his knees, 43 And said to his servant, **Go up now, look toward the sea. And he went up, and looked, and said, There is nothing. And he said, Go again seven times. 44 And it came to pass at the seventh time, that he said, Behold, there ariseth a little cloud out of the sea, like a man's hand.** And he said, Go up, say unto Ahab, Prepare thy chariot, and get thee down that the rain stop thee not. 45 And it came to pass in the mean while, that the heaven was black with clouds and wind, and there was a great rain. And Ahab rode, and went to Jezreel.*

Remember, this story was used in the Book of James Chapter 5, about *The Prayer of Faith* saving the sick. Therefore, we must examine what Elijah did when he prayed about the rain and how this applies to *The Prayer of Faith*. There are great secrets to be learned by studying what Elijah did regarding *The Prayer of Faith*.

Remember, Elijah prophesied to Ahab that it would not rain again, except at his word when he met with him the first time.

1 Kings 17:1 (KJV)
*1 And Elijah the Tishbite, who was of the inhabitants of Gilead, said unto Ahab, As the Lord God of Israel liveth, before whom I stand, **there shall not be dew nor rain these years, but according to my word.***

Elijah was standing on the Word of the Lord and the Holy Scriptures that God would cause it to rain again if the people repented. Elijah only prayed for it to rain after the people repented when the fire of God fell on the sacrifice. *The Prayer of Faith* can only be offered by standing on God's Word and His promises that He will heal. While standing on God's promises to heal, the sick person must repent of all sins for God to heal them. Once their sins are confessed, and a vow is made to quit sinning, the person will receive healing through *The Prayer of Faith*, according to the promise of God.

There is another secret that can be found when Elijah prayed for it to rain. Elijah kept sending his servant back to the sea until he saw a cloud. Elijah sent his servant back seven times, and it wasn't until the seventh time his servant saw a cloud the size of a man's hand. When Elijah heard this, he knew his prayer was answered, and it would rain. The secret that is revealed in sending his servant back is that when offering *The Prayer of Faith*, we cannot give up too soon when praying for the sick. It might take some time and warfare to get the sick person healed. Unfortunately, too many ministers give up too quickly, which is why many people are not healed when *The Prayer of Faith* is spoken. Elijah knew that although God promised it to rain again, he had to be persistent in prayer to get God's promised Word to manifest. Just because God made the promise, it doesn't mean it will come to pass without someone offering *The Prayer of Faith*.

Whenever *The Prayer of Faith* is offered, we must keep believing God and speaking to the mountain until the person is healed. Sometimes it might just be a small sign in their body, but the person praying *The Prayer of Faith* must stay at it until a sign manifests. Elijah didn't stop offering *The Prayer of Faith* until he saw a sign that he had broken through, and God was manifesting His Word. Elijah stayed focused and persisted in *The Prayer of Faith* until God's power manifested by sending a cloud the size of a man's hand. When it comes to *The Prayer of Faith*, it is vital to be persistent in prayer until the answer manifests.

We can see this truth of being persistent in prayer until the promise of God's Word manifests in one story of Jesus praying for someone blind. When Jesus first prayed for the man with the laying on of hands, he said he saw men walking as trees. Then Jesus laid hands on him again, and he fully received his sight. Jesus did not stop praying for the man until he was fully healed.

> *Mark 8:22-26 (KJV)*
> *22 And he cometh to Bethsaida; and they bring a blind man unto him, and besought him to touch him. 23 And he took the blind man by the hand, and led him out of the town; and when he had spit on his eyes, and put his hands upon him, he asked him if he saw ought. 24 **And he looked up, and said, I see men as trees, walking. 25 After that he put his hands again upon his eyes, and made him look up: and he was restored, and saw every man clearly.** 26 And he sent him away to his house, saying, Neither go into the town, nor tell it to any in the town.*

Now let's reread James 5:14-18, and I will point out some more important facts and secrets when praying *The Prayer of Faith*.

James 5:14-18 (KJV)

*14 Is any sick among you? let him call for the elders of the church; and let them pray over him, anointing him with oil in the name of the Lord: 15 **And the prayer of faith shall save the sick,** and the Lord shall raise him up; and if he have committed sins, they shall be forgiven him. 16 Confess your faults one to another, and pray one for another, that ye may be healed. The effectual fervent prayer of a righteous man availeth much. 17 Elias was a man subject to like passions as we are, and he prayed earnestly that it might not rain: and it rained not on the earth by the space of three years and six months. 18 And he prayed again, and the heaven gave rain, and the earth brought forth her fruit.*

Below are important facts and secrets from this passage:

1. If you are sick, you are to call for the Elders of the Church.

2. Elders are to anoint with oil the sick person when praying for them because oil represents the Holy Spirit, and we know the Holy Spirit is the One performing the healing.

3. Only The Prayer of Faith saves the sick and not any other prayer. Prayers that are filled with fear, doubt, and unbelief won't save the sick.

4. When the sinner confesses their sin, they will be forgiven and healed when prayed for.

5. The sinner must make a vow to quit sinning.

6. The Prayer of Faith must be offered effectually and fervently, like how Elijah prayed for the rain.

7. One of the most profound secrets to The Prayer of Faith is that just because God gives a promise, it still takes someone like Elijah to pray persistently in faith until God manifests His Word.

8. The Elders must be righteous men. The Elders have also made a vow to quit sinning and are not living in sin.

9. When praying for the sick, we must be persistent like Elijah praying for it to rain. When offering The Prayer of Faith, you can't give up too early and think God didn't hear you. You must persist until the healing manifests.

The Elders in the Church who offer *The Prayer of Faith* to save the sick must be bold and persistent in their faith and not give up until they get a breakthrough. We have to be bold and aggressive like Elijah, who knew how to lay hold of the promises of God and not give up until he saw God perform His Word. God is looking for people of faith who will not give up easily just because they don't see the miracle come to pass the first time they speak to a mountain. We have to force the miracle of healing to manifest with bold, uncompromising, and persistent faith when praying *The Prayer of Faith*.

The Bible says the Kingdom of Heaven suffers violence, and the violent take it by force. Therefore, we must be tenacious about our faith and hold on like bulldogs until we see God perform His Word. This is one of the most important secrets we can learn when praying *The Prayer of Faith*.

Matthew 11:12 (KJV)
*12 And from the days of John the Baptist until now **the kingdom of heaven suffereth violence, and the violent take it by force.***

The final question that must be asked is why doesn't God just heal the sick person after they confess their sin and make a vow to stop sinning? Why does it take *The Prayer of Faith* from a Church Elder to save the sick? The answer is it takes a Church Elder or someone of faith to manifest God's promises because God gave man dominion on the earth, and God will only work through someone who has dominion on the earth to accomplish His plans and purposes.

Psalm 8:4-6 (KJV)
*4 **What is man, that thou art mindful of him?** and the son of man, that thou visitest him? 5 For thou hast made him a little lower than the angels, and hast crowned him with glory and honour. 6 Thou madest him to have dominion over the works of thy hands; thou hast put all things under his feet:*

For God to manifest His Word on the earth, He needs someone to give Him the authority to operate. God is given authority to operate and fulfill His Word by people using their faith. A person of faith allows God to use His faith to get things done on the earth. This is why Jesus had to come as a man and take dominion as a man to allow God to take dominion back on the earth. This is also why you never see God doing any miracles in the Old Testament without a man or woman of God being involved. *The Prayer of Faith* allows God to fulfill His promise to perform miracles and heal people.

In conclusion, many secrets are revealed about *The Prayer of Faith* in James, Chapter 5. This is a foundational chapter for administering healing and working miracles in the Church. We must learn there is more than what meets the eye when reading how *The Prayer of Faith* is offered up. A vow must be made to not sin in the future while a confession of past sins is being made. Once sin is dealt with, the Elders must speak to the sickness with persistent and bold faith until the repentant sinner is healed. Elijah is the perfect example of not giving up until God manifests His Word. God is looking for people who will take Him at His Word and boldly pray to see His Word manifest. Never give up or back down when praying ***The Prayer of Faith!***

CHAPTER 13

Persistent Faith

Persistent faith cannot be overlooked when believing God for an answer to a prayer. A person of strong faith doesn't idly stand around hoping for God to answer their prayer, but boldly keeps praying until God answers them. Faith-filled Christians know God must be convinced they truly believe Him before He will answer them. People of faith don't take no for an answer when it comes to the promises of God. In this chapter, I will reveal what it means to have persistent faith and why we should never give up when seeking God for an answer to our prayers.

God is looking for people of faith who will not give up when taking Him at His Word. Unfortunately, too many people start in faith and end up in doubt when they don't see a quick answer to their prayer. Faith, however, is eternal and never quits or gives up because faith knows God always comes through for those who believe. Once you understand this truth, you can learn how to receive many answers to your prayers from God.

Jesus taught a powerful parable about a persistent widow who went before an unjust judge to avenge her of her adversary. In this parable, the unjust judge avenged the widow of her adversary, not for the sake of justice, but because she wore him out by continually coming to him for his help. The persistent widow's determination persuaded the unjust judge to avenge her of her adversary. She had an adversary coming against her, and she knew she had to keep bugging the unjust judge until he made a judgment in her favor.

Let's read this parable together, and I will reveal powerful truths to understand better what Jesus taught about being persistent when praying to God.

> *Luke 18:1-8 (KJV)*
> *1 And he spake a parable unto them to this end, that men ought always to pray, and not to faint; 2 Saying, There was in a city a judge, which feared not God, neither regarded man: 3 And there was a widow in that city; and she came unto him, saying, **Avenge me of mine adversary.** 4 And he would not for a while: but afterward he said within himself, Though I fear not God, nor regard man; 5 **Yet because this widow troubleth me, I will avenge her, lest by her continual coming she weary me.** 6 And the Lord said, Hear what the unjust judge saith. 7 **And shall not God avenge his own elect, which cry day and night unto him, though he bear long with them? 8 I tell you that he will avenge them speedily.** Nevertheless when the Son of man cometh, shall he find faith on the earth?*

This parable gives great insight into the mind of God concerning faith and prayer. Jesus revealed the persistent attitude people need to have when praying to God. He also revealed that God determines to answer someone's prayer based on persistence and not justice. God is not moved by prayer alone; He is moved to act when prayer is mixed with persistence.

We shouldn't faint when praying, rather, we must wear God out by continually coming to Him to be avenged of our adversary.

Praying is not the issue in this parable, but fainting is the issue when believing God for His help. So, what does the word *faint* mean? *Faint* means to be weak, lose courage, fail in heart, and be weary. A person who faints grows weary and gives up in the face of trials or opposition while waiting on God for an answer to their prayer. If you faint and give up and stop praying, you cannot expect God to answer you.

In the Book of Proverbs, King Solomon said that if you faint on the day of adversity, your strength is small.

> *Proverbs 24:10 (KJV)*
> *10 If thou faint in the day of adversity, thy strength is small.*

The definition of the word for *faint* in this Proverb means to fail, become disheartened, wax feeble, be slothful, relax, withdraw, and be quiet. In the Hebrew language, it gives a picture of a bowstring being loosened. It also portrays a person discharging their responsibilities to the Lord. A person who faints on the day of adversity lacks courage, loses heart, and has small strength.

In this same Proverb, the word for *strength* means valiant, might, power, ability, and dominion. It also means the ability to produce something or perform in battle. A strong person is tough in mind and spirit and faces adversity with courage. God is looking for those who will be strong when adversity comes their way and will not run or back down from a fight. A person strong in faith knows there is always a battle to get their prayers answered.

In this life, we also have an adversary named satan, and if we want to be delivered, we also must be like this persistent widow before God. God wants us to wear Him out when we are praying to be avenged of our adversary, just like this widow wore out the unjust judge. God wants to see persistence in our faith that won't quit or give up in the face of opposition. God will answer your prayers not based upon the need of a problem, but because of the tenacity of your faith to keep asking without giving up.

The Apostle Peter taught that when we pray, we are to cast all our care upon the Lord because He cares for us. He also taught that we must be sober and vigilant because our adversary, the devil, walks about like a roaring lion seeking whom he may devour. Peter went on to say we were to resist satan steadfast in the faith.

> *1 Peter 5:7-9 (KJV)*
> *7 Casting all your care upon him; for he careth for you. 8 Be sober, be vigilant; because your adversary the devil, as a roaring lion, walketh about, seeking whom he may devour: 9 Whom resist stedfast in the faith,* knowing that the same afflictions are accomplished in your brethren that are in the world.

The definition of the word *steadfast* means to be solid, immovable, stable, sure, and strong. God commands you to be strong in battle and to steadfastly resist the devil in your faith. When the enemy attacks you with a storm of life, he is after your faith. God wants to see if you will stand strong in your faith during the storm. If you have been obeying the Word of God, you will be prepared with your faith to stand against any storm the devil may challenge you with.

Jesus never said that challenging storms would never come in this life. Instead, Jesus taught we should prepare for storms to come, which is like being a wise home builder who built his house upon a rock. When you obey the teachings of Jesus, you are building your life upon a rock, and you will survive the demonic storms of life. People who are unwise and weak in faith disobey God's Word and don't prepare for future demonic storms. When the storm comes, their home is destroyed.

Matthew 7:24-27 (KJV)
24 Therefore whosoever heareth these sayings of mine, and doeth them, I will liken him unto a wise man, which built his house upon a rock: 25 And the rain descended, and the floods came, and the winds blew, and beat upon that house; and it fell not: for it was founded upon a rock. 26 And every one that heareth these sayings of mine, and doeth them not, shall be likened unto a foolish man, which built his house upon the sand: 27 And the rain descended, and the floods came, and the winds blew, and beat upon that house; and it fell: and great was the fall of it.

The Bible also describes demonic storms as an evil day in the Book of Ephesians, Chapter 6. The evil day is when the devil and his evil hosts come against you to destroy you. God commands us to be strong on that day and stand against these adversaries trying to destroy our lives. The only way to stand on an evil day is by putting on the whole armor of God and praying in the Spirit.

Ephesians 6:10-18 (KJV)
10 Finally, my brethren, be strong in the Lord, and in the power of his might. 11 Put on the whole armour of God, that ye may be able to stand against the wiles of the devil. 12 For we wrestle not against flesh and blood, but against principalities, against powers, against the rulers of the darkness of this world, against spiritual wickedness in high places. 13 Wherefore take unto you the whole armour of God, that ye may be able to withstand in the evil day, and having done all, to stand. 14 Stand therefore, having your loins girt about with truth, and

*having on the breastplate of righteousness; 15 And your feet shod with the preparation of the gospel of peace; 16 Above all, taking the shield of faith, wherewith ye shall be able to quench all the fiery darts of the wicked. 17 And take the helmet of salvation, and the sword of the Spirit, which is the word of God: 18 **Praying always with all prayer and supplication in the Spirit,** and watching thereunto with all perseverance and supplication for all saints;*

After you put on the whole armor of God to withstand the evil day, you are commanded to pray with all prayer and supplication in the Spirit. Standing in the evil day with your armor on means you're also praying in the Spirit for God to avenge you of your adversary. When you have faith and stand strong in your prayer, God will speedily answer and avenge you, just like the unjust judge avenged the persistent widow.

Luke 18:7-8 (KJV)
7 And shall not God avenge his own elect, which cry day and night unto him, though he bear long with them? 8 I tell you that he will avenge them speedily. Nevertheless when the Son of man cometh, shall he find faith on the earth?

Persistent prayer cannot be underestimated in the Christian walk. God is looking to see if you will have an unwavering faith that will not back down on the evil day. God will honor anyone with persistent faith, and the devil fears a man or woman of God who won't stop praying to God for an answer. The devil will try everything to wear the saints out, but strong saints resist him until they win. The more persistent and demanding you are in your prayers to God, the more speedily He will avenge you of your adversary.

Another analogy that can be used in standing strong in prayer is the picture of being on a ship and surviving the waves of a storm. When a ship and its crew are going through a storm, they need every member on board to *Hold*

Fast. Each crew member must also hold fast to a rope, so they are not thrown overboard. This means when times get tough, one needs to *Hold Fast* and ride out the storm with courage and strength.

When riding out a storm, *Hold Fast* to everything God has taught you from His Word, and never give up when praying to God. Remember, no storm lasts forever, and the sun always comes out no matter how fierce the storm rages against you. Those who *Hold Fast* to their faith in God will survive every demonic storm, and God will avenge them of all their adversaries.

Here are some Scriptures that command us to *Hold Fast:*

> *1 Thessalonians 5:21 (KJV)*
> *21 Prove all things; **hold fast** that which is good.*
>
> *2 Timothy 1:13 (KJV)*
> *13 **Hold fast** the form of sound words, which thou hast heard of me, in faith and love which is in Christ Jesus.*
>
> *Titus 1:9 (KJV)*
> *9 **Holding fast** the faithful word as he hath been taught, that he may be able by sound doctrine both to exhort and to convince the gainsayers.*
>
> *Hebrews 4:14 (KJV)*
> *14 Seeing then that we have a great high priest, that is passed into the heavens, Jesus the Son of God, let us **hold fast** our profession.*
>
> *Hebrews 10:23 (KJV)*
> *23 Let us **hold fast** the profession of our faith without wavering; (for he is faithful that promised;)*
>
> *Revelation 2:25 (KJV)*
> *25 But that which ye have already **hold fast** till I come.*

Revelation 3:3 (KJV)
*3 Remember therefore how thou hast received and heard, and **hold fast**, and repent. If therefore thou shalt not watch, I will come on thee as a thief, and thou shalt not know what hour I will come upon thee.*

Revelation 3:11 (KJV)
*11 Behold, I come quickly: **hold that fast** which thou hast, that no man take thy crown.*

As a Christian, you must be strong in the Lord to survive evil days and the storms of life. The widow woman showed strong faith and survived the storm when she didn't give up asking the unjust judge to avenge her of her adversary. God is looking for those who will be strong, hold fast, never let go of their faith, and never back down from a fight. God is also looking for those who will wear Him out when praying to Him with their persistent faith during the worst storms of their life.

Jesus ended the parable of the persistent widow by asking if the Son of Man would find faith when He returned. This statement reveals that being persistent in prayer has everything to do with our faith. This statement also reveals what Jesus is looking for.

Luke 18:7-8 (KJV)
*7 And shall not God avenge his own elect, which cry day and night unto him, though he bear long with them? 8 I tell you that he will avenge them speedily. **Nevertheless when the Son of man cometh, shall he find faith on the earth?***

When Jesus returns to the earth, He will seek persistent faith-filled praying saints. These are the ones He will avenge of their adversaries, which we know is the devil, the antichrist, and wicked sinners left on the earth during the Great Tribulation. During the Great Tribulation, the devil and the antichrist will attack the saints of the Most High, but God will protect those Saints who kept believing in Him to avenge them of their adversary. Jesus will return at an appointed time and avenge His persistent, faith-filled believers from every adversary.

In the Book of Luke, Jesus taught another parable about being persistent in prayer when one of His disciples asked Him to teach him how to pray. In this parable, Jesus used the analogy of a man going to a friend in the middle of the night, needing food for another one of his friends who came to him. At first, his friend doesn't want to help him but ends up giving him food not based upon him being his friend but for his persistence in asking. After Jesus spoke this parable, He taught about asking, seeking, and knocking. Jesus also taught about our Heavenly Father giving the Holy Spirit to His children who ask. Let's read this powerful passage of Scripture to gain greater insight into persistent prayer.

Luke 11:1-13 (KJV)
*1 And it came to pass, that, as he was praying in a certain place, when he ceased, one of his disciples said unto him, **Lord, teach us to pray, as John also taught his disciples.** 2 And he said unto them, When ye pray, say, Our Father which art in heaven, Hallowed be thy name. Thy kingdom come. Thy will be done, as in heaven, so in earth. 3 Give us day by day our daily bread. 4 And forgive us our sins; for we also forgive every one that is indebted to us. And lead us not into temptation; but deliver us from evil. 5 And he said unto them, Which of you shall have a friend, and shall go unto him at midnight, and say unto him, Friend, lend me three loaves; 6 For a friend of mine in his journey is come to me, and I have nothing to set before him? 7 And he from within shall answer and say, **Trouble me not:** the door is now shut, and my children are with me in bed; I cannot rise and give thee. 8 **I say unto you, Though he will not rise and give him, because he is his friend, yet because of his importunity he will rise and give him as many as he needeth.** 9 And I say unto you, Ask, and it shall be given you; seek,*

and ye shall find; knock, and it shall be opened unto you. 10 For every one that asketh receiveth; and he that seeketh findeth; and to him that knocketh it shall be opened. 11 If a son shall ask bread of any of you that is a father, will he give him a stone? or if he ask a fish, will he for a fish give him a serpent? 12 Or if he shall ask an egg, will he offer him a scorpion? 13 If ye then, being evil, know how to give good gifts unto your children: how much more shall your heavenly Father give the Holy Spirit to them that ask him?

In this parable, Jesus is teaching again that God does not answer prayers based on someone's needs. Instead, God answers prayer based upon persistent and demanding faith. Jesus taught His disciples to wear God out by continually coming to Him in persistent prayer to receive answers. Only through persistent prayer do we get our prayers answered by God. Unfortunately, most Christians and ministers don't understand this aspect of God, and that is why many prayers go unanswered. Many people give up too quickly when asking God for an answer.

Jesus taught that there were three levels of praying to God for an answer:

1. Ask – This word means to make a specific request and gives the picture of a beggar to a giver or a child to a parent. This person won't stop begging or asking until they get what they want.

2. Seek – This word gives a picture of someone searching for something and won't stop until they find what they are looking for. To seek means you are diligent and relentless until you find what you are looking for.

3. Knock – This word means to strike, pound, or thump on a door. This word gives reference to someone pounding with shameless persistence until the door is opened.

When you pray to God, you are to ask, seek, and knock. First, we ask, then we seek, and finally, we keep knocking until God answers us. When you ask, you are diligently looking for an answer. When you seek, you are aggressively searching for an answer. When you knock, you keep knocking and wear out God until He answers! God wants to give good gifts to His children, but these gifts will only come if we are earnestly persistent in our faith-filled prayers by asking, seeking, and knocking.

We see the truth of God looking for persistence in prayer in the story of the Canaanite woman coming to Jesus and asking Him to deliver her daughter from a vexing devil. Jesus did not respond to this woman until her persistence and faith broke through. This woman was a Gentile and had no covenant with God or right to inherit God's blessings, which is why Jesus ignored her at first. It wasn't until after the death, burial, and resurrection of Jesus Christ that salvation was opened to all the Gentiles. This woman was able to access the Covenant of God through Jesus with her persistent faith. This shows how important our faith and persistence in prayer are to God and how it can move Him to answer you.

Let's read this amazing story of her faith and persistence:

Matthew 15:21-28 (KJV)
*21 Then Jesus went thence, and departed into the coasts of Tyre and Sidon. 22 And, behold, a woman of Canaan came out of the same coasts, and cried unto him, saying, Have mercy on me, O Lord, thou son of David; my daughter is grievously vexed with a devil. 23 **But he answered her not a word.** And his disciples came and besought him, saying, **Send her away;** for she crieth after us. 24 But he answered and said, I am not sent but unto the lost sheep of the house of Israel. 25 Then came she and worshipped him, saying, Lord, help me. 26 But he answered and said, It is not meet to take the children's bread, and to cast it to dogs. 27 And she said, Truth, Lord: yet the dogs eat of the*

*crumbs which fall from their masters' table. 28 **Then Jesus answered and said unto her, O woman, great is thy faith: be it unto thee even as thou wilt. And her daughter was made whole from that very hour.***

Jesus knew this Canaanite mother wouldn't back off or give up asking for help. The Canaanite woman *asked* for help, *sought* help, and kept *knocking* until Jesus helped her. This level of persistence and faith caused Jesus not only to respond, but also caused Him to compliment her by saying she had great faith. After Jesus commended her faith, her daughter was delivered from the vexing devil. Jesus was moved not because of her daughter's need but by this mother's faith and persistence. Many people have needs, but needs do not move God; He is only moved by persistent faith.

With the understanding of persistence in our prayers of faith, we can see why Elijah praying for rain was used as an example of praying *The Prayer of Faith* in the last chapter. Elijah persisted in praying *The Prayer of Faith* and kept sending his servant back seven times until he saw a cloud. Elijah wasn't going to stop praying until he received an answer from God. Elijah knew that although God promised it would rain again, it would take his persistent faith in prayer to get God to manifest His Word.

1 Kings 18:41-45 (KJV)
*41 And Elijah said unto Ahab, Get thee up, eat and drink; for there is a sound of abundance of rain. 42 So Ahab went up to eat and to drink. And Elijah went up to the top of Carmel; and he cast himself down upon the earth, and put his face between his knees, 43 **And said to his servant, Go up now, look toward the sea. And he went up, and looked, and said, There is nothing. And he said, Go again seven times. 44 And it came to pass at the seventh time, that he said, Behold, there ariseth a little cloud out of the sea, like a man's hand. And he said, Go up, say unto Ahab, Prepare thy chariot, and get thee down that the rain stop thee not. 45 And it came to pass in the mean***

while, that the heaven was black with clouds and wind, and there was a great rain. And Ahab rode, and went to Jezreel.

A person with persistent faith is not idly sitting back and hoping for God to answer their prayers. Instead, a person with persistent faith grabs the bull by the horns and wears God out until He answers them. God is looking for this type of audacious faith, and this is the type of faith Jesus taught and desires for us to have. Persistent, unwavering faith pleases God. God will pass over a billion people and seemingly ignore them, observing and looking for someone with steadfast faith to answer their prayers.

When the Patriarch Jacob was returning to the land of Israel after being gone for over 20 years, he had an incredible experience with God that teaches us amazing truths about being persistent in prayer. God told Jacob it was time to return to the Promise Land. Jacob had gone away to his uncle Laban, who lived in another country, to find a wife. During the 20 years of being gone, God blessed Jacob with wives, children, and great riches.

As Jacob got closer to the Promise Land, he was told by his servant that his brother Esau was approaching with four hundred men. The news of Esau approaching frightened Jacob because before he left the land of Israel 20 years before, Esau had plotted to kill him. Esau planned to kill Jacob because Jacob deceived his father, Isaac, into giving Jacob the firstborn blessing that was entitled to him. Isaac was blind at the time and could not discern it was Jacob who deceived him into giving the birthright blessing to him instead of Esau.

The night before Jacob was to meet up with his brother, Jacob was alone and had an unforgettable encounter with God. Jacob wrestled all night with what the Bible says was a Man in this encounter, but we know the

Man was God. Jacob would not let go of this Man, which was God, until He blessed Him. God blessed him because he wouldn't let go, and God changed his name from Jacob to Israel, which means *Triumphant with God,* or *Wrestles with God.* Let's read this profound story, and then I will elaborate more on what this story means to us today.

> *Genesis 32:24-32 (KJV)*
> *24 **And Jacob was left alone; and there wrestled a man with him until the breaking of the day.** 25 And when he saw that he prevailed not against him, he touched the hollow of his thigh; and the hollow of Jacob's thigh was out of joint, as he wrestled with him. 26 **And he said, Let me go, for the day breaketh. And he said, I will not let thee go, except thou bless me.** 27 And he said unto him, What is thy name? And he said, Jacob. 28 **And he said, Thy name shall be called no more Jacob, but Israel: for as a prince hast thou power with God and with men, and hast prevailed.** 29 And Jacob asked him, and said, Tell me, I pray thee, thy name. And he said, Wherefore is it that thou dost ask after my name? **And he blessed him there.** 30 And Jacob called the name of the place Peniel: for I have seen God face to face, and my life is preserved. 31 And as he passed over Penuel the sun rose upon him, and he halted upon his thigh. 32 Therefore the children of Israel eat not of the sinew which shrank, which is upon the hollow of the thigh, unto this day: because he touched the hollow of Jacob's thigh in the sinew that shrank.*

Jacob wrestling with God is a beautiful example of a man in a dire situation who had persistent faith and wouldn't let go of God until He blessed him. Jacob knew if he were to survive and not be killed by his brother Esau, he would need a miraculous blessing of God's protection. So, when God saw Jacob would not let go, He blessed him and changed his name to Israel, which meant that he was one who, as a prince, had power with God and men and prevailed. The next day, Jacob was delivered from the hand of his brother Esau and went on to prosper in the *Promise Land.*

This story reveals how we are to lay hold of God in our time of need and not let go until He blesses us. God had already promised Jacob to bless him when Isaac spoke a blessing over him, but Jacob didn't sit back and hope for God to bless him. Jacob was persistent in his faith when seeking God's blessing, even to the point of wrestling with God all night. This story is a shining example for us today when seeking God for a blessing or an answer to prayer. We cannot sit back and hope for God to bless us just because we are Christians. We, as Christians, need to lay hold of God by crying out to Him day and night for a blessing. Those who cry out to God in persistent faith will be the ones who will inherit the *Precious Promises* of God found in His Word.

In contrast to Jacob holding on to God for a blessing, Esau, his brother, sold his birthright to Jacob on a day he fainted in need of food. Esau saw no value in his Divine birthright, and the Bible says he despised his birthright when he sold it to Jacob. Esau was the firstborn son of Isaac and was entitled to the Blessing of Abraham, but Esau, being the godless man he was, despised his birthright when he fainted from being hungry for food. The story of Esau selling his birthright because he fainted is an analogy of people fainting and not inheriting the blessing of God. If you faint when waiting on God, you will be like Esau and not inherit the blessing of God and you will not receive an answer to your prayer.

Genesis 25:29-34 (KJV)
*29 And Jacob sod pottage: and Esau came from the field, **and he was faint**: 30 And Esau said to Jacob, Feed me, I pray thee, with that same red pottage; **for I am faint**: therefore was his name called Edom. 31 And Jacob said, **Sell me this day thy birthright**. 32 And Esau said, Behold, **I am at the point to die: and what profit shall this birthright do to me?** 33 And Jacob said, Swear to me this day; and he sware unto him: **and he sold his birthright unto Jacob**. 34 Then Jacob gave Esau*

*bread and pottage of lentiles; and he did eat and drink, and rose up, and went his way: **thus Esau despised his birthright.***

Later, when Esau sought his father's blessing, he was rejected, though he sought it carefully with tears.

> *Hebrews 12:16-17 (KJV)*
> *16 Lest there be any fornicator, or profane person, **as Esau, who for one morsel of meat sold his birthright.** 17 For ye know how that afterward, when he would have inherited the blessing, he was rejected: for he found no place of repentance, though he sought it carefully with tears.*

Before I end this chapter, I want to leave you with a profound thought. It is God Himself who has persistent faith. This is why God is looking for persistent faith. God never faints, gives up, quits, or gets weary. The Prophet Isaiah revealed this truth about God in a famous prophecy. In this prophetic Word, God reveals Himself imparting this same type of attitude of never fainting or growing weary in those who wait upon Him. As we wait upon the Lord in prayer, He renews our strength so we can walk and not faint. Before God revealed this truth in this passage of Scripture, He referred to Jacob, whose name was changed to Israel.

Let's read this prophetic passage to gain insight into God Himself and how He strengthens those who wait upon Him.

> *Isaiah 40:27-31 (KJV)*
> *27 Why sayest thou, **O Jacob, and speakest, O Israel,** My way is hid from the Lord, and my judgment is passed over from my God? 28 **Hast thou not known? hast thou not heard, that the everlasting God, the Lord, the Creator of the ends of the earth, fainteth not, neither is weary?** there is no searching of his understanding. 29 **He giveth power to the faint; and to them that have no might he increaseth strength.** 30 Even the youths shall faint and be weary, and the young men shall*

*utterly fall: 31 **But they that wait upon the Lord shall renew their strength; they shall mount up with wings as eagles; they shall run, and not be weary; and they shall walk, and not faint.***

On the night Jesus went to the cross, He persistently prayed to God, and God strengthened Him with a visitation from an angel. The strength Jesus received from God through this angel empowered Him to endure the cross. Jesus also warned His disciples to pray so they wouldn't enter into temptation. Unfortunately, the disciples didn't pray but instead fell asleep, and when Jesus was taken, they all ran because they didn't receive strength from God as Jesus did. If they had persisted in prayer, they could have stood strong with the Son of God during the biggest trial of His life.

Luke 22:40-46 (KJV)
*40 And when he was at the place, he said unto them, **Pray that ye enter not into temptation.** 41 And he was withdrawn from them about a stone's cast, and kneeled down, and prayed, 42 Saying, Father, if thou be willing, remove this cup from me: nevertheless not my will, but thine, be done. 43 **And there appeared an angel unto him from heaven, strengthening him. 44 And being in an agony he prayed more earnestly: and his sweat was as it were great drops of blood falling down to the ground.** 45 And when he rose up from prayer, and was come to his disciples, he found them sleeping for sorrow, 46 And said unto them, **Why sleep ye? rise and pray, lest ye enter into temptation.***

We are commanded not to faint when praying, because prayer is where God strengthens us. If you persist in your prayers and do not faint, God will come and place His strength inside you. Too many people give up too soon when praying and never experience the strength of God being imparted to them. If you persist in prayer, God will strengthen you. When the strength of God is imparted to you, your faith will be strengthened; with this strong faith, you will receive your answer from God.

In conclusion, Jesus taught God is only moved to answer prayers for people with persistent and demanding faith. This truth may shock some, but this is the secret to how to get your prayers answered by God. If you go to God with persistent and demanding faith, He will avenge you of your adversary speedily and help you in your time of need. Never back down, quit, get discouraged, or grow weary when praying and waiting on God for an answer. It may seem like God isn't hearing your prayer, but the reality is that He is waiting to hear your persistent faith. When you pray in persistent faith, you are imitating God, who will strengthen and bless you. The only way to inherit the blessing of God is to have a persistent demanding faith that will never stop until God answers your prayer. God is looking for those who will pray without ceasing with persistent and demanding faith, and won't let go of Him until they get an answer.

1 Thessalonians 5:17 (KJV)
17 Pray without ceasing.

CHAPTER 14

The Trial of Your Faith

Why Christians and people go through fiery trials is very complex and difficult for some to comprehend. As a result, some people end up accusing God or falling away when their faith is tested. However, *The Trial of Your Faith* should lead you to a stronger faith and closer walk with God. In this chapter, I will give a deeper understanding of why we go through trials and how God designs the fiery trial to build within you a stronger faith and bring you closer to Him.

The Bible describes our faith like gold, and just like gold is refined in the fire, so our faith is refined in fiery trials.

> *1 Peter 1:6-9 (KJV)*
> *6 Wherein ye greatly rejoice, though now for a season, if need be, ye are in heaviness through manifold temptations: 7 **That the trial of your faith, being much more precious than of gold that perisheth, though it be tried with fire,** might be found unto praise and honour and glory at the appearing of Jesus Christ: 8 Whom having not seen, ye love; in whom, though now ye see him not, yet believing, ye rejoice with joy*

unspeakable and full of glory: 9 Receiving the end of your faith, even the salvation of your souls.

To better understand this passage, one must ask why the Apostle Peter used gold being tried with fire as to faith being tested? In ancient times, gold was purified by being heated in a melting pot. Once the gold was heated into a liquid form, the impurities found in the gold would rise to the top and could be separated from the gold. Gold that has been heated and separated from all impurities is see through, like clear transparent glass.

The Bible says that the heavenly Jerusalem and its streets are pure gold and look like clear glass.

> *Revelation 21:18 (KJV)*
> *18 And the building of the wall of it was of jasper:* ***and the city was pure gold, like unto clear glass.***

> *Revelation 21:21 (KJV)*
> *21 And the twelve gates were twelve pearls: every several gate was of one pearl:* ***and the street of the city was pure gold, as it were transparent glass.***

God uses fiery trials to refine our faith like gold being refined in a fire to remove all impurities from our character. The fiery trial drives up all impurities within you so they can be removed. The impurities God seeks to purify us from are fear, worry, doubt, and unbelief. The hotter the fire and the longer someone stays in a trial, the more impurities will be burned off and removed. Finally, when all these impurities are burned out, all that will remain is pure faith and trust in the Lord.

If you remain faithful to God in the middle of your fiery trial, God will purify your faith like gold. Most people want to get out of the trial as fast as possible and don't realize the value of what is taking place in their fiery trial. If you want pure, transparent faith like gold, you must stay in the fiery trial as long as possible. Make sure you repent of all fear, worry, doubt, and unbelief when going through a fiery trial.

The Bible says that whatsoever is not of faith is sin.

> *Romans 14:23b (KJV)*
> *23 ...for whatsoever is not of faith is sin.*

Fiery trials burn anything and everything out of us that is not of faith. Fear is one of the main impurities God is looking to burn out of His people. Fear is the opposite of faith. Fear has its foundations in believing lies from the devil, saying God will not be there for you in your time of need. However, God is so good and trustworthy that He does not tolerate being doubted. Therefore, God will put His people through fiery trials, so they cast out all fear. The Bible says that perfect love casts out fear because fear has torment.

> *1 John 4:18 (KJV)*
> *18 There is no fear in love; but perfect love casteth out fear: because fear hath torment. He that feareth is not made perfect in love.*

The Bible also says that the devil used the fear of death to keep people in bondage. One of the main reasons Jesus came to earth was to destroy the devil, which had the power of death. When Jesus died, was buried, and rose again, He took back the power of death from the devil.

> *Hebrews 2:14-15 (KJV)*
> *14 Forasmuch then as the children are partakers of flesh and blood, he also himself likewise took part of the same; that through death he might destroy him that had the power of death, that is, the devil; 15 And*

deliver them who through fear of death were all their lifetime subject to bondage.

People fear many things, but death is the ultimate fear because once someone dies, this life is over, and all hope of things getting better is gone. Death to the natural man is the worst outcome that could happen to them. People also fear extended torment that leads to death. However, anyone with strong faith in God doesn't fear death. Christians know that when they die, they will live eternally with God in a glorified body.

When God allows someone to go through a fiery trial, He goes after any fear in their heart. The only way to remove this fear is to put them through a fiery trial and make them face their fear. When someone goes through a fiery trial, and God shows up in the middle of their trial, their faith is increased. This is why the Bible says I sought the Lord, and He delivered me from all my fears.

Psalm 34:4 (KJV)
4 I sought the Lord, and he heard me, and delivered me from all my fears.

The only way to deliver someone from all their fears is to make them face their fears. The only way to make someone face their fears is to put them in trial after trial, which drives up fear in their heart. In the military, they call this *Habituation*. In military terms, *Habituation* means putting someone in a situation repeatedly until they conquer their fear or fear is burned out of them.

An example of *Habituation* is when a person fears heights, their drill instructors will make them jump out of a plane repeatedly until all fear of heights is burned out of them. In Christian terms, if you are afraid of something and not living in faith, God will repeatedly put you through a fiery trial until that fear is burned out of you. Until you are free from fear, God will keep putting you through a fiery trial.

Another example of fear is the fear of public speaking. According to studies, many people rank public speaking as one of their greatest fears. So, if God calls you to be a preacher, God will have to burn the fear of public speaking out of you. God will do this by having you repeatedly speak publicly until all fear of public speaking is burned out of you.

Now, let's investigate some stories in the Bible where people went through a fiery trial, and God dealt with their fears. The best story from the Bible to start with is the story of Job. Job is notoriously known for having gone through one of the fieriest trials known to man. In one day, the devil killed all his children, burned up all his sheep with fire from Heaven, destroyed his camels, and killed almost all his servants.

> *Job 1:12-19 (KJV)*
> *12 And the Lord said unto Satan, Behold, all that he hath is in thy power; only upon himself put not forth thine hand. So Satan went forth from the presence of the Lord. 13 And there was a day when his sons and his daughters were eating and drinking wine in their eldest brother's house: 14 And there came a messenger unto Job, and said, The oxen were plowing, and the asses feeding beside them: 15 And the Sabeans fell upon them, and took them away; yea, they have slain the servants with the edge of the sword; and I only am escaped alone to tell thee. 16 While he was yet speaking, there came also another, and said, The fire of God is fallen from heaven, and hath burned up the sheep, and the servants, and consumed them; and I only am escaped alone to tell thee. 17 While he was yet speaking, there came also another, and said, The Chaldeans made out three bands, and fell upon the camels, and have carried them away, yea, and slain the servants with the edge of the sword; and I only am escaped alone to tell thee. 18 While he was yet speaking, there came also another, and said, Thy sons and thy*

*daughters were eating and drinking wine in their eldest brother's house:
19 And, behold, there came a great wind from the wilderness, and smote
the four corners of the house, and it fell upon the young men, and they
are dead; and I only am escaped alone to tell thee.*

All these terrible things befell Job in one day, and then on another day, the
devil smote Job with boils from the top of his feet to the crown of his head.

Job 2:7-8 (KJV)
*7 So went Satan forth from the presence of the Lord, **and smote Job
with sore boils from the sole of his foot unto his crown. 8 And he
took him a potsherd to scrape himself withal;** and he sat down among
the ashes.*

Why did God allow satan to put Job through this fiery trial? God told
satan that Job was a perfect and upright man who feared God and shunned
evil. It appeared there wasn't anything that needed to be burned out of
Job. So, why did God allow Job to go through this fiery trial?

Job 1:6-8 (KJV)
*6 Now there was a day when the sons of God came to present themselves
before the Lord, and Satan came also among them. 7 And the Lord said
unto Satan, Whence comest thou? Then Satan answered the Lord, and
said, From going to and fro in the earth, and from walking up and
down in it. 8 And the Lord said unto Satan, **Hast thou considered my
servant Job, that there is none like him in the earth, a perfect and
an upright man, one that feareth God, and escheweth evil?***

This passage of Scripture reveals God did not put Job through this fiery
trial because he was sinning. So why did God put Job through this fiery
trial? You have to read a little further, where Job starts to talk to find the
answer to this question. Job reveals something in his speech, which gives a
major clue as to why he went through this fiery trial, and it had everything
to do with fear.

Job 3:25 (KJV)
25 For the thing which I greatly feared is come upon me, and that which I was afraid of is come unto me.

Job admitted out of his mouth that he feared all these terrible things happening to him. This means he was not living in faith and trusting God in these areas. So, God had to place him in a fiery trial to perfect Job's faith. God made Job face his fears head-on. Later, in the Book of Job, God blessed Job with more than he had before he went through this fiery trial, so Job must have conquered his fears. We never find in the Scriptures that Job went through another fiery trial like this again.

Job 42:12-17 (KJV)
12 So the Lord blessed the latter end of Job more than his beginning: for he had fourteen thousand sheep, and six thousand camels, and a thousand yoke of oxen, and a thousand she asses. 13 He had also seven sons and three daughters. 14 And he called the name of the first, Jemima; and the name of the second, Kezia; and the name of the third, Kerenhappuch. 15 And in all the land were no women found so fair as the daughters of Job: and their father gave them inheritance among their brethren. 16 After this lived Job an hundred and forty years, and saw his sons, and his sons' sons, even four generations. 17 So Job died, being old and full of days.

There is another story in the Bible where a man named Jairus went through a fiery trial during the ministry of Jesus. Jairus' daughter had fallen sick, and Jairus went to Jesus for Him to heal her. However, when Jesus was on the way to his house to heal his daughter, Jairus received a report that his daughter had died and not to bother Jesus anymore.

Mark 5:21-23 (KJV)
21 And when Jesus was passed over again by ship unto the other side, much people gathered unto him: and he was nigh unto the sea. 22 And,

*behold, there cometh one of the rulers of the synagogue, Jairus by name; and when he saw him, he fell at his feet, 23 **And besought him greatly, saying, My little daughter lieth at the point of death: I pray thee, come and lay thy hands on her, that she may be healed; and she shall live.***

Let's look at what Jesus said to Jairus when he received the evil report that his daughter had died.

Mark 5:35-36 (KJV)
*35 While he yet spake, there came from the ruler of the synagogue's house certain which said, Thy daughter is dead: why troublest thou the Master any further? 36 **As soon as Jesus heard the word that was spoken, he saith unto the ruler of the synagogue, Be not afraid, only believe.***

Right in the middle of the worst fiery trial that Jairus could go through, Jesus tells him not to be afraid, but only believe. If you look at this from Jairus' perspective, he went to God, and the situation didn't get better, but it got worse. When we look at this from Jesus' perspective, Jesus knew the situation would get better if he had faith and didn't fear. Jesus then goes to Jairus' house and raises his daughter from the dead. Jairus must have conquered his fear and had faith because his daughter was raised from the dead.

Mark 5:37-43 (KJV)
*37 And he suffered no man to follow him, save Peter, and James, and John the brother of James. 38 And he cometh to the house of the ruler of the synagogue, and seeth the tumult, and them that wept and wailed greatly. 39 And when he was come in, he saith unto them, Why make ye this ado, and weep? the damsel is not dead, but sleepeth. 40 And they laughed him to scorn. But when he had put them all out, he taketh the father and the mother of the damsel, and them that were with him, and entereth in where the damsel was lying. 41 **And he took the damsel by the hand, and said unto her, Talitha cumi; which is, being***

interpreted, Damsel, I say unto thee, arise. 42 And straightway the damsel arose, and walked; for she was of the age of twelve years. And they were astonished with a great astonishment. 43 And he charged them straitly that no man should know it; and commanded that something should be given her to eat.

I know this may be a hard truth for some people to grasp about God allowing people to go through fiery trials to remove any fear in them. However, the best way for God to remove fear is to have someone face their worst fears; when they face that fear head-on, it can be cast out of them. If faith pleases God, and whatsoever is not of faith is sin, then we need to allow God to burn all impurities out of us. God will not stop this process until all fear, worry, doubt, and unbelief is removed from us.

The Book of James says that God puts people through trials to perfect their faith and patience. The goal of the trial is to make you perfect and entire, wanting nothing.

James 1:2-4 (KJV)
2 My brethren, count it all joy when ye fall into divers temptations; 3 Knowing this, that the trying of your faith worketh patience. 4 But let patience have her perfect work, that ye may be perfect and entire, wanting nothing.

There is a powerful story in the Book of Daniel of three young Hebrew men who stood against the King of Babylon. The King of Babylon had made an idol of himself and demanded that anyone who would not bow down to it should be thrown into a fiery furnace. These three Hebrew men refused to be afraid and bow down, so they were thrown into the fiery furnace. However, God showed up in the middle of the fiery furnace and didn't allow the fire to harm these powerful, faith-filled men. God will always show up in your fiery trial and deliver you when you face your fears and believe Him.

Daniel 3:14-27 (KJV)

14 Nebuchadnezzar spake and said unto them, Is it true, O Shadrach, Meshach, and Abednego, do not ye serve my gods, nor worship the golden image which I have set up? 15 Now if ye be ready that at what time ye hear the sound of the cornet, flute, harp, sackbut, psaltery, and dulcimer, and all kinds of musick, ye fall down and worship the image which I have made; well: but if ye worship not, ye shall be cast the same hour into the midst of a burning fiery furnace; **and who is that God that shall deliver you out of my hands?** *16 Shadrach, Meshach, and Abednego, answered and said to the king, O Nebuchadnezzar, we are not careful to answer thee in this matter. 17 If it be so, our God whom we serve is able to deliver us from the burning fiery furnace, and he will deliver us out of thine hand, O king.* *18 But if not, be it known unto thee, O king, that we will not serve thy gods, nor worship the golden image which thou hast set up.* *19* **Then was Nebuchadnezzar full of fury, and the form of his visage was changed against Shadrach, Meshach, and Abednego: therefore he spake, and commanded that they should heat the furnace one seven times more than it was wont to be heated.** *20* **And he commanded the most mighty men that were in his army to bind Shadrach, Meshach, and Abednego, and to cast them into the burning fiery furnace.** *21 Then these men were bound in their coats, their hosen, and their hats, and their other garments, and were cast into the midst of the burning fiery furnace. 22 Therefore because the king's commandment was urgent, and the furnace exceeding hot, the flames of the fire slew those men that took up Shadrach, Meshach, and Abednego. 23 And these three men, Shadrach, Meshach, and Abednego, fell down bound into the midst of the burning fiery furnace. 24 Then Nebuchadnezzar the king was astonished, and rose up in haste, and spake, and said unto his counsellors,* **Did not we cast three men bound into the midst of the fire?** *They answered and said unto the king, True, O king. 25* **He** *answered and said, Lo, I see four men loose, walking in the midst of the fire, and they have no hurt; and the form of the fourth is like the Son of God. 26 Then Nebuchadnezzar came near to the mouth of the burning fiery furnace, and spake, and said, Shadrach, Meshach, and Abednego, ye servants of the most high God, come forth, and come hither. Then Shadrach, Meshach, and Abednego, came forth of the midst of the fire. 27 And the princes, governors, and captains, and the king's counsellors, being gathered together, saw these men, upon whose bodies the fire had no power, nor was an hair of their head singed, neither were their coats changed, nor the smell of fire had passed on them.*

God didn't keep Shadrach, Meshach, and Abednego from this fiery trial, but showed up in the middle of the fire and delivered them. God's glory is revealed by delivering you from your fears and not keeping you from your fears. How strong do you think the three Hebrew men's faith grew when God showed up in the fiery furnace with them? The best way to get fear out of someone and grow their faith is to be with them and deliver them miraculously when facing the very thing they fear. God has not promised to keep us from all trouble, but to deliver us from trouble if we set our love upon Him.

Psalm 91:14-16 (KJV)
*14 Because he hath set his love upon me, **therefore will I deliver him: I will set him on high, because he hath known my name.** 15 He shall call upon me, and I will answer him: **I will be with him in trouble; I will deliver him,** and honour him. 16 With long life will I satisfy him, and shew him my salvation.*

The Bible also says that many are the afflictions of the righteous, but the Lord delivers them out of them all.

Psalm 34:19 (KJV)
19 Many are the afflictions of the righteous: but the Lord delivereth
him out of them all.

Once you understand this truth about God, you will no longer fear what you are going through, but will have faith in God to show up and deliver you. The Bible is filled with stories of God showing up and delivering people during their fiery trials. The whole ministry of Jesus was Him showing up with God's power and healing people from the trials they were facing. Jesus didn't keep people from fiery trials; He saved them in their trials. All the people who Jesus healed had faith and were not living in fear. Their faith and the absence of fear brought God's healing deliverance to them. If you have faith in God and do not fear what you are going through, God will deliver you, too.

The truth of God testing people's faith and making them face their fear cannot be better seen than in the story of the sickness and death of Lazarus. Lazarus became sick, and they called for Jesus to heal him, but Jesus purposely waited two days before He went to Bethany, where Lazarus lived. Within those two days of Jesus not going to Bethany, Lazarus died. Why didn't Jesus rush over to Bethany and heal Lazarus as soon as He heard he was sick?

John 11:1-6 (KJV)
1 Now a certain man was sick, named Lazarus, of Bethany, the town
of Mary and her sister Martha. 2 (It was that Mary which anointed the
Lord with ointment, and wiped his feet with her hair, whose brother
Lazarus was sick.) 3 Therefore his sisters sent unto him, saying, Lord,
behold, he whom thou lovest is sick. 4 When Jesus heard that, he said,
This sickness is not unto death, but for the glory of God, that the Son of
God might be glorified thereby. 5 Now Jesus loved Martha, and her

*sister, and Lazarus. 6 **When he had heard therefore that he was sick,
he abode two days still in the same place where he was.***

For some Divine reason, Jesus waited two days before going to Bethany,
knowing Lazarus was going to die.

John 11:11-14 (KJV)
*11 **These things said he: and after that he saith unto them, Our
friend Lazarus sleepeth; but I go, that I may awake him out of sleep.**
12 Then said his disciples, Lord, if he sleep, he shall do well. 13 Howbeit
Jesus spake of his death: but they thought that he had spoken of taking
of rest in sleep. 14 **Then said Jesus unto them plainly, Lazarus is
dead.***

When Jesus finally arrived at Bethany, Martha, the sister of Lazarus, said,
if You had been here, my brother would not have died.

John 11:21 (KJV)
*21 **Then said Martha unto Jesus, Lord, if thou hadst been here, my
brother had not died.***

Mary, also a sister of Lazarus, said that if Jesus had been there, her brother
would not have died.

John 11:32 (KJV)
*32 Then when Mary was come where Jesus was, and saw him, she fell
down at his feet, saying unto him, **Lord, if thou hadst been here, my
brother had not died.***

Before Jesus raised Lazarus from the dead, He said that if they believed,
they should see the glory of God. So, Jesus was working on their faith the
whole time.

John 11:40 (KJV)
*40 Jesus saith unto her, **Said I not unto thee, that, if thou wouldest** **believe, thou shouldest see the glory of God?***

The only way you will see the glory of God is if you have faith and defeat your fear. Those who have faith in God will always see God deliver them in the middle of their fiery trial. Jesus ended up raising Lazarus from the dead, and what they feared didn't come to pass. Yes, Lazarus died, but rose again. What do you think happened to everyone's faith who saw this miracle? Lazarus was dead for four days, and his body had the stench of death. Jesus proved everyone's fear wrong.

Yes, Lazarus died, but that was not the final outcome. Jesus conquered death and changed the reality of what could have been grievous for everyone involved. We cannot please God without faith, and there is no such thing as untested faith. If you are going to go down the journey of faith, you will be tested. However, God will show up in every test if you have faith in Him and help you conquer *all* your fears. The fiery trial of your faith allows God to show you His power, and that you can trust Him. If you have faith and do not fear, God will always be there for you.

Another purpose for a fiery trial is resistance and endurance training. Resistance training is any exercise where you lift or pull against a weight to increase strength. Endurance training is any exercise intended to increase your stamina. The longer someone is in a fiery trial, the more their faith strengthens, and their spiritual endurance increases. Our faith is strengthened when we keep the faith as we go through a fiery trial. Our patience increases, giving us greater endurance the longer we stay in the trial. When the fiery trial is over, your faith will be stronger, and you will have more endurance to outlast the devil.

Don't expect your life to be free from fiery trials if you are going to live by faith. The very nature of faith demands that it be put into a situation to prove itself. You cannot prove you have faith unless you are put into a fiery trial where you can flex your muscle of faith. God is not afraid to allow you to face your fears, even if it means you will die. God is the God of resurrection, and His power is revealed in the middle of people's worst circumstances. Once you come to terms with this fact and are no longer afraid of your trials, you will come out on top every time and be more than a conqueror.

The faith of Jesus was even tested when He went to the cross. When Jesus endured the cross, He became our glorious example of how to overcome any fiery trial we may face.

Hebrews 12:1-4 (KJV)
1 Wherefore seeing we also are compassed about with so great a cloud of witnesses, let us lay aside every weight, and the sin which doth so easily beset us, and let us run with patience the race that is set before us, 2 **Looking unto Jesus the author and finisher of our faith; who for the joy that was set before him endured the cross, despising the shame, and is set down at the right hand of the throne of God. 3 For consider him that endured such contradiction of sinners against himself, lest ye be wearied and faint in your minds. 4 Ye have not yet resisted unto blood, striving against sin.**

The primary purpose of a trial is to put you in a desperate situation where it can only take a miracle from God to rescue you. Desperate situations that need a miracle from God are where true faith thrives. Some people cower in these situations, whereas a person of faith boldly faces the situation, knowing God will come through for them. You are called to boldly face every trial you go through and believe God to deliver you. Nothing is impossible to them that believe.

You can either be someone who lives in fear of being tested, or you can choose to be someone who passes every test with strong faith. God is looking for those who will step up to the plate and be a strong person of faith who is ready and willing to pass every test that comes their way. They're prepared to pass the tests and thrive when tested. This strong person of faith is free from fear, worry, doubt, and unbelief. This is a whole new way of approaching the trial of your faith.

When God tested Abraham to offer his promised son Isaac as an offering, he stepped up to the plate and obeyed God.

Genesis 22:1-9 (KJV)
*1 And it came to pass after these things, that God did tempt Abraham, and said unto him, Abraham: and he said, Behold, here I am. 2 And he said, Take now thy son, thine only son Isaac, whom thou lovest, and get thee into the land of Moriah; and offer him there for a burnt offering upon one of the mountains which I will tell thee of. 3 And Abraham rose up early in the morning, and saddled his ass, and took two of his young men with him, and Isaac his son, and clave the wood for the burnt offering, and rose up, and went unto the place of which God had told him. 4 Then on the third day Abraham lifted up his eyes, and saw the place afar off. 5 And Abraham said unto his young men, Abide ye here with the ass; and I and the lad will go yonder and worship, and come again to you. 6 And Abraham took the wood of the burnt offering, and laid it upon Isaac his son; and he took the fire in his hand, and a knife; and they went both of them together. 7 And Isaac spake unto Abraham his father, and said, My father: and he said, Here am I, my son. And he said, Behold the fire and the wood: but where is the lamb for a burnt offering? 8 And Abraham said, **My son, God will provide himself a lamb for a burnt offering:** so they went both of them together. 9 And they came to the place which God had told him of; and Abraham built an altar there, and laid the wood in order, and bound Isaac his son, and laid him on the altar upon the wood.*

Abraham was ready to sacrifice his son, but God stopped him and told him not to do it. The Bible says the Angel of the Lord told him not to lay a hand upon him and that now He knew Abraham feared God, seeing he did not withhold his only son from Him. God also provided a ram to be offered as a sacrifice instead.

Genesis 22:10-18 (KJV)
*10 And Abraham stretched forth his hand, and took the knife to slay his son. 11 And the angel of the Lord called unto him out of heaven, and said, Abraham, Abraham: and he said, Here am I. 12 **And he said, Lay not thine hand upon the lad, neither do thou any thing unto him: for now I know that thou fearest God, seeing thou hast not withheld thy son, thine only son from me.** 13 And Abraham lifted up his eyes, and looked, and behold behind him a ram caught in a thicket by his horns: and Abraham went and took the ram, and offered him up for a burnt offering in the stead of his son. 14 And Abraham called the name of that place Jehovahjireh: as it is said to this day, In the mount of the Lord it shall be seen. 15 And the angel of the Lord called unto Abraham out of heaven the second time, 16 And said, By myself have I sworn, saith the Lord, for because thou hast done this thing, and hast not withheld thy son, thine only son: 17 That in blessing I will bless thee, and in multiplying I will multiply thy seed as the stars of the heaven, and as the sand which is upon the sea shore; and thy seed shall possess the gate of his enemies; 18 And in thy seed shall all the nations of the earth be blessed; **because thou hast obeyed my voice.***

Abraham's faith was tested, and he came out on top. The Bible says in the Book of Hebrews that Abraham believed God would raise his son Isaac from the dead, even if he sacrificed him. God had told Abraham earlier that Isaac was the promised seed; therefore, Abraham knew this had to be a test. Abraham had strong faith in God and showed it in all that he did.

Hebrews 11:17-19 (KJV)
*17 By faith Abraham, when he was tried, offered up Isaac: and he that had received the promises offered up his only begotten son, 18 Of whom it was said, **That in Isaac shall thy seed be called: 19 Accounting that God was able to raise him up, even from the dead;** from whence also he received him in a figure.*

It is no fun to go through a trial, but it is rewarding when God uses it to purify your faith. No trial is easy, and it will take all the faith you can muster to pass the test. So many people complain or get upset with God when they face challenging times, not knowing the challenging times are where you grow the most in life. Instead of being like people who do not know the Lord, use the fiery trial to strengthen your faith and grow in God. Once the trial is over and you pass the test, you will be thankful you remained faithful to God. Anyone who passes all the tests that God challenges them with ends up having a faith that can shake all hell and overcomes the world.

1 John 5:4 (KJV)
*4 For whatsoever is born of God overcometh the world: **and this is the victory that overcometh the world, even our faith.***

In conclusion, your faith will be tried and tested. God uses the test not only to grow your faith but also to prove your loyalty to Him. So many people complain when going through a fiery trial and show disloyalty to God. When tested with a fiery trial, God is looking for those who will conquer their fear, worry, doubt, and unbelief. Choose to be a person who will have faith and believe God in your fiery trial. When you pass the fiery test of your faith, you will become a person who pleases God. Never fear when your faith is being tested because you will glorify God with your purified faith when you pass the test.

Job 23:10 (KJV)
10 But he knoweth the way that I take: **when he hath tried me, I shall come forth as gold.**

CHAPTER 15

≈—❧—≈

Smith Wigglesworth Quotes

Smith Wigglesworth was a man of God who lived during the early 19th century. He was raised as a Methodist, but later in life, he was filled with the Holy Spirit and became a part of the Pentecostal movement. Smith's ministry was filled with many miracles, and it is recorded that he raised over 14 people from the dead. He was also called the Apostle of Faith because he was known for having great faith in God.

I became a Christian on July 9th; my birthday is on July 26th. On my birthday, my faith-believing grandma gave me a book about Smith Wigglesworth, called *The Secret of His Power*. This book revolutionized my whole Christian life from that point forward. God also spoke to me and told me I would receive the mantle of Smith later in my life. I am now entering what God prophetically spoke to me over 30 years ago. I am adding Smith Wigglesworth quotes to this book because of his ministry's impact on me. I pray his quotes on *Faith* and the *Word of God* bless you as they have blessed me over the years.

FAITH QUOTES

I am not moved by what I see or feel, but by what I believe.

God will pass over a million people just to find someone who believes Him.

I am not here to entertain you, but to get you to the place where you will laugh at the impossible.

I'd rather die believing than live doubting.

Fear looks, Faith jumps.

Unbelief can be very blind, but faith can see through a stone wall.

Inactivity of faith is a robber, which steals blessings.

It is one thing to say you have faith, and another thing to be in a tight corner and prove it.

Great faith is the product of great fights.

Great testimonies are the outcome of great tests. Great triumphs can only come out of great trials.

All lack of faith is due to not feeding on God's Word.

I believe there is only one way to all the treasures of God, and that is the way of faith.

I can get more out of God by believing Him in one minute than by shouting at Him all night.

The only reason for healing not to occur was a lack of faith.

Believers were designed to operate in what is called the law of faith.

I believe that all lack of faith is due to not feeding, drinking, thinking, speaking, and singing God's Word.

Without faith, you have nothing. You cannot be saved without it. You cannot be healed without it.

When faith lays hold, impossibilities must yield.

God wants to give you a faith that shakes hell!

It is like receiving a gift; you don't know that you have it till you act in faith.

How can one come to possess great faith? Now listen, here is the answer to that: first, the blade, then the ear, then the full corn in the ear. Faith must grow by soil, moisture, and exercise.

The end of all real faith always is rejoicing.

There is no limit to what our limitless God will do in response to a limitless faith.

Faith never fears, faith thrives in the greatest conflict, faith moves even things that cannot be moved.

Faith never fails to obtain its objective.

If there is anything in your heart which is in the way of condemnation, you cannot pray the prayer of faith.

Ask for what you want; believe, receive from God, and thank God for it.

God wants us all to have an audacity of faith that dares to believe for all that is set forth in the Word.

There are two kinds of faith. There is the natural faith. But the supernatural faith is the gift of God.

Nothing in the world glorifies God so much as the simple rest of faith in what God's Word says.

Faith is an act.

A prayer without faith is without accomplishment.

Being hard-hearted, critical, or unforgiving will hinder faith quicker than anything.

Your life must be one of going from Faith to Faith.

To the man of faith, there is not a thing that is not opportunity.

Faith is better than feelings, and if you have faith, you will have all the feelings you can feel.

Thousands have missed wonderful blessings because they have not had faith to move out and begin in the natural, in faith that the Lord would take them into the realm of the supernatural.

Desire toward God and you will have desires from God and He will meet you on the line of those desires when you reach out in simple faith.

Believe that when you come into the presence of God, you can have all you came for. You can take it away, and you can use it, for all the power of God is at your disposal in response to your faith.

Faith is the audacity that rejoices in the fact that God cannot break His own Word.

Faith is not agitation. It is quiet confidence that God means what He says, and we act on His Word.

Faith is just the open door through which the Lord comes. Do not say, "I was saved by faith" or "I was healed by faith." Faith does not save and heal. God saves and heals through that open door.

Two things will get you to leap out of yourselves into the promises of God today. One is purity, and the other is FAITH, which is kindled more and more BY PURITY.

No wavering. This is the principle: He who believes is definite. A definite faith brings a definite experience and a definite utterance.

Real faith has perfect peace and joy and a shout at any time. It always sees the victory.

Purity is vital to faith.

There is nothing that our God cannot do. He will do everything if you will dare to believe.

I know this, no man looks at appearances if he believes.

Dare to believe, and then dare to speak, and you shall have whatsoever you say if you doubt not.

There are boundless possibilities for us if we dare to act in God and dare to believe.

There are many who call themselves believers who are extremely unbelieving.

Brothers and sisters, as you ask, BELIEVE.

I saw that God wants us so badly that He has made the condition as simple as He possibly could—Only Believe.

When the gift of Faith is in operation, you know ahead of time what the Holy Spirit is going to do.

When we believe God, all things are easy.

To the man of faith, everything that is contrary to the will and the Word of God is nothing but an opportunity to prove that God is true.

The man who believes God has it.

WORD OF GOD QUOTES

Let everything about you be a lie but let the Word of God be true.

Some people read their Bibles in Hebrew, some in Greek; I like to read mine in the Holy Ghost.

There are four principles we need to maintain. First, read the Word of God. Second, consume the Word of God until it consumes you. Third, believe the Word of God. Fourth, act on the Word.

There is power in God's Word to make that which does not exist appear.

Libraries make swelled heads, but the Word of God makes enlarged hearts.

Faith cometh by hearing and hearing by the Word of God, not by reading commentaries.

If a thing is in the Bible, then it is so; it is not even to be prayed about; it is to be received and acted upon.

The Word of God has not to be prayed about, the Word of God has to be received.

The Word of God is eternal and cannot be broken. You cannot improve on the Word of God, for it is life, and it produces only life.

It is one thing to know the Word, and another thing to be captive to the Word. You are either captive to the Word, or captive to the world.

This blessed Book brings such life and health and peace, and such abundance that we should never be poor anymore.

You have to bring your mind to the Word of God and not try to bring the Word of God to your mind.

If I read the newspaper, I come out dirtier than I went in. If I read my Bible, I come out cleaner than I went in, and I like being clean!

I find nothing in the Bible but holiness, and nothing in the world but worldliness. Therefore, if I live in the world, I will become worldly; on the other hand, if I live in the Bible, I will become holy.

None of you can be strong in God unless you are diligent and constantly hearkening to what God has to say to you through His Word.

Fill your head and your heart with the Scriptures. As you do this, you are sowing in your heart seeds, which the Spirit can germinate.

Believers are strong only as the Word of God abides in them.

If you will receive the Word of God, you will always be in a big place.

Never compare this Book with other books. Comparisons are dangerous. Never think or say that this Book contains the Word of God. IT IS the Word of God. It is supernatural in origin, eternal in duration, inexpressible in value, infinite in scope, regenerative in power, infallible in authority, universal in interest, personal in application, and inspired in totality. Read it through, write it down, pray it in, and pass it on. It is the Word of God.

CHAPTER 16

Vince Baker Quotes

I used to read and study other men of God's quotes until one day, God told me I should write my own quotes. From then on, I received powerful quotes from God. All the quotes in this chapter came to me from spending time with the Holy Spirit. Whenever I received a quote from God, I would quickly write it down, so I didn't lose it. I believe great quotes can pack a lot of power in times of need. I learned you can draw a lot of strength and wisdom from a great quote. A high-powered quote from God is like a powerful weapon against the enemy. You can also learn a lot about a person by the quotes they come up with or think about regularly.

Below is a list of quotes God gave me on *Faith* and the *Word of God*. I pray these quotes inspire you in your walk with God as they have inspired me.

FAITH QUOTES

Faith doesn't take no for an answer when it comes to the promises of God.

Even if God anointed you with a double portion of His Spirit, if you don't have faith, it won't do you a bit of good.

Faith doesn't see delays or having to wait on God for an answer to a prayer as a problem.

The main difference between someone weak in faith and strong in faith is what they think in their heart.

If you have faith, you will have a good time while everybody else is stressed out.

Faith violently takes by force what is promised to it in the Word of God.

Faith loves to get right in the middle of the worst situations and believe God for a miracle.

Faith knows that even if it gets down to the wire, God will always come through.

Unbelief is thinking, feeling, speaking, and believing you don't have something that God said you have.

Faith is not afraid of ANYTHING!

If it wasn't for Jesus, we wouldn't have any faith.

Faith is something unique and not everyone has it.

Faith always has the last laugh.

The more faith you have, the more God can use you.

The secret to strong faith is being able to overcome all opposition and resistance until the Word of God manifests.

It's impossible to defeat faith.

Faith not only believes God can perform a miracle, but persistently bugs God until He does.

Faith demands that God keeps His Covenant.

Faith makes no room for self-pity, but aggressively and thankfully inherits the promises of God.

Faith is always optimistic and thankful.

Faith never thinks of itself or says it is a victim.

Faith keeps believing when all others have given up all hope.

Faith puts a demand on God to fulfill His Word.

The worse things get, the more faith laughs.

As far as faith is concerned, it doesn't matter if things get worse.

It's thinking the thoughts of God found in His Word that makes you strong in faith.

God is looking for someone that He can develop to the point where the whole world marvels and talks about their faith.

Never, never, never speak any thoughts of fear, doubt, and unbelief.

Once you use your faith and receive a miracle from God, you are never the same.

Real faith never gives up.

Faith is bold like a lion.

Faith is strong and very courageous.

Faith has guts, intestinal fortitude, and a strong backbone.

Anyone strong in faith will be extraordinary.

Always remember that when you are believing God for a miracle, God is in the same boat with you.

Faith knows how to believe its way out of a rock and a hard place.

Faith only connects with faith.

Have faith in God and not in your faith.

Your faith must unite with God's faith for faith to work.

Some people think they have strong faith until they are tested with a fiery trial.

The trial of your faith not only reveals where your faith is at but is used to perfect your faith.

Faith will keep speaking to a mountain until it moves.

Mountains don't listen to weak, little, or dead faith.

Faith understands that mountains don't always like to obey.

Death cannot defeat faith.

Nothing can defeat faith.

Faith never gets discouraged.

Faith hunts for, and eradicates, negative thoughts.

Faith never worries about something it has no control over.

Faith doesn't worry about ANYTHING!

Demons only obey Christians with strong faith.

I would rather have great faith than a big ministry.

Faith laughs in the face of impossibilities.

If you want to please God, you must learn everything you can about faith.

Faith is eternal and never quits or gives up.

The devil is only afraid of Christians who are strong in faith.

Faith is not bound by space and time, and never stops believing God.

Faith knows that just because there is a delay, it doesn't mean that God will not keep His Word.

Faith knows how to hang on to God's promises, even if things look bad.

Faith is the language of God, therefore if you are going to speak to God, you must speak to Him in faith.

God's creative ability is His faith at work.

Faith laughs in the face of danger.

Faith stays joyous during an attack, because it knows beyond a shadow of a doubt that God will come through every time.

When a situation goes from bad to worse, faith keeps believing God until it gets the victory.

Faith turns defeat into victory every time.

Until you see fear, doubt, unbelief, and worry as a sin, you will not grow in your God given faith.

Faith loves a challenge, and always arises to the occasion.

Faith always defeats all opposition.

You can't kill faith.

The preaching of faith is the secret to having a revival.

The anointing can only match your level of faith.

Strong faith fights through all opposition and contradiction until it manifests the Word of God.

Real faith understands there is an enemy who will stop at nothing to keep the Word of God from manifesting.

Faith ignores anything and everything that would try to lie and say that God's Word is not true.

If you want to have great faith in God, you must settle into the fact that you will be tested.

Faith only focuses on the truth of God's Word until it manifests.

Faith never backs down from a fight.

When all looks lost, faith keeps going.

Faith will always come out on top of any test thrown at it.

Faith is not afraid of the time it may take for God to manifest His Word.

Your inward eye of faith allows you to plainly see the path of God for your life that no one else can see.

Keep your foot on the throttle of your faith, and you will see your prayers answered speedily.

You cannot access the blessings of the Kingdom of God without faith.

Faith is a measure of Spiritual Authority and Power given by God through obedience decreed by spoken words.

Faith knows God has answered its prayer and doesn't stop believing, even if things get worse.

We have to use our faith in God to give God the authority to use His faith to help us in our situation.

Faith starts and ends in what is revealed in the Scriptures.

If you always stay in the low-level living of fear, doubt, and unbelief, you will never come into the powerful potential of living by faith, where miracles and Divine answers to your prayers occur on a regular basis.

Once you've quit worrying, you've opened yourself up to living by faith.

A guilty conscience will ruin your chance of speaking by faith and getting your prayers answered by God.

You cannot speak to mountains by faith and expect them to move if you doubt God and His Word in your heart.

Patience is vital to faith.

Faith loves to pray for people in terrible conditions and see them healed.

Faith never complains but is always thankful for all things.

Faith in God is a mental toughness that enables you to believe and muscle your way through adversity and come out on top every time.

You have to learn how to enter by faith the Covenants God made with Abraham, David, and Christ to receive blessings from God.

The prayer of faith can change the world.

You can't be in faith and worry at the same time.

When you have faith, you will always have tangible answers from God Almighty.

Faith will blind you to your problems and open your eyes to only God's answers.

Strict adherence to the Words of Christ creates an unshakeable faith in the believer.

Your faith will leap over all of your limitations once you get a full revelation of God's sovereignty, power, ability, and willingness to help you.

Fear, doubt, worry, and unbelief are the enemies of God.

God cannot stand not being believed in because everything about Him is inherently good, and He has the power to do anything.

Great peace comes upon those who truly believe and trust in God.

You can miss out on many blessings from God by not believing in Him and what He says.

There is no end to what God will do for those who trust and believe in Him.

Faith is more than just mere optimism.

Nothing can stop the will of God when you pray the prayer of faith.

Bad news is a test to see if you will back off your faith and start worrying.

Faith breaks through the wall of worry.

The key to real faith is to stay just as excited during the time of testing as when miracles are manifesting.

Your faith needs to be continually exercised to become stronger.

Tough and contrary situations are opportunities and blessings to exercise and strengthen your faith.

Before you can possess strong faith, all your worries must be dealt with.

Don't expect to have great faith if you are unwilling to do the work in reading, studying, and practicing the Word of God.

Faith can walk through a minefield of fear, doubt, worry, and unbelief and come out unscathed.

Learning to live by faith is more beneficial than a high-paying job.

Worry will put you on the defensive, but faith puts you on the offensive.

Miracles don't just happen on their own; someone has to have faith.

Bad news fears men and women of God who walk by faith.

I don't want to hear how much faith you have; I want to see you get out on the battlefield of life and prove how much faith you have.

If you have strong faith in God, you can live like a king or queen while the rest of the world is going through hell.

You can't tackle life problems with little, weak, or dead faith.

The just live by faith and not by random luck.

There is nothing you cannot believe for and nothing you cannot do when you have faith in God.

God will do anything and everything to help a faith-filled man or woman of God.

It's not hoping that gets things done, but knowing by faith it is done, that gets things done.

You will experience exactly what you believe.

Jesus did not perform any miracles for people where someone was not actively involved with their faith for the miracle to manifest.

If you could see the future, you would have more faith in the present.

The only thing that can stop God's power is the lack of faith.

You cannot turn the world upside down with weak faith.

Faith is the original blueprint, design, and framework by which all of Heaven operates.

God wants to get us to the place where we fully believe Him without seeing anything with our naked eye.

The devil is no match against someone who knows the Word of God and is strong in faith.

Faith is not afraid to fight the devil over God's Word being true.

I don't want you to tell me how much faith you have; I want you to show the devil how much faith you have by defeating him in every battle.

WORD OF GOD QUOTES

The Father, the Son and the Holy Spirit are found in the Word of God, and when you get the Word of God in you, the Father, the Son and the Holy Spirit will be found in you.

When people don't do what God's Word says and fail, they still blame God or someone else for their failure.

Just because someone reads their Bible doesn't mean they are listening to the voice of the Holy Spirit.

Sometimes I wonder if people are reading the same Bible as I am.

The more I read the Bible, the more I clearly see that God wants to work miracles.

I don't want just to know the Word; I want to know the God of the Word.

One thought from God's Word can change your life forever.

All failure comes from a lack of understanding God's Word.

If you are not being challenged by the Word of God, you are not hearing the Word of God.

Read the Bible through the eyes of faith, or you will end up with wrong interpretations.

Adhering to, keeping, and obeying the Words of Christ will make you great and carry you into eternity.

I don't just want to know the Scriptures; I want to know the Holy Spirit who inspired the Scriptures.

There is a place where you can get to in your obedience to the Word of God that nothing can shake you.

The closer you get to God, the slower and deeper you read the Bible.

You have to keep all the Words of Christ to experience the Father.

Nothing excites me more than studying God's Word and being in His presence.

Nothing can replace the Word of God in your life.

The Word of God speaks to the heart, cleanses the soul, and transforms the mind.

Changing your thoughts to line up with the thoughts from God's Word is what changes you, not just reading your Bible.

No book or sermon can replace reading and studying God's Word for yourself.

It's not just reading the Word of God that changes you, what changes you is when you understand and obey what you read in the Word of God.

Obeying all the Words of Christ is the only way you can prove your love for the Father.

If you truly want to be made free, you need to eat up the Word of God.

It's important to keep your mind on the Word of God because of all the evil forces and voices in this world that try to distract and pull you off course from doing God's will.

There's a lot of preaching these days that is just self-help and motivational speaking, not the Word of God.

No weapon, enemy, or foe can withstand a strike from the sword of God's Word delivered by a man or woman of God.

Whoever does the will of God and obeys His Word is my true family.

You have to spend a lot of time meditating on God's Word and thoughts to grow up and mature in Christ.

Some people are bothered by what the Bible says. I am bothered by people who are bothered by the Word of God.

It amazes me how people can read the same Bible and walk away with two or more totally different interpretations.

It takes years to refine and polish the Word of God inside of you.

You have to boldly live the Word of God.

You will find God when you meditate on the Word of God.

God is looking to bless anyone who hears, understands, meditates on, and does the Word of God.

You cannot base your belief system on your experiences or the experiences of others. It must be based completely upon the Word of God.

It's not how much you read or know of the Bible that matters, but how much you conform to the teachings of the Bible in your life that matters.

CHAPTER 17

Final Faith Thoughts

Faith is one of the most powerful and fascinating subjects you can learn from the Word of God. Anyone who walks, talks, and lives by faith is powerful and will be highly favored by God. Nothing can stand in the way of a powerful person of faith who knows how to claim in prayer what is promised to them in the Word of God.

Faith is easy for some to grasp and much more challenging for others to learn. Some people are filled with more faith than others, but anyone can grow in their faith. To succeed in your faith, you must be ready to face challenges and grow in your knowledge of God's Word. You will also have to face all your fears, doubts, worries, and unbelief to become a strong person of faith.

One of the wonderful aspects of Jesus is that He is always there to help grow and develop your faith. We can see in the Word of God that Jesus always helped people while He ministered on the Earth, even when they were weak in their faith or had little faith. If He saw someone willing to step out in whatever faith they had, He would honor that faith and help to make it grow. The end goal of Jesus, however, was to make them strong in their faith.

The beauty of God is that He can take ordinary people and turn them into a legend by faith. A person of faith has learned to not walk, talk, live, or think like others. God wants to remove the shackles of low-level thinking, believing, speaking, and living from His people. A person of faith has learned from God to live in a higher realm of thinking, speaking, and acting.

God said that His thoughts are not our thoughts, nor are His ways our ways. A person of faith lives in the higher thoughts and ways of God.

Isaiah 55:8-9 (KJV)
8 For my thoughts are not your thoughts, neither are your ways my ways, saith the Lord. 9 For as the heavens are higher than the earth, so are my ways higher than your ways, and my thoughts than your thoughts.

God wants to develop your faith to where you will move mountains and shake all hell. God desires to transform you from an unbeliever into someone who laughs at the impossible with their faith. You may start in your Christian walk with little or no faith, but by the time Jesus is finished developing your faith, you will believe Him for the impossible. God is waiting for a generation of believers who will turn the world upside down with their faith.

Jesus was shocking people's minds with all the miracles He performed with His faith and with the faith of those who believed what He preached. Faith in the message of the Gospel of the Kingdom will always cause miracles to occur. If you are not seeing mind-blowing miracles, you are not seeing the Kingdom of God manifested on Earth.

Matthew 9:35 (KJV)
*35 And Jesus went about all the cities and villages, teaching in their synagogues, **and preaching the gospel of the kingdom, and healing every sickness and every disease among the people.***

The preaching of the Gospel and the Kingdom of God was never intended to be preached without miracles, signs, and wonders following. Jesus commanded that when His disciples preached the message of the Kingdom, they were to heal the sick, cleanse the lepers, raise the dead and cast out devils.

Matthew 10:7-8 (KJV)
7 And as ye go, preach, saying, The kingdom of heaven is at hand. 8 Heal the sick, cleanse the lepers, raise the dead, cast out devils: freely ye have received, freely give.

After Jesus rose from the dead, He commanded His disciples to preach the Gospel and that signs would follow the preaching of the Word. The signs only followed those who believed.

Mark 16:15-20 (KJV)
*15 And he said unto them, Go ye into all the world, **and preach the gospel** to every creature. 16 **He that believeth** and is baptized shall be saved; but **he that believeth not** shall be damned. 17 **And these signs shall follow them that believe; In my name shall they cast out devils; they shall speak with new tongues; 18 They shall take up serpents; and if they drink any deadly thing, it shall not hurt them; they shall lay hands on the sick, and they shall recover.** 19 So then after the Lord had spoken unto them, he was received up into heaven, and sat on the right hand of God. 20 **And they went forth, and preached every***

where, the Lord working with them, and confirming the word with signs following. Amen.

God never intended that His Gospel be preached without signs following. God is in the business of performing miracles, signs, and wonders. However, it is the duty of those who hear the Gospel message to believe. It is God's duty to perform miracles. The only way for God to perform miracles is for both the people preaching the Gospel and those hearing the Gospel must have faith. Faith is the key for God to perform miracles.

The Old Testament is filled with stories of God performing miracles for those who believed. God is the same God who did miracles in the Old and New Testaments. People who received miracles in the Old Testament also had faith. God has always been looking for faith since He created the World.

Men like Abraham, Moses, Joshua, Elijah, Elisha, Samuel, King David, and all the Old Testament prophets had faith and blew people away with the miracles God performed through them. God is looking for men and women of faith who will believe Him for miracles once again. God knows that once someone sees a miracle; they are never the same. Mind-blowing miracles change people, and miracles can only occur by faith. This is why faith is so important to God.

God is looking for people with a strong faith who laugh at the impossible. Laughing at the impossible started when God told Abraham he would have a son in his old age. Abraham laughed because he knew having a child would take an astounding miracle for him and his wife to conceive in their old age. Abraham and Sarah were well past the age of having kids when God told them they would have a child.

Genesis 17:15-17 (KJV)
*15 And God said unto Abraham, As for Sarai thy wife, thou shalt not call her name Sarai, but Sarah shall her name be. 16 And I will bless her, and give thee a son also of her: yea, I will bless her, and she shall be a mother of nations; kings of people shall be of her. 17 **Then Abraham fell upon his face, and laughed,** and said in his heart, Shall a child be born unto him that is an hundred years old? and shall Sarah, that is ninety years old, bear?*

When Sarah heard God make the promise to Abraham that Sarah would bear a child in her old age, she also laughed within herself. However, her laugh was more in joyful unbelief. When God confronted her about laughing within herself in disbelief, she denied she laughed because she was afraid.

Genesis 18:9-15 (KJV)
*9 And they said unto him, Where is Sarah thy wife? And he said, Behold, in the tent. 10 And he said, I will certainly return unto thee according to the time of life; and, lo, Sarah thy wife shall have a son. And Sarah heard it in the tent door, which was behind him. 11 Now Abraham and Sarah were old and well stricken in age; and it ceased to be with Sarah after the manner of women. 12 **Therefore Sarah laughed within herself,** saying, After I am waxed old shall I have pleasure, my lord being old also? 13 **And the Lord said unto Abraham, Wherefore did Sarah laugh,** saying, Shall I of a surety bear a child, which am old? 14 **Is any thing too hard for the Lord?** At the time appointed I will return unto thee, according to the time of life, and Sarah shall have a son. 15 **Then Sarah denied, saying, I laughed not; for she was afraid. And he said, Nay; but thou didst laugh.***

Sarah proclaimed when Isaac was born that everyone who heard God gave them a child in their old age would laugh with them. The name Isaac means laughter.

Genesis 21:5-7 (KJV)
*5 And Abraham was an hundred years old, when his son **Isaac** was born unto him. 6 **And Sarah said, God hath made me to laugh, so that all that hear will laugh with me.** 7 And she said, Who would have said unto Abraham, that Sarah should have given children suck? for I have born him a son in his old age.*

God knows His miracles are so astounding that all we can do is laugh in faith at them. God loves when people laugh at the impossible. God has been making people laugh at the impossible for years. Only God can come out of nowhere and save the day with a miracle that confounds the natural mind. God is in the habit of making the natural man laugh at what is impossible. Performing miracles and making people laugh in faith is easy for God.

When you learn to laugh at the impossible with your faith in God, you, too, can be called a Friend of God like Abraham.

James 2:23 (KJV)
*23 And the scripture was fulfilled which saith, **Abraham believed God,** and it was imputed unto him for righteousness: **and he was called the Friend of God.***

You might go through a tough trial of faith, but if you will laugh at the impossible, God will come through for you. A person of strong faith believes God, despite what is happening around them. Strong faith has joy unspeakable because they see they have the answer before it manifests. Strong faith always receives what they believe God for. Only God can make someone laugh when they are going through hell, because they believe God will deliver them, and He does every time.

The message in the Bible is clear that God is looking for faith so He can perform miracles. Once you learn this truth, your life will never be the same. You will enter a new world where nothing is impossible. Your limitless faith will enable God to do limitless miracles. Faith has always been the key to entering into all God has for us.

This book has been an incredible journey in the exploration of faith. I wrote this book as a guide to help anyone who has chosen the walk of faith, and although it may be challenging, it is also very rewarding. It will take everything you have to walk and live by faith, and it is not for the faint of heart. Walking and living by faith also takes a lot of wisdom and understanding of the Word of God. If you want to please God and see Him perform miracles, you must learn everything you can about faith.

Here are some of the most powerful truths and secrets I have learned about faith:

1. Faith comes by hearing the Word of God.
2. It only takes a mustard seed size of faith for it to work.
3. Faith is based on a Covenant with God.
4. Faith inherits all the Precious Promises of God.
5. Faith is led by the Holy Spirit.
6. Faith believes in the Power of God.
7. Faith is always thankful and never complains.
8. Faith speaks what it believes, and what it speaks comes to pass.
9. Faith speaks to mountains, and mountains obey faith-filled words.
10. Faith is teachable.
11. Faith understands the Word of God.
12. Faith feeds on the Word of God.

13. Faith is forgiving.

14. Faith conquers fear and is courageous.

15. Strong faith has no fear, worry, doubt, or unbelief.

16. There is always a good fight to faith.

17. Faith never backs down from a fight.

18. Faith laughs at the impossible.

19. Faith not only needs a challenge but thrives when challenged.

20. Faith is not afraid of the devil.

21. Anyone with strong faith will be extraordinary.

22. Wherever there is faith, there will be miracles.

23. Faith is rare on the Earth.

24. Faith can be measured and can grow.

25. Faith can be perfected.

26. Faith is backed by works.

27. Faith is dead without works.

28. Faith can be seen.

29. Even if someone dies, faith keeps believing in the God of resurrection.

30. Faith always receives an answer from God.

31. Faith is fully persuaded that God will perform His Word.

32. Faith is the substance of things hoped for, the evidence of things not seen.

33. Faith makes all things possible and makes a way where there is no way.

34. The Prayer of Faith works whenever fully understood.

35. Faith is persistent and never gives up.

36. Faith is eternal and never stops believing God.

37. Faith is patient and knows Kingdom answers take time.

38. Faith stands the test of time.

39. Faith takes hard work, and faith works hard.

40. Faith is not afraid to be tested and passes every test.

41. Faith pleases God and knows God is looking for someone with faith.

42. God will pass over a billion people to find someone with faith.

43. Faith opens the door to the supernatural realm of God.

44. Faith sees what others don't see.

45. Faith is not moved by what it sees or hears in the natural.

46. Faith sees into the unseen realm.

47. Faith can see the invisible God.

48. Faith is faithful to God.

49. Faith in Jesus will get you into Heaven and heal your body.

50. Faith is humble before God.

51. God has the Greatest and Strongest Faith.

52. God used His faith to create everything.

53. God operates His entire Kingdom by faith, and faith is the way of life in Heaven.

54. Strong faith gives glory to God.

55. Jesus is looking for faith, and faith is looking for Jesus.

Faith is one of the most fascinating and important subjects you can ever study in the Bible. It cannot be underestimated how important our faith is to God. No one can be saved or receive a miracle without faith. With this being said, you must learn to grow and exercise your faith daily because it is only by faith can we please God and see Him perform mighty miracles.

Hebrews 11:6 (KJV)
6 But without faith it is impossible to please him: for he that cometh to God must believe that he is, and that he is a rewarder of them that diligently seek him.

Knowing how important faith is to God, we should strive to have a faith that is talked about by the entire World.

Romans 1:8 (KJV)
*8 First, I thank my God through Jesus Christ for you all, **that your faith is spoken of throughout the whole world.***

In conclusion, it is imperative that we have faith if we are going to please God. God is looking for people who will take faith to the next level. I believe there is a generation that will take God at His Word before Christ returns and shake hell with their faith. I have written this book to help people grow and develop their faith. Once your faith matures, you will see the God of the Bible perform miracles in your life. God is waiting for you to believe and come into all that He has called you to be. *HAVE FAITH IN GOD!*

There is no limit to what God can do with a person of Faith!

Testimony

I want to put before you the difference between our faith and the faith of Jesus. Most people in this place have come to where they have said, "Lord, I can go no further. I have gone so far, and I can go no further. I have used all the faith I have, and I have to stop now and wait."

Thank God we have the faith we do, but there is another faith. I remember one day being in northern England and visiting some sick people. I was taken to a house where a young woman was lying on her bed. Her reason had gone, and many things were manifested there that were satanic, and I knew it.

She was only a young woman, with a beautiful child. Then the husband, a young man, came in with a baby, and he leaned over to kiss his wife. The moment he did, she threw herself onto the other side of the bed, just as a lunatic would do, with no consciousness of the presence of her husband. That was very heartbreaking. Then he took the baby and pressed the baby's lips to the mother. Again, she responded wildly. I asked a sister who was attending her, "Have you had anyone to help?"

"Oh," she said, "we have had everything."

But I said, "Have you no spiritual help?"

Her husband stormed out and said, "Help? Do you think we believe God after we have had seven weeks of no sleep and of maniac conditions? You are mistaken. You have come to the wrong house."

Then a young woman of about eighteen just grinned at me and went out the door. That brought me to a place of compassion for the woman. Something had to be done, no matter what it was. Then with all my faith, I penetrated the Heavens, and I was soon out of that house, I will tell you, I never saw a man get anything from God who prayed on the earth. If you get anything from God, you will have to pray to Heaven; for it is all there.

If you are living in the earthly realm and expect things from Heaven, they will never come.

And as I saw, in the presence of God, the limitations of my faith, there came another faith, a faith that could not be denied, a faith that took the promise, a faith that believed God's Word. And from that presence, I came back again to earth, but not the same man. God gave a faith that could shake hell and anything else. I said, "Come out of her, in the name of Jesus!" And she rolled over, fell asleep, and woke in fourteen hours, perfectly sane and whole.

Smith Wigglesworth

About The Author

Vince Baker was born in Southern California and later lived on 17 acres just north of Sacramento. As a child, Vince was raised as a Southern Baptist. Vince was always drawn to the Lord and even said he wanted to be a preacher at an early age.

Vince's life was uneventful until one day, he encountered God while driving in his car at the age of 17. God manifested Himself to Vince in such a powerful way that his life would never be the same. After this experience, Vince became a Christian and dedicated his life to the Lord. In that same month, Vince received a book from his Christian Grandma called *The Secret of His Power*. This book was about a famous miracle-working evangelist named Smith Wigglesworth. God used this book to prepare Vince for ministry. God also used the testimony of Smith, found in another book called *Apostle of Faith,* to talk to him about things He wanted to do through him in his later years.

Vince went to a Christian High School his senior year. At this school, Vince was introduced to a seasoned Evangelist who took local churches to feed the poor and evangelize. Vince found out he lived near the Evangelist and started traveling with him. During this time, Vince became his right-hand man and saw many amazing miracles on the streets through this ministry. This ministry was called to train the Church on how to evangelize with power. Vince was able to travel up and down the west coast, ministering to the homeless and helpless while equipping the Church. Vince has a big heart for the poor, homeless, and hurting people.

Within a short time, Vince heard from God to attend Bible College. Through confirmation from God and a miracle of his tuition being paid for, Vince studied the Bible more deeply at this Bible College. Vince's foundational training from the Word of God during this time was priceless. Vince ended up graduating as the Valedictorian from this Bible College.

After Bible College, Vince started ministering to children at a Christian school, taught Sunday School, and functioned in the local Church. Vince later moved into full-time ministry and was an assistant Pastor at a local Church for five years during the mid-'90s.

As an assistant Pastor, Vince visited a Church where the Prophet Kim Clement was ministering. Prophet Kim Clement pulled Vince out of the crowd and prophesied over him. In that prophecy, God spoke to Vince through the Prophet Kim Clement that He would use him mightily and that he needed to prepare himself.

Presently, Vince works in the marketplace, where he is the CEO and part-owner of Agora Advantage. God called Vince to the marketplace, but Vince knew he would be called back into full-time ministry later in life. Agora Advantage has been a fantastic opportunity where Vince has grown in many ways. As a sign from God, Vince was voted in as the CEO of Agora Advantage on the Day of Pentecost.

As Vince neared the prophesied time that God would bring him back into full-time ministry, he began seeking the Lord more deeply. During this time, Vince had another unforgettable encounter with God regarding the

Ark of the Covenant. God gave Vince a vision of four men carrying the Ark of the Covenant up onto an altar in a large Church. The Holy Spirit spoke to Vince and said, "Wherever you read Ark of the Covenant in the Old Testament, think Holy Spirit. Wherever you read Holy Spirit in the New Testament, think Ark of the Covenant. Put the two together, and you will know Me." Vince studied these two subjects everyplace he could find them in the Bible and received tremendous insight into understanding the Holy Spirit.

God also revealed to Vince a prophetic way to study the Bible from this experience. Vince spent years in the Word of God, studying different subjects of the Bible as the Holy Spirit led him. At the leading of the Holy Spirit, Vince researched every place a word or phrase was found from the Old and New Testaments. Vince has currently done over four hundred of these studies, some of which took months to complete. The revelations that came out of these studies were priceless and life changing. Vince wrote all these teachings and revelations down. Many of these word studies make up many of the truths he writes and preaches about in his books and messages today. Vince found that when you study a subject everywhere it is in the Bible, you can receive the full counsel of God on that subject. Vince also received many dreams and visitations from God during this time.

Vince has a unique calling where he can preach, teach, prophesy, move in the gifts of the Spirit, bring healing, and perform miracles by the power of the Holy Spirit. Vince is called to help the body of Christ come into their destiny and High Calling.

Currently, Vince resides in Northern California with his wife, Eunice, and their two dogs, enjoying the blessings of God.

Invite Vince to Speak

Visit

www.VinceBakerMinistries.com

ADDITIONAL BOOK BY
<u>VINCE BAKER</u>

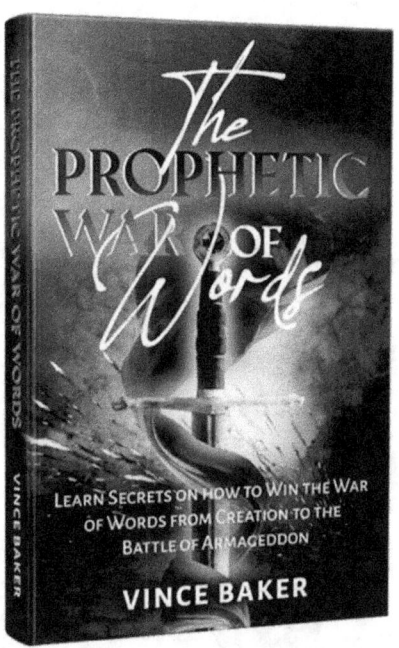

www.amazon.com/author/vincebaker
www.VinceBakerMinistries.com

ADDITIONAL BOOK BY
<u>VINCE BAKER</u>

ADDITIONAL BOOK BY
<u>VINCE BAKER</u>

ADDITIONAL BOOK BY
<u>VINCE BAKER</u>

www.amazon.com/author/vincebaker

www.VinceBakerMinistries.com

ADDITIONAL BOOK BY
VINCE BAKER

www.amazon.com/author/vincebaker

www.VinceBakerMinistries.com

www.ingramcontent.com/pod-product-compliance
Lightning Source LLC
Chambersburg PA
CBHW071713120626
46550CB00001B/219